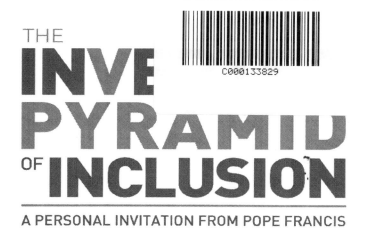

THE
INVE
PYRAMID
OF **INCLUSION**

A PERSONAL INVITATION FROM POPE FRANCIS

An interactive and practical workbook

DES McCABE

NEW ACTIVITY
PUBLICATIONS

Published by New Activity Publications
(a not-for-profit publisher)

ISBN 978-1-904969-61-7

www.invertedpyramid.info
www.desmccabe.com

DEDICATION

For those of all beliefs and none.
This is an invitation to each of us
to find a better way to work together.

CONTENTS

SECTION 3: The Inverted Pyramid in all our Workplaces   165

Section Three invites us to explore the application of the Inverted Pyramid methodology in our various workplaces, from businesses and organisations to public sector bodies, charities, education and government agencies. What challenges and opportunities of inclusion are different sectors facing?

SECTION 4: CASE STUDY: Future Church and Pope Francis   249

Section Four offers us a ringside seat in a 'live' case study as Pope Francis tries to turn the Catholic Church upside down. With our understanding of the Inverted Pyramid methodology in a range of sectors, we can now look at what Francis is doing. It's not going to plan... so what should he do next?

SECTION 5: Future Work – the Emerging Inverted Pyramid Workplace   297

What does the emerging Inverted Pyramid workplace look like for us? How can we invert our leadership thinking, transform our Human Resources departments and provide training? Section Five invites us to play a key role in building an Inverted Pyramid workplace of the future that meets the needs of everyone.

SECTION 6: Personal Review and Action Plan   351

Section Six helps us to review our priorities, create a personal Action Plan and explore how we can begin today, with others, in a new way. What are the Inverted Pyramid opportunities for each of us? How can we begin to develop initiatives with colleagues in our organisations and communities?

APPENDICES

INTRODUCTION

Ellis Mottur, Assistant Secretary for Trade Development at the US Department of Commerce, pulled down a large map of Northern Ireland in his Washington office and asked me 'Now, where is Killowen where you live?' He saw immediately the significance when I pointed to the shore of Carlingford Lough which looks over to the Cooley mountains in the Republic of Ireland. I was literally on the Northern Ireland border.

It was 1997 and the 'Troubles' in Northern Ireland were moving into a 'Peace Process'. My colleague Tim Bourke and I were privileged to work with the governments of the US and Ireland in the formative stages of the Good Friday agreement.

A key part of this choreography was the Northern Ireland Act (1998), which was introduced to address equality, particularly with regard to different religious beliefs. The purpose of the legislation was to ensure that all public bodies treated everyone equally, especially in relation to employment and the workplace.

The Northern Ireland Authorities asked me to develop a training workshop to help bring all public sector bodies up to date. Can you imagine anything more exciting than having to attend a three-hour workshop on religion and European legislation?!

I worked closely with the fledgling Northern Ireland Interfaith Forum in the development of the workshop, and members contributed information on the beliefs and day-to-day practices of their tradition, including Islam, Hinduism, Sikhism, Judaism, Buddhism and the Baha'i faith. These were all hidden minorities in Northern Ireland at the time.

1

The workshop was a success, and for three years I personally trained staff in health trusts, government departments, colleges, police, fire, et cetera across Northern Ireland. It was really a personal development programme because it enabled people to shift away from the old Northern Ireland mindset of Catholic versus Protestant. Individuals were able to reflect not only on a broader spectrum of religion and belief, but also on their personal spirituality and what they wanted to see in a more caring Northern Ireland, where we looked after each other.

Similar legislation on religion and belief was then introduced in the UK, and the British Government asked me to provide similar training. Diversiton was born, and the religion and belief workshop was licensed across six areas in England, Scotland and Wales. The Republic of Ireland also came on board at the same time.

It was against the backdrop of 9/11 that diversity arrived in 2001, and the focus shifted dramatically to difference as international terrorism, anti-Muslim sentiment and immigration fostered anxiety and led to negative stereotyping. Indeed, many people still think of skin colour, religion or ethnicity when the word *diversity* is used.

Diversity is that which makes each of us unique, including our skills, experience and personal values. Diversity is our DNA. Diversity, which should have been about cherishing (and leveraging) our uniqueness, became a label to allocate us into separate groups.

In the last ten years, *inclusion* has grown as a concept in the workplace, potentially as a way of addressing this separation. The hope is that inclusion will encourage people to respect each other and work better together.

So, it's been interesting watching this cumulative development take place, from equality through diversity and now to inclusion. These three separate and distinct constructs have effectively merged in many of our HR departments. There are around 2.5 million people on

LinkedIn with the initials 'DEI' or 'EDI' in their job title (I'll leave you to work out what the letters stand for).

Before continuing with this evolving and cumulative approach and adding more letters, perhaps we should think about what we've created with LGBTQQIP2SAA (lesbian, gay, bisexual, transgender, queer, questioning, intersex, pansexual, two-spirit, androgynous, asexual). An alternative or additional approach may be to look at what we want to achieve when we talk about inclusion. Someone once said that you have to start with the end result in mind. What does the end result look like when we talk about inclusion? What are our objectives? What are the expected outputs?

Pope Francis starts at the end when he says that we need a much kinder, more collaborative world, where people look after each other. Looking specifically at the Catholic Church back in 2015, Francis wanted to turn the traditional hierarchal organisation structure upside down. He called for 'servant leadership' where the bishops and clergy are at the 'bottom' and the people are at the 'top'. He called this an Inverted Pyramid.

This book explores the methodology behind how the Inverted Pyramid works and discusses the application across all areas of society. Armed with these new perspectives, we can then look at where Francis has got to with his planned reform of the Catholic Church. He began his global roll-out plan in 2021 and called it a process of Synodality (journeying together). But all has not gone to plan.

Inclusion must allow us to move beyond our work 'boxes' and work together in new ways, wherever we are. At the heart of this Inverted Pyramid methodology, Pope Francis offers an invitation to a personal development process. This puts each of us in the driving seat and can lead to new thinking (and new ways of working) for business, in education, in terms of community development and a different approach to what we call Human Resources.

This is a call for each of us to take part and to journey together from here, to build a better world for everyone.

Specifically, the aims of this book are:

- To articulate the difference between equality, diversity and inclusion
- To explain the difference between a traditional organisation structure and an Inverted Pyramid process
- To explain what Dual Responsibility is and why it matters
- To help us to recognise the difference between transactional working and interpersonal relationship building
- To give us the opportunity to reflect on our own personal approach to building inclusion using the Inverted Pyramid Exercises throughout this book
- To document a practical methodology for realising the Inverted Pyramid concepts of inclusion, caring for others and collaborative working
- To demonstrate how we can be key drivers for building a world of inclusion
- To explore how organisations and businesses can develop *community* and so build inclusion
- To reflect upon the aims of Pope Francis and the challenges for the Catholic bishops as a practical ongoing 'live' Inverted Pyramid case study
- To map out a practical framework for building inclusion from where we are now, in our workplaces, communities and homes
- To encourage each of us to create our own personal Action Plan and so to proactively build our own Inverted Pyramid of Inclusion.

Inclusion and the Inverted Pyramid

Section One explains exactly what the Inverted Pyramid is and how it can work for all of us. This methodology suggests that we urgently need to turn our current thinking 'upside down'. What is inclusion all about? How can we truly build inclusivity in our workplaces and in our world?

CHAPTER 1

Inclusion is a personal development process – start here

Overview

I was intrigued when I read that Pope Francis had used the phrase 'Inverted Pyramid' in his efforts to reform the Catholic Church. For the last 12 years my colleague Jimmy Ryan and I have been running programmes on implementing the 'upside down triangle'. It's a similar approach.

Jimmy and I have worked with thousands of individuals looking for a better way to build their future, as well as many businesses and public sector bodies wanting to promote inclusion and create stronger communities. We have seen first-hand the Inverted Pyramid methodology transforming individual lives as well as a multitude of organisations.

Much of the learning we have gathered along the way may be helpful and worth sharing as others seek to carve out a more collaborative and supportive way forward.

The Inverted Pyramid process can move us from a transactional to an interpersonal way of working. So much of our daily lives and activities are about doing things and getting things done. We have become slaves in many ways – to our employers, work culture and just living day by day.

Later in the book we will return to what the Church should do next, but before that, we need to understand what the Inverted Pyramid is and how it can work for each of us.

We will explore how we can build a new way of working and living together through a global model of inclusion. We will look at how this relates to the businesses and organisations that we work in, and also at how we can support our children. We will see how we can build community with a personal approach that each of us can lead and be part of.

There's no magic wand here. We all have to think and behave differently. We need to teach people in our organisations about this new way of working. We need to be explicit about the behaviours, attitudes, values and language that underpin this collective endeavour.

Every member of staff, every child and every community must have the opportunity to be part of the process of journeying together. This book will help us explore and so share the key messages. You will find out later how to become part of our global network of licensed trainers, if you would like to share this methodology. It doesn't matter where you live or work. The needs of the world are urgent and well documented, and so we must share this approach as quickly as possible.

Purpose of this book

The intention of this book is to set out a range of ideas, questions and concepts which encourage each of us to develop our own Inverted Pyramid process.

The book seeks to offer guidance and assistance in five key areas:

1. To offer a practical handbook on the methodology of the Inverted Pyramid of Inclusion. What is it? How does it work?
2. To provide opportunities for discussion on the application of the Inverted Pyramid to different types of organisation. How can the Inverted Pyramid be applied to our workplace, our business or our group?
3. To illustrate how we can all help to build inclusion with, through and beyond our organisation or business. What is our individual role in all of this?
4. To give each of us an opportunity to reflect at a personal level on our own journey of inclusion. How can we develop our understanding of the key themes, issues and concepts around collaboration and community?
5. To encourage everyone to work together to build our Inverted Pyramids from here, and so become active players in building a global world of inclusion. What is our Action Plan?

We have a lot to get through! And this book is only a start. It's an invitation to work together as we develop and roll out activities, and share our learning in each of the five key areas above.

From this moment onwards, I see us as co-authors in our Inverted Pyramid global community: to add to what we find here, share our experience in the sector or roles we know well, add our own case studies, develop our Inverted Pyramid activities and encourage others to journey with us.

This book seeks to encourage dialogue with everyone, irrespective of their background, location or belief. For how are we going to reach out to everyone and build a world of inclusion if we do not have conversations with those who are different to us, build new relationships and work together in better ways?

The heart of the Inverted Pyramid is about inclusion in our world, so we will be looking at business, community, education and religion, all within this one book. This will help us to gain an understanding of how others are addressing challenges and opportunities with the Inverted Pyramid. And if we are to build a kinder, more interconnected and collaborative world, then we need to work much better across sectors and structures. The Inverted Pyramid process is the key mechanism for enabling this to happen.

So, as you read the book, enjoy the opportunity to place yourself within an environment that may be less familiar to you. Try to look at the concept of an Inverted Pyramid within those sectors that you wouldn't normally associate yourself with, be it education, religion, government, business or perhaps even your own new role as a hybrid individual worker. Put yourself in the mindset of other organisations and structures; their learning and challenges may not be so different from yours. You may be surprised at the fabric of connections available as you build your Inverted Pyramid.

Getting out of our own work 'box' to look from another perspective is important, and so too is getting out of our familiar vocabulary. We know that each sector has its own jargon and terminology, but if we are to be inclusive of all others, we need to be able to talk about God, love, kindness and business in the same sentence. Indeed, as we shall see, the Inverted Pyramid itself will introduce us to a host of new concepts such as *Dual Responsibility*, the *Social Meitheal* and the *Mexican Wave of Kindness*. Take the opportunity to explore what the Inverted Pyramid means for your relationships, especially with those who are different in some way and those who may need your help.

Most of all, use this book as a personal development opportunity to build your understanding of the Inverted Pyramid in your own life. The book can offer opportunities not only for collaboration and inclusion in their fullest sense, but also to build our future and fulfil the roles we are truly capable of.

For Pope Francis, becoming a Servant Church means empowering and actively encouraging us to reach out and to journey in the service of others. It doesn't matter what our background, experience or beliefs are. Francis is putting forward an Inverted Pyramid model and process for everyone. It's a framework that enables us to work together, based on caring for and looking after each other.

Of course, we do not have to be a member of any faith system or religious tradition to promote the idea of collaboration with others. Those in the business, education, health, industry, voluntary and public sectors are all in prime position to help build a kinder and more collaborative world.

Indeed, the Inverted Pyramid framework, as we shall see, provides a real opportunity for all of us to break down and move beyond the barriers that currently divide society, particularly on the basis of wealth, opportunity, sector, faith, location or personal background.

Francis has made a personal move by stepping out from his 'top job' in a traditional hierarchal organisation to stand as a single person encouraging the Church and all others to work with him. He is creating his own personal Inverted Pyramid and inviting us, whether we are in our homes, workplaces or communities, to journey with him. This is a different type of leadership and a different way forward.

Inclusion is a personal development process

Inclusion is a personal development process. It starts with each of us. So many organisations see inclusion as an organisational strategy or bolt-on. They see it as something that we do to others.

But if we are to truly build an inclusive world then we have to remember Gandhi's famous words:

11

'Be the change that you want to see in the world.' We are that change. We have to be not just initiators but partners in the process of building inclusion with others.

This calls for a radical shift in how we think about inclusion. Inclusion is an interpersonal development process. It starts with us constantly reaching out to all others, regardless of who they are and irrespective of our situation, role, job or position. It impacts our business and organisation processes, strategies and policies. It means that we have to behave and work with others in a very different way. Inclusion isn't easy. But if we don't start, then who will?

Inverted Pyramid Exercises (IPEs)

The Inverted Pyramid is an invitation for each of us to reach out beyond 'now' and to see our lives, the world and what we truly are in a bigger way.

To help this aspect of our personal (and spiritual) development, I have included some IPEs throughout the book. These are little resting points on our journey. They are built around the principles of Saint Ignatius's Spiritual Exercises, in which he invites us to go beyond our role as onlooker in the story and to become actively involved. Ignatius would call on us to see ourselves as players in the evolution of the Inverted Pyramid and to be part of the story. We all have a specific role to play.

Try to take a few moments to think about the reflection questions at the end of each exercise. How do the questions relate to you and your own situation?

Getting the most from this book

- **Journal**
  Please use a journal or notebook from here onwards. This will become your personal Inverted Pyramid handbook, a useful reference document and a place to capture your thoughts and ideas. Think about the content and what it means for you personally, your current role and relationships, the work you do, your future and indeed all that you are as a person. (There are spaces to write in the book as you go along if you prefer this.)

- **This is a workbook**
  This is not intended to be a rulebook! It is a set of ideas and topics for discussion and application. Take what is useful for you or your organisation and use this.

- **Journey with me**
  When you find points that you disagree with, please treat these as an opportunity to move the discussion forward. This helps us continue to map out the new landscape of inclusion together. Don't forget to write down what you think I've missed or questions that I didn't address – and let me know. Let's keep working together on this.

- **Personal development programme**
  Treat this book as your own personal development programme. Each chapter is a module. Use the opportunity to record your thoughts, ideas and questions.

- **Get the complete picture**
  Please do not read in isolation the one or two chapters that you identify with most. It is only by working through the entire process that you will begin to build a fuller understanding of the landscape of inclusion.

- **Inverted Pyramid Exercises**
  Take a couple of minutes to reflect on the IPEs scattered throughout this book. These short reflections may offer us a different perspective. They are designed to take us out of 'reading mode' and to encourage us to think in a personal way about our journey.

- **Time to harvest**
  At the end of each chapter there is an opportunity to capture any thoughts, ideas, questions or action points that you want to note and take forward. You will gather these for your personal Action Plan at the end of the book. Play with the possibilities! The process of capturing your thoughts in writing supports your learning and the development of practical initiatives.

- **Regularly review all your notes**
  Keep your journal with you and begin to allow your Inverted Pyramid ideas to become reality in all aspects of your life and work. What are the key messages coming through for you? What pointers or actions do they suggest for you at a personal, work or spiritual level? How are they influencing your thinking about your current organisation and situation? And how is all this relevant to your current life, career and future?

- **Action Plan**
  At the end of this book, you'll have an opportunity to pull together all your ideas into an Action Plan. The points above can help you to make this real, relevant and effective as you move forward from here. Enjoy!

INVERTED PYRAMID EXERCISE

Are you ready to leave your tent?

THE TENT

It is no longer enough
to sit inside the tent
and call on people to join us,
and hope that they will come.

Sometimes we must go outside
of the tent and walk with others
so that we can move forward together,
in a new way.

PERSONAL DEVELOPMENT REFLECTION
1. What is your Tent?
2. A tent is typically pyramid-shaped. Can you invert this? How can you go outside?

CHAPTER 1: Time to harvest

Please take a moment to reflect and capture any initial thoughts, ideas, questions or action points that you wish to note and take forward. You will be able to gather these from each chapter for your personal development Action Plan at the end of the book.

Notes

1 ....

2 ....

3 ....

4 ....

5 ....

CHAPTER 2

How can we build a world of inclusion?

This chapter is all about exploring the landscape of DEI in our workplaces. What exactly are the differences and links between diversity, equality and inclusion?

What is DEI?

DEI is a collective term for diversity, equality and inclusion. This is a great question because nowadays we tend to lump these three topics together as if they were essentially the same subject. I think it's important to recognise that they are very different concepts, and if we are to bring them together, we need to be clear about the relationship between them. They may be connected but they all have very different priorities and associated activities.

In recent years there has been a huge growth in the number of people working in this area. Indeed, some 2.1 million people on LinkedIn have a current job with DEI in the title. We can see how this has come about: organisations have tried to respond to personal, social and political events which have transformed society and the way we see ourselves, others, migration, gender, sexuality, identity, racism, well-being, mental health and much more. We've come a long way from the equality legislation of 20 years ago.

Why is inclusion not working?

Many organisations are struggling to make inclusion a reality in the workplace. HR departments have worked systematically through diversity, equality and inclusion over the last two decades, and most have all their policies and procedures in place. And yet, so little has really changed. Why is inclusion so challenging? Why do we struggle to engage and empower all our staff? And most importantly, what can we do to change all of this and make inclusion a reality, not just in our workplace but also in our world?

The first thing that may help is to clarify what exactly diversity, equality and inclusion are.

Equality is essentially a legislative framework targeting key issues such as belief, sexuality, gender, race, et cetera. Equality labels people and groups by these characteristics in an effort to raise awareness, minimise discrimination and promote equality of treatment in the workplace.

Whereas equality is a narrow legal framework, diversity is our amazing individual toolbox! Some talk about difference but our diversity includes our skills, knowledge, backgrounds, talents, experiences, passions and interests. Our diversity is all that we are, from shoe size to fear of flying to the way that we make scrambled eggs. Our diversity is what makes us unique human beings. As you can see, diversity includes our equality characteristics and so much more.

Our diversity gives us the opportunity to share all that we are and so make a real difference to those around us. Diversity opens up countless possibilities for us to contribute and add value, if we can just find others to work with and come up with an opportunity to engage with them. Our diversity toolkit can help us to grow and become all that we should be.

But it's not as simple as this because the world does not offer people all the opportunities that they should have. So many of us fail to reach our potential. Some of us are stuck in the house on our own, some in workplaces that fail to see our potential. Others live in war zones, have no home or go hungry every night.

And this is where inclusion comes in. Inclusion is about how we enable everyone to play the fullest part that they can. And we do this by creating links, working together and looking after each other so that everyone does well. Inclusion is the process and result of leveraging our skills and experience to benefit everybody, inside and outside our organisation. Diversity and equality are two practical components of inclusion. Inclusion is bigger than HR, bigger than our organisation and bigger than all of us together.

Inclusion is both a personal development process whereby we each play our part in making our world a better place, and also interpersonal because this is how we make it real. Inclusion happens through our interactions, and the difference we make in each other's lives.

Inclusion uncovers our uniqueness (personal characteristics, DNA and experience), and seeks to wield all of this for a kinder, fairer and more peaceful world. This is the personal development opportunity to build meaningful interpersonal relationships. And this is the purpose of inclusion, for each of us to become all that we can be by looking after everyone together.

If our inclusion strategy is simply a subset of our business objectives then it's clear that we are not actively working to meet the needs, aspirations and potential of all our people. Our inclusion activities become simply another element of our business development strategy.

Inclusion means that we bring everyone together and do not exclude others, irrespective of our differences. Inclusion means that we look for ways to promote participation and collaboration. It means that we look for ways to access and develop the skills, knowledge and expertise that each person has, to benefit the whole organisation and the wider community.

Building awareness of inclusion in our workplaces

One of the challenges to building inclusion is in helping people to understand what inclusion is and navigating through the noise of the DEI landscape. Are we really saying that topics with labels familiar to DEI specialists, such as unconscious bias, bystander intervention, gender expression and microaggressions, are the only tools we have to define the landscape of inclusion? Of course these are all important, but what is the big picture that we are all working towards?

So often, we see a lot about equality issues but very little about inclusion. I think we might be missing something important here. Surely we should be discussing the real challenges of increasing migration and its effect on major economies? The political rhetoric around this is largely negative and has already manifested itself in race hate incidents. What about global inequality and climate change, which are dramatically affecting the livelihoods (and homes) of people everywhere? Or the impact of the war in places such as Ukraine, Afghanistan, Syria, Yemen, Somalia and Iraq? Isn't world peace an inclusion issue? Staff and skills shortages, especially in the health sector, are directly impacting on quality of life in many areas. Fuel poverty and the mainstreaming of food banks have highlighted the cost of living as a real inclusion priority for many. Families with working parents are increasingly finding themselves in a situation and categorised in a way that they never imagined. The widening gap between rich and poor, and also global starvation, form an uncomfortable but real context for any discussion on inclusion.

We therefore need to be mindful that HR does not become too insular, politically correct, 'woke' or focused on niche equality issues. We must not miss the priority of inclusion for everyone.

All of these inclusion challenges are feeding directly into our daily political agenda and economic policies in a big way. We should all be working together on these issues if we are to build inclusion and ensure that no one is left behind. We could be in for a tough few years, with public expenditure cuts, inflation, a global recession, health care crises, wars, household bills and more…

Including people in inclusion

Inclusion can be a positive force for good in our world. It can be a combined, collaborative and cumulative effort enabling people to help each other through these difficult periods. Our workplaces must become supportive and welcoming. At an interpersonal level, we must be more mindful of each other, more thoughtful in our language and a little bit more patient with each other, for we do not know what people are struggling with. This is inclusion in action.

One of the key challenges for HR personnel is, 'How do we make inclusion relevant for all members of staff? How do we engage individuals in building a more inclusive workplace and to navigate some of the bigger issues in our world? What are the positive behaviours and messages we can share? How can we as individuals help to make our workplaces (and the world) a kinder and more caring place?' I think we need a bigger perspective and to get people out of their HR bubbles.

I believe we can help to educate and inform, and we can encourage others to ask questions. Inclusion is, after all, a personal development process. The alternative is that we all just sit and wait for DEI to do something.

Questions for all staff

As you read through this book, please reflect on the following questions:

- What are our inclusion objectives for this year?

- What exactly will we do to build inclusion?
- How will we engage every one of our colleagues?
- How will we develop, build and own new inclusion initiatives?
- What will our staff be able to do differently?
- How will we measure progress and success?

We will come back to these questions later in the book.

INVERTED PYRAMID EXERCISE

Can we have inclusion for strawberries?

STRAWBERRIES

It's time to encourage
inclusion for strawberries.
You see, years ago we could just
buy a punnet of strawberries.

Now we have labelled our
favourite summer fruit,
separating former friends and family
into at least four categories.

Those at their peak
come with the highest price.
Those in their later days
get rapidly discounted,
and have a reduced label
plastered across their front.

Those with disabilities
are called 'wonky', as we highlight
some perceived 'imperfection'.
And those who have less
become Essentials, or Own Brand.

PERSONAL DEVELOPMENT REFLECTION
Find and celebrate what might be seen as different or imperfect in
something that you encounter today.

Can you see separate inclusion and equality activities in your organisation?

Many people still confuse inclusion with equality. When they talk about inclusion, they think about representation in the workplace. Have we enough women in senior roles? Are ethnic minorities properly represented in all areas? Are we discriminating against any of our rapidly expanding categories of employees?

All of this is about equality legislation. It's looking to ensure that staff are not discriminated against because of their age, gender reassignment, marriage or civil partnership status, pregnancy or maternity leave, disability, race (including colour), ethnic or national origin, religion or belief, sex and sexual orientation.

Inclusion, however, starts with each person, not a set of characteristics. Inclusion is how we maximise the potential of each person to contribute to the well-being of all others. Inclusion seeks to explore, capture and build upon all that makes us who we are. Inclusion is therefore limitless in its possibilities in terms of how we might link up and work together.

DIVERSITY AND INCLUSION

Diversity has been described by some
as the reflection of God in the world
for many people believe that
we are all made in His likeness.

Each of us is a unique piece
needed for this complete picture of God
or of our own understanding of all that is.
Inclusion is therefore our mission.

PERSONAL DEVELOPMENT REFLECTION
1. How is our piece unique?
2. Why are we necessary?

So, what's the link between diversity and inclusion?

Our modern world does not cope well with diversity and difference. People who appear different to us or act in a different way are often more likely to be excluded, ignored or marginalised. We are conditioned to think in a lesser way about those from a poorer upbringing, who are badly dressed, who speak with a foreign accent. Instead of cherishing their individual nature, behaviour or perspective, we often diminish them and therefore exclude all that they are. We might ignore or dismiss them because of this aspect of who they are.

We tend to feel safe and secure in our group conformity or organisation's culture and the predictability of the normal, whether at work, socially or in our deeper relationships with others.

For us to see and accept others as they truly are requires us to step out of our comfort zone. It means that we have to break from the norm of the group to highlight, accept and embrace the one who appears different in some way – unless of course, our group norm happens to be acceptance of those who are different.

If I were to talk in the next management meeting about God in the workplace, discuss Heaven and the afterlife, put forward suggestions as to how we should be addressing local poverty or building a world of love, I'm not sure I would last too long.

Some years ago, the focus was very much on diversity, whereas now the emphasis is more around inclusion. Diversity highlighted the key differences shared by many of us in terms of race, religion, sexuality and so on. Highlighting these differences, however, also carries the danger of increasing or reinforcing the barriers between groups.

The true challenge for diversity was to unleash the potential for individual development and organisational growth within each person. Diversity could have been the engine for innovation and creativity, as opposed to its perception as a safety net or insurance policy. We know that promoting difference is not always a good thing, especially when we classify people as asylum seekers or ex-prisoners, for example.

We are not playing to the person's strengths in these cases. We are actually limiting their potential by emphasising one difference. And as I said, each of these people have their own strengths and abilities. I have met many migrant pharmacists, marketing managers and social media specialists.

What is productive inclusion?

Inclusion is much more than simply *including*. It's much more than trying to involve everybody. Inclusion in the active promotion of every person for the benefit of everyone. Inclusion is a process that expands the possibilities of the entire group by realising the potential of each person.

INVERTED PYRAMID EXERCISE

Did you finish your blueberry muffin?

BLUEBERRY MUFFIN

A man in a yellow jumper
is sitting on the bench
just in front of me.
He seems to be asleep.

Around him is a collection of holdalls,
carrier bags and a pull-along case.
It seems like all his possessions
are there with him.

I am sitting with my Americano
and blueberry muffin.

After a while my man gets up slowly,
unable to really stand up straight.
He begins to load himself, like a donkey,
with all his bags.

He's clearly done this many times,
for bags are draped over his shoulders
and around his back
leaving his hands free for
the final bags and the pull-along case.
Off he shuffles.

Twenty minutes later he comes back,
all his bags neatly packed
into one shopping trolley.
He heads off slowly down the street.

A police car arrives
and travels alongside him,
clearly checking out the situation.
My man stops as the police get out.
He follows them, with his trolley,
to the police station.

Writing this, I finish my Americano
and blueberry muffin.

PERSONAL DEVELOPMENT REFLECTION
1. What should I have done?
2. What should I do now?

Building the jigsaw of full inclusion

It's difficult to build a jigsaw if we can only see the back of the pieces, which are all the same light blue colour. And many appear to be the same shape too, so it's pure guesswork as to where each piece belongs within the picture. It could take forever to complete the jigsaw.

However, even children know that if we turn the pieces over, we can see that each piece has a unique image and contribution to make, and so we can immediately begin to understand how they all fit together. We can complete our jigsaw.

INVERTED PYRAMID EXERCISE

What is the jigsaw of everyone?

THE JIGSAW

Without us, this world
would be incomplete.
Like a thousand-piece jigsaw
our absence is
all that we would see.
That one empty space.

It is because we are here
that everything is complete,
and all is as it should be.

We are irreplaceable.
We are the ones that make
everything worthwhile.
We are the ones that we all need.
For without us
our jigsaw is nothing.

And when we understand this,
we understand inclusion.
We understand everything.

PERSONAL DEVELOPMENT REFLECTION

1. What does your piece of the Jigsaw look like? Draw it.
   Describe it.
2. What is the overall picture on the jigsaw of everyone?

And so it is within our organisations. If we only see people in their (light blue) employee role, how can we ever fit them together in the best way possible? How can we enable people to work best together if we don't understand half of their capabilities and personal priorities?

It's only when we turn the pieces over and really get to know our colleagues that we can start to see where the pieces could best fit, and the true extent of what we can create together. It is then that we can start to build our jigsaw of full inclusion.

INVERTED PYRAMID EXERCISE

How can we make inclusion a reality?

INCLUSION

Inclusion is made real
through the rain
watering all of our crops
wherever they may be.
No preconditions,
no preferences,
reliably and consistently.

Inclusion is made real
through the sunshine
warming all of us
wherever we may be.
No preconditions,
no preferences,
reliably and consistently.

Inclusion is made real
through each of us
reaching out to others
wherever they may be.
No preconditions,
no preferences,
reliably and consistently.

PERSONAL DEVELOPMENT REFLECTION

1. At a personal level, who are you reaching out to?
2. Does your workplace have an inclusion policy? Does it focus on everyone or only on certain categories of people? How might you begin to change this?

CHAPTER 2: Time to harvest

Please take a moment to reflect and capture any initial thoughts, ideas, questions or action points that you wish to note and take forward. You will be able to gather these from each chapter for your personal development Action Plan at the end of the book.

Notes

1 ....

2 ....

3 ....

4 ....

5 ....

CHAPTER 3

What is the Inverted Pyramid of Pope Francis?

In this chapter we will outline the ten key principles that Francis has given for the development of his Inverted Pyramid Church and begin to reflect on what these might mean for each of us in the work that we do. And we will take a deeper look at how the Inverted Pyramid approach might work in our daily lives.

What is the Inverted Pyramid?

Pope Francis has a practical plan for building a world of inclusion. He is seeking change, for the Catholic Church to become more servant-led, with the idea of turning his organisation upside down, creating an Inverted Pyramid. But in laying out this framework, Francis is also inviting every organisation, business and hierarchal structure in the world to become more 'bottom-up'.

His model of global inclusion is based on three core concepts: working with others, looking after everyone and journeying as one. And it all begins with us. For at the heart of this global transformation is an invitation to each of us to create and grow our own personal Inverted Pyramid.

Together, we can grow our Inverted Pyramids from wherever we are. And then we can link all our Inverted Pyramids together in new ways.

It's a personal relationship approach rather than a corporate strategy. We can work together to build a global community of inclusion.

The Inverted Pyramid methodology is a completely different way of journeying together and using our skills and experience in a much more positive, creative and mutually supportive way. We need to bring joy back to everyday life. We need some good news on our phones and TV screens.

Inverted Pyramid relationships are driven by values of kindness and caring for one another. But do not make the mistake of thinking that this is a 'soft' option, for it is quite the opposite. When we work positively together with a spirit of friendship within our Inverted Pyramids, we are called to use all the skills, experience, knowledge and expertise that we have been given.

We are at last able to bring our own sense of passion and purpose fully to the work that really matters to us and to help others to do the same. We are no longer confined to bringing only part of ourselves to work. We are no longer trapped within traditional outdated hierarchal management structures with the same people and relationships. Francis has created a framework where we can live and work in a different way, help each other and create a better world for everyone.

It's a practical plan driven by the urgency that we have around us. We desperately need collaboration rather than competition, community rather than conflict. We need different and better connections. We need greater cooperation and companionship.

The last twenty years have shown us that we cannot continue to live in our own little bubbles and forget about everybody else. The idea that 'as long as we are okay, everything is okay' is no longer credible. We can no longer simply rely on an outdated economic model of the rich getting richer at the expense of the poor getting poorer. We cannot continue to destroy our environment simply to make more money. Nuclear conflict, global warming, food poverty and pandemics are all a reality.

If we don't change the way that we are, what will change? And who will bring about this change? Francis is giving us the tools that we need. He's inviting us to begin today, for we are the architects of inclusion.

So do not think of the Inverted Pyramid as something that our organisation will sort out and all will be well in the world. For inclusion is not simply about policies and processes. It's about how each one of us can work in a different way.

A bottom-up approach

When Pope Francis talked about an Inverted Pyramid and the idea of turning the Church upside down, many people in all sorts of organisations could identify with this bottom-up approach. The linking of servant leadership, empowerment and collaboration are the foundations of inclusion.

An Inverted Pyramid Church

In his homily on 17 October 2015, Pope Francis put forward a vision of the Church which he described as an 'Inverted Pyramid'. The traditional organisation structure has the Pope at the top of this pyramid, followed by cardinals, bishops and clergy, until we get to the laity at the bottom. Francis's vision was that the bishops and clergy would be servants of the people, with the laity at the top. Francis wants this renewal to come from below so that 'those who exercise authority are called "ministers", because, in the original meaning of the word, they are the "least of all"'.[i]

Throughout his pontificate, Pope Francis has repeatedly called for a synodal church, one where bishops, priests and people 'walk together' in a common mission. Francis sees synodality as what '...God expects of the Church in the third millennium'.[ii]

A two-year worldwide process of synodality began at the Vatican on 10 October 2021.

Ten key principles for the development of an Inverted Pyramid world

Francis outlined the following principles for this methodology:

1. We must journey together

The Book of Acts of the Apostles tells of a worldwide journey that started in Jerusalem, passed through Samaria and Judea, then on to the regions of Syria, Asia Minor, Greece and, of course, Rome.

2. We must work together with all others in new ways

Pope Francis calls on the clergy to get out of their seats and to journey in this way:

'*There is a certain resistance to moving beyond the image of a Church rigidly divided into leaders and followers, those who teach and those who are taught; we forget that God likes to overturn things: as Mary said, "He has thrown down the rulers from their thrones but lifted up the lowly" (Lk 1:52). Journeying together tends to be more horizontal than vertical; a synodal Church clears the horizon where Christ, our sun, rises, while erecting monuments to hierarchy covers it. Shepherds walk with their people: we shepherds walk with our people, at times in front, at times in the middle, at times behind. A good shepherd should move that way: in front to lead, in the middle to encourage and preserve the smell of the flock, and behind, since the people too have their own 'sense of smell'. They have a nose for finding new paths for the journey, or for finding the road when the way is lost. I want to emphasize this, also for the bishops and priests of the diocese. In this synodal process, they should ask: "Am I capable of walking, of moving, in front, in between and behind, or do I remain seated in my chair, with mitre and crozier?"'* [iii]

We are all shepherds. We are all called to walk 'in front, in between and behind' the flock. Francis sees us as no longer stuck in fixed roles. This is an important phrase when we come to look at the practical implementation and methodology of playing our part in the Inverted Pyramid. This will be our guiding principle on *how* we journey together and on *what* we do as we journey.

3. We must seek to include everyone

'Don't limit yourself to those who come to church or think as you do – they may be no more than 3, 4 or 5 percent. Let everyone come in... Go out and meet them, let them question you, let their questions become your questions. Journey together: the Spirit will lead you; trust in the Spirit. Do not be afraid to engage in dialogue and even to be taken aback by what you hear, for this is the dialogue of salvation. Don't be disheartened; be prepared for surprises.'[iv]

Taken together with Pope Francis's condemnation of clericalism and endorsement of 'co-responsibility', this seems to indicate that a major goal of the Synod is to disassemble the relationship between the laity and the clergy, moving toward a flatter, less hierarchal and more equal structure. The aim of this is to effectively give the laity (what we used to call) co-responsibility for all aspects of the operation and future development of the Church.

4. We must explain and ensure that the Inverted Pyramid is not about reforming internal Church structures

'Leave no one behind or excluded. It will be good for the Diocese of Rome and for the whole Church, which is not strengthened simply by reforming structures (that is the great illusion!) or by giving instructions, offering retreats and conferences, by issuing guidelines and programmes. All those things are good, but as part of something else, namely our rediscovery that we are a people meant to walk together, with one another and with all humanity.'[v]

5. We are a listening people

One of the things we learn in basic communication skills is that effective listening depends on showing a response to what is said to us. We must acknowledge the other person. We must nod or smile. We must make eye contact. We must engage with them. Otherwise, our listening simply becomes an information-gathering session. It does not progress to an ongoing discussion. It is not the foundation for building new relationships. At the heart of a listening Church we must have discussion, the development of new relationships and individual action, for how else are we going to build a Church for the third millennium?

So, it is important to differentiate a listening *Church* from a listening *people*. If we are to engage with others then we must do so at an individual and interpersonal level. If we 'listen' from a bureaucratic, administrative and hierarchal perspective then we are making a clear statement that we do not want to have discussions between bishops and people; we do not want to develop new types of relationships within our Inverted Pyramid; we do not want to encourage or empower others to take action, for this must be controlled by the bishops.

6. We must offer the Inverted Pyramid as a real alternative to the world

'A Synodal Process is a time to dialogue with people from the worlds of economics and science, politics and culture, arts and sport, the media and social initiatives. It will be a time to reflect on ecology and peace, life issues and migration. We must keep the bigger picture in view to fulfil our mission in the world.'[vi]

For what we are doing (and have done) in the world is simply not working. Global warming, poverty, migration, war, food shortages, increasing social inequality show us that we are interconnected. We see immediately the impact of one event in the world translated into our lives. Our 'firefighting' approach seems to lurch us from one world crisis to the next. We desperately need a different way of journeying together, one that offers us hope, friendship and real joy.

7. We must show action – not words

'*Love is shown more in deeds than in words.*' This is a common quote from St Ignatius Loyola, where he stresses that our love for each other is not simply about good intentions toward another person, but what we do to make things better for those who need our help.

8. The Inverted Pyramid is not about religion!

It's about creating a better, kinder and more caring way of working together, here and now. It's about building relationships, a better world and safer future for our children and grandchildren.

The Inverted Pyramid approach is so much more than the bishops trying to sort out the Catholic Church. It cannot be a tactic to try to save the institutional Church. It is not a piece of sticking plaster.

The Inverted Pyramid belongs to every organisation and to each of us. For, as we shall see, the Inverted Pyramid *is* each of us. The Inverted Pyramid is our path of personal development, our methodology for genuine and sustainable collaboration and our framework for building an inclusive world.

9. We do not need permission

The Inverted Pyramid turns the traditional hierarchal structure on its head. Instead of waiting for others to act or give us permission, Francis is calling on each of us to reach out, work together and build a world of inclusion. The Inverted Pyramid methodology provides a framework which helps us to link with others, to utilise our skills and experience, and to grow and develop in all areas of our lives.

The Inverted Pyramid is a personal development process. It's a business and organisation development process. It's a relationship process. It's a spiritual development process. It's a process that helps to build a safer, kinder and more inclusive world in which we all look after each other, our planet and our future together.

10. The Inverted Pyramid is all about each of us

Firstly, Francis chose his papal name after St Francis of Assisi, who was well known for looking after the little ones in society. The Pope's first priority is the poor, whoever they may be. He famously wants a 'poor Church for the poor' that reflects the love of Christ for the forgotten.

Secondly, Francis is renowned for his commitment to practical peace-building. This is about building a peaceful world where we work and collaborate on this vision.

Thirdly, Francis is seeking not only to build community among all peoples, but indeed with all creation. He talks about our common home, our relationship with the environment and the implications for the poorest in society.

Just as Francis of Assisi was called to 'rebuild God's Church,' his namesake's call to us is to reform the way we work together and the structures preventing us from building a world of inclusion, and also to reimagine our role in the world. The Inverted Pyramid might just be the most radical and far-reaching concept for the world since the time of Jesus himself.

A False Start

The process has two initial phases: a series of consultations held in local dioceses from October 2021–April 2022, followed by one held at the continental level from September 2022–March 2023. It will culminate in the 16th Ordinary General Assembly of the Synod of Bishops (the 'Synod on Synodality', which was originally planned to take place in October 2023. The Pope recently decided to split this into two parts with the second part a year later.

The bishops submitted the *National Synthesis Document* in June 2022, drawing together the emerging conclusions of this phase in preparation for the next stage of the process. The Synod of Bishops' Office received the summaries from all the world's 114 bishops' Conferences, synthesising the experiences, questions, discussions and insights that emerged from their parishes and dioceses.

The second or 'continental' phase of the process began in September 2022, during which the Synod of Bishops' Office group together the bishops' Conference reports by continent before drafting a document highlighting the priorities and core issues which will emerge on a broader scale.

Each continental document will go back to the local bishops' Conference for forwarding to the local, parish and diocesan levels for a period of reflection, listening, dialogue and discernment that responds to and enriches the document from the Synod Office. Those responses will then be returned to the Synod of Bishops' Office and will form the foundation for building the working document for the general assembly of the Synod of Bishops in October 2023 and 2024.

The 16th Ordinary General Assembly of the Synod of Bishops will be held in two sessions, spaced one year apart: the first from October 4 to 29, 2023, the second in October 2024.

The current process, designed and implemented by the bishops, gives people little say in decision-making, planning and organising, taking the initiative, addressing priorities, developing local strategies etc. The laity have been asked to sit and wait some 18 months to see what the bishops decide. So much for engagement and empowerment.

Responding to Francis

In response to Francis's call, the Catholic Church tried to implement an Inverted Pyramid approach by introducing a process of Synodality developed by the bishops. The worldwide consultation offered the opportunity for people to engage at a local level, but there were some shortcomings with its design.

First, the process treated people as subjects rather than as partners. In other words, people were asked preformatted questions. The Church was simply gathering information so that the bishops could redesign from the top. Secondly, only a small percentage (of Catholics) took part, presumably those most committed to the Church. It certainly did not seek to be fully inclusive in terms of reaching out to the whole world. And thirdly, after the sessions many people were asking, 'What happens next? What do we do now?' They were not allowed to take ownership or influence the development of the process, as would be integral to an Inverted Pyramid approach. They were once again left stranded at the bottom of the pyramid. Francis must be tearing his hair out!

Back to our Case Study

We all need to think through the process of how we might work together in an Inverted Pyramid way. We need to understand what we mean by an Inverted Pyramid organisational approach and how it can work in practice. We need to train people to understand their roles, responsibilities and opportunities within the new arrangements.

How do we as individuals behave differently in an Inverted Pyramid organisation? What do we actually do? How do we work together? How do we build at a local level and online? How do we ensure that everyone is included in this process? How do we connect different Inverted Pyramids in our communities and across the world?

And, if this is a truly bottom-up process, how do we address the traditional mindset of control and authority that exists in all sorts of organisations? How do we map out our transition from a hierarchal approach to one which is empowered by those we seek to serve? How do we ensure that this is truly servant leadership in line with the vision of Francis? These are just some of the questions that we will discuss in this book. And then, I hope, we can begin our Inverted Pyramid journeying together.

Work it Out!

At the same time as Pope Francis was writing about the Inverted Pyramid, Jimmy Ryan and I were managing a range of independent *Work it Out!* pilots for Diversiton across both the public and private sectors. At the heart of the *Work it Out!* model is an engagement and working together process using an upside down triangle – or Inverted Pyramid – approach. The training was based on my book from 2011 of the same name.

We were also working with the Minister of the Department for Rural and Community Development in the Republic of Ireland to implement a programme to support people in local deprived communities using the *Work it Out!* methodology.

Following a successful pilot in 2017 in Clonmel, the Irish government provided three years of special project funding to Diversiton to build an inclusive bottom-up approach to empowering local people who were looking to develop their future, find work, start a business, support their local community – or who were just stuck. It was a broad mix! The process enabled people to build their futures not by chasing jobs but by focusing on their core skills and interests and working together to help each other succeed.

Jimmy and I worked with communities in County Waterford and County Tipperary. The pilots refined a clear methodology of how we can bring people together from different backgrounds, different age groups and different experiences to work collaboratively together for a common purpose. The aim of the Inverted Pyramid is to help people to build a career, develop their future together and ultimately to become more of what they really wanted to be and to do what was most important to them.

The first year of the project was in Carrick-on-Suir which had a large migrant population at the time, and integration was a key aspect of this. This was followed by further local area-based initiatives in Tipperary Town and Roscrea. In parallel with this, Diversiton delivered a range of Inverted Pyramid initiatives within local councils and for a range of companies who were keen to build effective inclusion strategies.

We followed a number of principles including being individually driven (bottom-up), accepting everyone who wanted to join (opting in), imposing no financial costs on participants and mixing everyone together. This was often quite a surprise to many, because there is an assumption that if we're training business people and migrants, for example, we should train them all in their own specific group types rather than blending them.

Much of the learning from the *Work it Out!* process is directly relevant to implementing an Inverted Pyramid methodology across all sectors, including community, business and education, as well as with individuals directly.

In Section Two we will explore the skills and behaviours for building our personal Inverted Pyramids, and in Section Three we will look more closely at the practical application of the methodology in various sectors. The *Work it Out!* Inverted Pyramid programmes continue to be delivered internationally and are now licensed to organisations, businesses and government agencies to help them to support those they work with.

CHAPTER 3: Time to harvest

Please take a moment to reflect and capture any initial thoughts, ideas, questions or action points that you wish to note and take forward. You will be able to gather these from each chapter for your personal development Action Plan at the end of the book.

Notes

1 ....

2 ....

3 ....

4 ....

5 ....

How does the Inverted Pyramid work?

The Inverted Pyramid

The typical management structure is a hierarchal 'pyramid' with the boss at the top and the staff organised beneath him or her in layers. Our roles are clearly defined, from the most 'senior' down to the least important. We are given titles and job descriptions that hold us in our place and ensure we fulfil our responsibilities. What we can and can't do is tightly controlled. We are accountable to the person we report to. We know who we shouldn't talk to and what we shouldn't challenge. Many of us work in this type of structure every day.

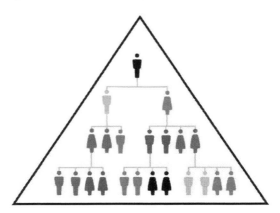

Traditional hierarchal management structure

With the Inverted Pyramid we turn the organisation structure upside down. We turn the triangle of control and authority on its head. Power is shared with each person. Individuals are now free to reach out and meet with all others, wherever they are, in order to work on priority projects and initiatives.

We don't wait to be told what to do because the process starts with us. We have a responsibility and are expected to use our skills and experience to reach out to others and to work together in a positive and proactive way. Individuals work collaboratively, create new initiatives and drive them forward together.

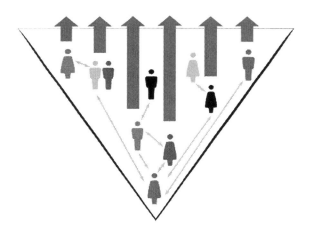

The Inverted Pyramid

In the traditional hierarchal structure, the limitations for action and pressure to conform are created by the organisational culture and reinforced by the accepted routines, reporting and ways of working. The pressures are all inwards, typically directed on our job roles and tasks.

With the Inverted Pyramid we are drawn upwards and outwards to others more freely. It's like taking the lid off a jar of bees. Our creative freedom is facilitated by the Inverted Pyramid way of working, allowing us to take greater personal responsibility. We are no longer limited by reporting lines but can contribute to the development of the organisation in a bigger way.

The Inverted Pyramid Process

1. It starts with each individual.
2. We reach out and link with others, get to know them and identify areas of common interest. We create our first Inverted Pyramid Team.
3. We work together (think of round tables). We have discussions, develop our ideas and formulate a way forward for our initiative.
4. We look to build wider collaboration and inclusion internally and externally. There is no 'top' of the Inverted Pyramid.

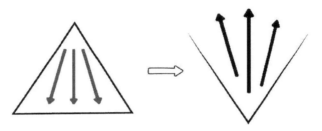

The traditional hierarchy AND the Inverted Pyramid

The traditional hierarchy in an organisation represents a STRUCTURE. The Inverted Pyramid, however, represents a PROCESS. The two do not conflict with each other and in fact are complementary.

The reporting structure facilitates the organisation's functioning and day-to-day operations. The development of more effective linkages, relationships and new initiatives comes through the Inverted Pyramid processes.

Whereas a normal focus of a traditional hierarchy is on the reporting relationships (represented by levels and titles), the focus of the Inverted Pyramid is on the connections between people, wherever they are, and the creation of tangible outputs from these.

We will discuss later the practicalities of putting this into place so that every organisation can have the best of both worlds.

What is the Inverted Pyramid way of working?

Our values, behaviours and ways of working, which underpin our activities, are set out below. Every member is committed to taking personal responsibility for each of the elements listed.

1. We are a proactive and collaborative community where everybody is equally important. We value each person and work to enable everyone to achieve what is important to them.
2. We help people to build themselves up. We encourage them. We congratulate them. We ask how they are. We are interested in what they are doing – always, at every opportunity.
3. We are continually grateful for the help and support of others. We recognise that others give of their time and expertise at no cost and we share our expressions of gratitude as often and as freely as we can. We know that the Inverted Pyramid is a precious gift and never take the activities, events, training or support for granted.
4. We share our successes, however small or insignificant these may seem to us. We recognise that they are building blocks for us and encouragement for others.
5. We link with others. This may be for a particular workpiece, because we are learning a new skill, because of something they need or because of where they live. There are many reasons to link up based on the needs of others, our mutual priorities and our own development.

6. We look after everyone in the group. We are kind. It's okay for someone to just be in the group, particularly if they're going through something difficult. The group is a place of friendship, support, respite and growth.
7. We attend meetings. It is our responsibility to participate in all meetings. Life happens and the odd miss is fine, but we are conscious that our input is needed to continue to build the community. If we are unable to be present at a meeting, we let others know. Indeed, we value the fact that someone else may be turning up simply because we are there.
8. We recognise that we all develop as individuals on our own path, in our own way, in our own time and at our own pace. We are not in competition with each other. Sometimes we have to be patient with others.
9. We always use positive language. Positivity is a cornerstone of our way of being. Irrespective of what may have happened or not happened, our approach is always to look forward.
10. We never try to sell to each other. We share our skills, knowledge, products and services at no cost to help others in our Inverted Pyramid Teams to succeed.
11. We bring in new people to our groups so that we can share with them and help them. We work actively to grow our Inverted Pyramids and to make their benefits available to others.
12. We build the Inverted Pyramid structure by looking for opportunities to develop and support local Inverted Pyramid Teams in new areas.
13. We promote each other. We introduce people who can help with the interests and plans of others. We like and share social media posts by others. We link to people from our websites.
14. We continue to grow and succeed by operating in this way at all times. If someone is not acting in accordance with the above points, we gently remind them of the expected Inverted Pyramid values and behaviour.

15. We read and act directly in line with this list of values and behaviours on a regular basis to ensure that each of us is fully playing our part and continually bringing new energy and focus to our teams. This is our personal audit, yardstick and commitment.

Linking with others

We can begin by building relationships with others to develop our understanding around needs, priorities and passions. In this way we begin to create our own personal Inverted Pyramid project, which in turn helps others to build theirs. Our personal Inverted Pyramid expands and blossoms upwards and outwards from us.

We can create Inverted Pyramid linkages in several key ways:

- **Idea-driven links**
  You have an idea and so you reach out to others to discuss this. From here you might develop your idea or project initiative further and add new people to your Inverted Pyramid Team.

- **Relationship-driven links**
  In relationship-driven links, you already know people such as friends or work colleagues. Through these friendships or work relationships you will hopefully find it easy to introduce a new idea, ask for opinions or seek advice on how to move your thinking forward.

- **Opportunity-driven links**
  Opportunity-driven links arise out of your reaction to something that happens, whether in your workplace, home life, local community or indeed the wider world.

- **Personally driven links**
  We all have skills and experience that can support others. We all have a passion for something. We can build our career in line

with our gifts and what's important to us by actively developing new and additional Inverted Pyramid Teams.

With the Inverted Pyramid structure, we are encouraged to reach out and discuss ideas, opportunities and challenges with our colleagues. As always, it starts with a personal relationship. So, we meet with different people, get to know them and form new groups to take forward, test and develop our ideas or suggestions.

Round Tables

We sit around the table, listen to each other and discuss ideas. Round tables are essential because they do not have someone in charge, sitting at the head of the table. Likewise on video calls, it is important to put people into breakout rooms so that they can get to know each other, build relationships and share ideas. These breakout rooms are virtual round tables.

Understanding responsibilities and roles

The Inverted Pyramid is not simply about turning your current organisation structure upside down. In Pope Francis's example, it is not about putting the Pope and the bishops at the bottom and the laity at the very top. If we do this, the laity are still waiting for permission to start that journey, or for approval to take action to filter up from the bottom of the Pyramid. Those traditionally at the top of the hierarchy are still 'in charge'.

The Inverted Pyramid is about us all as individuals being 'centre stage', with the opportunity to act, to reach out, to build links, to serve others and to grow our business or Church together. It doesn't matter if we are a priest or a businessperson or a teacher or a mother. We are all called to act in our own way, where we are now.

It is from where we are now that we build our Inverted Pyramid projects and develop our communities. Our roles and projects may all be different, but our responsibilities are the same. Our process of linking and connecting is the same. Inclusion calls on us to reach out from where we are now to help all others.

Put your hands together

If you make a Λ shape with your hands, you can easily see how we can become trapped within a traditional hierarchal structure. If you make a **V** shape with your hands, you can see how we can all be open to each other and grow upwards together.

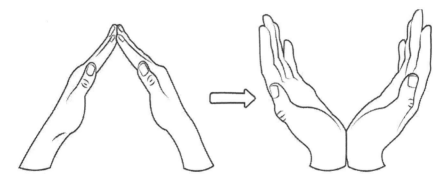

Not structure but process – equal engagement

The idea of an Inverted Pyramid is useful for emphasising the concept or idea of a servant organisation, but we have to distinguish this from the process of how we actually achieve it. Whereas we were 'trapped' before at the bottom of a hierarchal structure, we are now free to grow and develop in our own way. What's more, we have a responsibility to do this.

Not organisational but relationship – servant leadership

The Inverted Pyramid allows us to move away from the concept of fixed tiers and levels of seniority which separate us in the traditional structure, for we all begin to grow our own Inverted Pyramid in the way that we meet and work with others. Fixed tiers and levels of seniority are replaced with an openness from everyone.

We are all servants of others, and it is through and with others that we journey. Our roles in the Church, business or education may support this interaction, but do not give us authority over others.

Bottom-up

The key phrase that matters here is 'bottom-up'. You can't have a bottom-up Church if the laity is at the top of the pyramid! The Inverted Pyramid is about our process of engagement, not a description of where we sit in an organisation framework.

The upward and outward trajectory of communication and links drives the cumulative growth and sustainability of our worldwide community of inclusion.

Understanding our connections

Our own individual journey with others starts when we accept the invitation and commence our process by reaching out.

Once this process begins, we can see how so much can open up to us in terms of possible

connections, conversations and initiatives. The double-headed arrows between people in the Inverted Pyramid demonstrate how we actively work with and alongside everyone by linking up with one or two others and listening, to create our Inverted Pyramid Teams. Each of us is invited to walk '*in front, in between and behind*' others in their own way, for every action that we take brings us closer to a global community of kindness and collaboration.

Our individual call

When we begin our journey with others, we too will be building our Inverted Pyramid of empowerment. Our Inverted Pyramid Teams will be identifying needs, creating initiatives, linking people together, discussing new ideas and working on the areas that matter to each of us.

But this is so much more than working together and building initiatives. While doing all of this, we will be developing new positive relationships that can support us now and in the future. It is this support structure that will help us when things get tough. Journeying together is a place of being beyond words and activity. It's a place of friendship, joy and love.

Who will be the first people that you reach out to as you build your Inverted Pyramid? What will you discuss? What would you like to see as the first initiative or project that you work on?

In the Inverted Pyramid, it all starts with us. It's all in our hands. And this is where we are right now. We are ready to connect with one or two people and begin our conversations. And from this, others will help us to build further links as we develop different ideas, projects, groups, initiatives, training.

Imagine when we have thousands and millions of individuals participating in this way. Imagine the energy and the impact generated. Imagine the good works that will be fulfilled. And imagine the message of love, compassion and mercy that spills out across the world, at a time when it is so urgently needed. The whole world can become one huge Inverted Pyramid made up of millions of pyramids.

This is where we all start, no matter who we are – reaching out to work with all others, to listen, to help, to support and to be of service through all that we are. It's the invitation of a lifetime.

The Inverted Pyramid is:

- A clearly defined way of looking after each other and working collaboratively
- A clear statement of personal responsibility for building a global community of love
- A framework for equal participation and full inclusion
- A recognition that each individual has a unique role to play in line with our gifts and talents
- An invitation to begin now.

The Inverted Pyramid is not:

- An organisation structure
- A model which separates people into levels or categories based on salary or seniority
- A framework in which people are managed by, or dependent upon, a hierarchal Church administration, corporate business model or indeed any external structure.

Values and intentions are great, but how do we turn these into actual day-to-day behaviours which form the fabric of who we are and how our organisation works? This is the challenge we will address later.

The Inverted Pyramid is not just a new model or approach. It's a whole new framework encompassing many other disciplines and allowing us to utilise what we already know in a much more effective and impactful way. It's a different way of thinking. And once we understand this, we start to build our overall competency in the way that we think, behave and work with others. It's also not a bolt-on HR initiative – it's a different way of working and of being.

If we try to implement this new way of working half-heartedly, we will see a clash with the old top-down methodology and control way of working. We will resort to old behaviours. The Inverted Pyramid process is embedded in the way that we communicate and seek to help each other. It is this positive act of reaching out and working together that is primary, not the systems, processes and frameworks of the traditional hierarchal pyramid.

The huge benefit is that we are all learning this together, and every organisation, irrespective of size, can inform and help us to build new approaches and new ways in. We simply need to link with others, not just in our own sector but especially in sectors that are different to ours.

Implementing the Inverted Pyramid approach

Many organisations are keen to build community, to become more outward-looking and better connected to those they serve, to build bottom-up processes and encourage staff to take greater responsibility. All of this is captured in the Inverted Pyramid approach. But we have to turn vague concepts and ideas into robust and effective working practices. And this is where the challenge is real.

The development of the Inverted Pyramid way of working is a process in itself. It hasn't arrived as a preformed, ready-packaged 'Let's implement this!' discipline. Rather, its form is an invitation for each of us to help develop, build and grow the process as we go. One of the frustrations for many organisations that I've worked with is that they want things all mapped out for them in advance. But because this process is owned and led by individuals, the direction, timescales and impact are personal to them, rather than part of some plan that the organisation might seek to impose. For that would take us back to a top-down approach.

Standard approach

Many years ago, when I was giving training courses on Religion and Belief within organisations, many managers wanted a set of rules to follow to help them do the right thing for each religious tradition. But it doesn't work like that. There are no textbook Hindus, Muslims or Jews. There are only people, and each person relates to their faith in their own way. Some are fervent believers, others much more relaxed in their approach. Some are very traditional, others more flexible.

And so, when a company asked me, 'Do we need a Prayer Room?' my answer was always, 'Well, have you asked the people concerned? For if you only have two Muslims in your business, then they may feel under a lot of pressure to pray five times every day! They may not want to stand out from their colleagues in this way. They may not welcome the responsibility of representing their faith tradition so openly.' We must remember that the interpersonal interaction always trumps the transactional process.

INVERTED PYRAMID EXERCISE

Are we all working together?

OURSELVES AND OTHERS

When we talk about personal development
we think about ourselves.
When we talk about inclusion
we think about others.
When we talk about the Inverted Pyramid
we think about all of us, and how we work together.

PERSONAL DEVELOPMENT REFLECTION

1. How would you describe the Inverted Pyramid to your colleagues?
2. How do you see the link between the Inverted Pyramid and personal development?

CHAPTER 4: Time to harvest

Please take a moment to reflect and capture any initial thoughts, ideas, questions or action points that you wish to note and take forward. You will be able to gather these from each chapter for your personal development Action Plan at the end of the book.

Notes

1 ....

2 ....

3 ....

4 ....

5 ....

CHAPTER 5

Dual Responsibility

At the heart of the Inverted Pyramid methodology is the concept of Dual Responsibility. In this chapter we will uncover the historical evolution of Dual Responsibility and what it means in practical terms for building a better way of working together.

Dual Responsibility

Dual Responsibility, as the name implies, means that we each have TWO responsibilities as part of building the Inverted Pyramid of Inclusion:

1. To care for ourselves and become all that is important to us. We do this with and through others, as we build our learning and grow our personal Inverted Pyramids (or Social Meitheal).
2. To care for everyone else in the world. We do this with every person that we connect with through our openness to them, showing interest in what they do and where they are at, being positive and supportive, suggesting ideas, offering help, building links and developing initiatives together.

Dual Responsibility means that we are responsible for making the most of the opportunity of life given to us. It requires us not only to make the best of the skills and gifts given to us but also to care equally for every other person in our family, group, business, community and, indeed, the world. Dual Responsibility give us the biggest canvas to paint with.

Dual Responsibility helps us to map out our sphere of influence, gives life to our creativity and so brings our thoughts and ideas to fruition. We cannot succeed in isolation.

Demolishing limiting beliefs

Dual Responsibility enables our thinking to become more outward-looking. When we only think about ourselves, we tend to play the same tape of limiting beliefs over and over in our head - ideas like:

- I am no good at...
- I haven't got enough money
- I will never find work in...
- That won't work for me...
- I will never lose weight...
- I can't get the sort of job I want...
- Nobody will hire me...
- I'm no good at this.
- I'll never be able to do that.

It is easy for us to build up and continually reinforce our own set of limiting beliefs. Many of us have been conditioned to have an attitude of scarcity rather than abundance, and so we limit ourselves not just with regard to our own potential, but also the impact that we can have with and through others. We try to work out why we are stuck, unable to shift our lives or make the changes that we can see are necessary.

But we do have a choice. When we decide to take responsibility to work together and help others, we find that we are now free to move forward with an outward-looking perspective. We look to solve problems and create options for others. We find ourselves being more proactive and positive. We suggest ideas that others may not have thought of. Why can't Person A link up with Person B to do something new? Here are some ideas for Person C. We become enablers. We become creative problem-solvers. We build our confidence. We develop our presentation skills. We become more by reaching out to help others:

- Could we...?
- Maybe John could link up with us and see if...?
- Why don't we look at...?
- Would it be possible to...?
- Maybe I could help with that...?

We shift into a collaborative project-helper mode as we learn about and from others, find out what they are trying to do, see where they are stuck and suggest ways forward. By taking responsibility for helping others, we free up our brain to explore more, to take on new challenges and to build success in new ways.

All of this in turn has two major impacts. Firstly, others do the same for our skills and situation. We now have a team suggesting ways to move forward, add value, address our priorities and work on what is important to us.

And secondly, our sense of value increases as we experience how others view our knowledge, abilities and potential. Working in a positive and collaborative way with those who look after us can help to unlock our potential and demolish our limiting beliefs. The shift from a solitary surviving mentality to one of an interpersonal facilitator is one that enables everything to change, for us and for others.

Collaborative working

The Inverted Pyramid methodology thrives when we all work together with a sense of Dual Responsibility. Dual Responsibility normalises and mainstreams the idea of helping others, by enabling us to feel comfortable stepping out of our own situation and providing an environment for effective collaborative living. We allow our brains the opportunity to be creative and to solve problems. We become more at ease with who we are. We encourage and welcome ideas from others.

We are grateful that others are offering their help, sharing their ideas and being supportive.

Dual Responsibility within the Inverted Pyramid way of working encourages us:

- to help and work with each other
- to be kind and compassionate, for we do not know what others are carrying
- to be positive and encouraging and so to empower others
- to share our skills, experience and ideas
- to help each other build a balance of paid and unpaid work to support ourselves, and
- to be successful in all that is important to us.

The age of mutual success

The old world of work was highly structured. Jobs existed for many years. People had long-term security in the one company or organisation. For many, their career plan could be predicted and they knew their path forward.

The new world of work is a deconstructed one and is moving rapidly away from the standard model of a typical hierarchal organisation (which does not see the care of others as its main priority). It's now more about individuals taking greater control and responsibility and connecting with others all over the world to build their futures, and much of this is facilitated by the Internet.

The hierarchal structure of organisations and societies that we were used to is now rapidly being replaced by new models, structures, frameworks, communities, teams and networks. It's a levelling up, not a dropping down.

It's all part of a different way of working and being.

The evolution of Dual Responsibility

The evolution of Dual Responsibility can be seen in numerous concepts and value systems, such as:

- the Golden Rule (Ethic of Reciprocity)
- the Platinum Rule
- the Social Meitheal
- Paying It Forward
- Giving Back
- Leaving A Legacy

We will touch briefly on each of these below and then address how we can 'normalise' and mainstream key behaviours that will help us to use deliberate acts of kindness as a core operating value to build our Inverted Pyramid of Inclusion.

The Golden Rule (Ethic of Reciprocity)

Religious groups and philosophical traditions can differ significantly in their beliefs and practices. However, there is near common agreement among all religions, philosophies and belief systems that each person should treat others as they would like to be treated. This is known as the Golden Rule, sometimes referred to as the Ethic of Reciprocity – the practice of exchanging and sharing with others for mutual benefit.

Here are some examples:

Bahá'í Faith: *Blessed is he who preferreth his brother before himself.* Baha'u'llah

Buddhism: *Hurt not others in ways that you yourself would find hurtful.* Udana-Varga 5:18

Christianity: *Do to others as you would have them do to you.* Luke 6:31, New International Version

Confucianism: *Do not do to others what you do not want them to do to you.* Analects 15:23

Hinduism: *This is the sum of dharma* [duty]: *do not do to others what would cause pain if done to you.* Mahabharata 5:1517

Humanism: *Don't do things you wouldn't want to have done to you.* British Humanist Society

Islam: *None of us* [truly] *believes until he wishes for his brother what he wishes for himself.* Number 13 of Imam Al-Nawawi's Forty Hadiths

Jainism: *In happiness and suffering, in joy and grief, we should regard all creatures as we regard our own self.* Lord Mahavira, 24th Tirthankara

Judaism: *...thou shalt love thy neighbour as thyself.* Leviticus 19:18

Native American Spirituality: *Do not wrong or hate your neighbour. For it is not he who is wrong, but yourself.* Pima proverb.

Roman Pagan Religion: *The law imprinted on the hearts of all men is to love the members of society as themselves.*

Shinto: *Be charitable to all beings; love is the representative of God.* Ko-ji-ki Hachiman Kasuga

Sikhism: *No one is my enemy, none a stranger and everyone is my friend.* Guru Arjan Dev : AG 1299

Sufism: *The basis of Sufism is consideration of the hearts and feelings of others. If you haven't the will to gladden someone's heart, then at least beware lest you hurt someone's heart, for on our path, no sin exists but this.* Dr. Javad Nurbakhsh, Master of the Nimatullahi Sufi Order

Taoism: *Regard your neighbour's gain as your own gain, and your neighbour's loss as your own loss.* T'ai Shang Kan Ying P'ien.

Zoroastrianism: *Whatever is disagreeable to yourself do not do unto others.* Shayast-na-Shayast 13:29

And some philosophers' statements:

Seneca: *Treat your inferiors as you would be treated by your superiors.* Epistle 47:11 (Rome, 1st century CE)

Plato: *May I do to others as I would that they should do unto me.* (Greece, 4th century BCE)

Kant: *Act as if the maxim of thy action were to become by thy will a universal law of nature.*

The Platinum Rule

The Platinum Rule adapts and extends the Golden Rule by focusing more fully on the other person. Instead of saying that we should treat others as **we** would like to be treated, the Platinum Rule encourages us to treat others as **they** would like to be treated.

This encourages us to be mindful of what is meaningful to others when we invite them to link and work with us. We should consider what is important to them and what is happening with them at this time. The Platinum Rule is particularly important when we look at building community within organisations.

The challenge in building inclusion is that reciprocity does not 'live within' (or indeed stagnate within) this small gathering of two or three people, but is magnified and extended as we continue to work together and reach on outwards to others. This is Dual Responsibility.

Dual Responsibility builds on the Platinum Rule by looking also at the collective benefit to the whole community or group. It is a clear value statement of how everyone can support the wider group or community as well as contributing to individual situations as we all look after each other.

The Social Meitheal

The word *Meitheal* (pronounced meh-hill) describes the old Irish tradition where from time immemorial, people in rural communities gathered on a neighbour's farm to help save the hay or some other crop. Each person would help their neighbour, who would in turn reciprocate. They brought different levels and types of skills, experience and equipment (technology) to the collective – some were better than others at specific activities, and over time, some became known locally as specialists in that area. They acted as a team and everybody benefited in some way. Those who prepared the food were equally as important as those out in the fields.

It is worth reflecting upon our modern corporate structure with its fabric of inequality defining each person by seniority, job title and remuneration – leading us to value individual contribution and respect staff in different ways.

Strong relationships and respect were built up by those in the Meitheal. They worked hard, were fed and watered, and these events were usually looked forward to as times of great fun and camaraderie. The Meitheal principle still lives on in many areas to the present time, where local groups are established on a bottom-up basis, driven by people journeying and working together for the common good.

It typifies some of the many great Irish community *sean fhocals* or proverbs such as *Faoi scáth a chéile a mhaireann na ndaoine*: *The people live in each other's shadow*, or *Ní neart go cur le chéile*: *There is no strength without coming together*.

A Social Meitheal also very aptly and succinctly describes the spirit that underpins and permeates the Inverted Pyramid way of being and behaving.

INVERTED PYRAMID EXERCISE

What can I share with others?

PAY IT FORWARD

The gifts
you have received
are here to be shared
with others.

The experience
you have been through
is here to be shared
with others.

The wealth
you have gathered
is here to be shared
with others.

The love
you are
is here to be shared
with others.

PERSONAL DEVELOPMENT REFLECTION

1. What are your gifts, experience, wealth and love?
2. How do you pay it forward?

Giving back

The Inverted Pyramid is limitless in its scope and reach. The Internet in particular has made amazing connections possible. This is a gift to our generation. We can link up with anyone, anywhere in the world with an opportunity of engagement, support and collaboration.

What this ultimately means is that we will no longer have to wait for traditional hierarchal organisations to sort out the issues in the world. We can work together to build multiple interconnected and overlapping creative structures that go to the heart of the things which are important to us.

INVERTED PYRAMID EXERCISE

Is it time to return all that has been lent to you?

GIVE BACK

Give back to the world
all that you have received
with interest,
before you die.

Share the love that
has been given to you.
Pass it all onto
future generations.

Inspire all others
with your encouragement,
your kindness and
how you help others.

Give back to the world
all your love
so that it can grow forever,
before it is too late.

Leaving a legacy

Some people leave a financial bequest in their will to benefit a good cause after they die. But our legacy is much more than the money we leave behind. Our legacy is the ongoing and cumulative impact of what we do, today and every day.

INVERTED PYRAMID EXERCISE

How can we build our legacy?

LEGACY MANAGER

Pick a project every day,
a priority activity
that you will focus upon.

It might be writing something
or fixing something
or creating something.

It could be helping someone
or talking to someone
or working with someone.

This will be our achievement
and success from today,
and every day from now on.

Pick a project today
and every day.
And watch your legacy grow.

PERSONAL DEVELOPMENT REFLECTION
1. What is your project for today?
2. What is your legacy from today, from this week and from this month?

Deliberate acts of kindness

Random acts of kindness are often spontaneous. We see someone in need and we reach out to help them. It is a reactive kindness. We have an endless supply of kindness within each of us to call on when we need it.

However, instead of being reactive (and random) in our kindness we can have a proactive (deliberate) approach to kindness. This is where we set out to be kind in every interaction. Our kindness spills over and flows freely into our interpersonal relationships.

Deliberate acts of kindness encourage and enable us to go beyond the transactional nature of many day-to-day interactions. Chatting with people, smiling, offering to help and encouraging others are amazing acts of kindness that we all have and can freely share.

We can choose in every interaction either to be kind or to be transactional. It costs nothing to smile, to ask how the person is or to offer to help. Kindness can help not only to bring a sense of humanity and human connection into other people's lives but also onwards into our world. Showing kindness to those we meet each day is our doorway to inclusion. Putting it simply, we cannot have inclusion if we are not kind to each other. Inclusion starts with us.

The Mexican Wave of Kindness

When we interact with someone in a spirit of kindness, we have an immediate impact on them and potentially on others too. Indeed, the impact for that person can be significant and may be seen in their subsequent interactions with those around them.

I am reminded of many football matches I have attended where the crowd creates a Mexican Wave in the stadium or arena, in which each person stands up and sits down in turn. By acting a split second after the person beside them, the individual movements create the impression of a large wave going around the stadium. And we know that waves have energy!

This wave has an energy for both giver and receiver, and potentially for others as well, as their combined goodness spreads onwards. When we bring hundreds, thousands and millions of deliberate acts of kindness together, we create an incredibly powerful, effective and indeed visual Mexican Wave of Kindness.

To build, grow and promote kindness as a force for good, we must be explicit about the goodness that we share. In other words, not only do we show kindness to others, we also encourage them to use their own stock of kindness. We have to ensure that the person that we help continues a 'chain reaction' and becomes part of the larger Mexican Wave, passing the behaviours and benefits of kindness onto others. This is how we leverage our own acts of kindness and connect to Dual Responsibility, for we are all responsible for looking after and helping each other.

When someone is kind to us, it is our turn to stand up and continue the Mexican Wave of Kindness so that eventually it spreads around the world.

Compound kindness

When we help someone, we can do this with the perspective of Dual Responsibility. For in helping you, I want both of us now to go on and continue to help many others. Together we can all build a helping community. For kindness is not just a personal commodity between two people but the (Mexican) wave of love that connects and flows between all of us.

And as you and I go on to help others, we can encourage them also to share their endless stock of acts of kindness with others. They too can join the community of the Inverted Pyramid. And now we can see how the Inverted Pyramid enables and invites us to build compound kindness on a scale we have never seen (or perhaps imagined) before.

And every single one of us can do this, irrespective of income, background, situation, status or experience. We can reach out to those beside us with deliberate acts of kindness, encourage each other and work together as part of a much bigger arena.

Kindness is the fuel of the Inverted Pyramid

The Inverted Pyramid, with its concepts of Dual Responsibility, connecting with each other and linking upwards and outwards to create inclusion, is essentially fuelled by kindness. And it is through kindness that we experience the generosity, thoughtfulness, practical help and love of others.

Kindness is an action that is freely available to each of us, to be used wherever and whenever we choose. We each have an inexhaustible stock of kindness acts in our warehouse ready for distribution. Kindness is an attribute of love itself.

Interpersonal asset

Up to now, our individual or isolated acts of kindness (often called random acts of kindness) could easily become dissipated and forgotten in our troubled world and everyday lives. However, our unending stock of deliberate acts of kindness offers us an interpersonal asset which is created when we help one another. Through the Inverted Pyramid approach, we can utilise and leverage this interpersonal asset to encourage others to create a Mexican Wave of Kindness with us and others that we go on to meet.

Every single person we get to know can help us to build a worldwide community of kindness. You see, kindness is the '*fabric of how we work together*', our '*explicit invitation to others to work with us*' and our asset '*for building love in our world*'.

The interpersonal asset of kindness helps to make the principles of Dual Responsibility, the Golden Rule, the Social Meitheal, Giving Back and Paying It Forward our regular approach to each other. Kindness is a deliberate way of being that drives our interactions with others as we build our global community of inclusion. The way that we work with others is kindness. Kindness is who we are.

And as we work together and build our fabric of kindness, we create greater strategic leverage for everyone.

CHAPTER 5: Time to harvest

Please take a moment to reflect and capture any initial thoughts, ideas, questions or action points that you wish to note and take forward. What are your main reflections from Section One?

Notes

1 ....

2 ....

3 ....

4 ....

5 ....

SECTION 2

Moving from Transactional Interactions to Interpersonal Relationships

The Inverted Pyramid offers a different way of interacting with others. How can we move from a *transactional* way of working to building sustainable *interpersonal relationships*? Section Two sets out the transformational skills and behaviours in our everyday interactions that enable us to build meaningful collaboration.

CHAPTER 6

Shifting from transactional behaviour to interpersonal relationships

Transactional, transformational, interpersonal

When we speak of transactional activity, we mean the series of steps required to complete a task or process, something like a recipe or the directions on a Google map.

The key operating framework of life in general (and certainly in organisations) is one of transactions. It's about getting things done. It's about the tasks and what we need to do. What we often miss out with this approach is the development of interpersonal relationships.

An interpersonal relationship means exactly what it says. It's a personal (not work) conversation and connection between (inter) two people. Interpersonal relationships are the foundation of inclusion.

The process of moving from transactional behaviours to interpersonal relationships is called **transformation**. It's how we can transform any transactional interaction, using our initiative or style of response. We initiate, take control or respond in an unexpected way. In other words, we step outside the transaction with, for example, a comment, a smile, a facial expression, a question, a gesture or an offer of help.

At the core of the Inverted Pyramid process is the shift from transactional activities to interpersonal relationships. This shift comes through transformational behaviour by each one of us. We are the drivers and facilitators of this process.

Let's look at a practical example.

Begging isn't just about money

Jenny, a good friend, told me this story recently: 'I just gave the tenner I had to a very old lady begging on a London Underground train. She was a hoot! She was saying, "Anyone got any food but not apples love, cos me teeth can't eat apples"! She then got off the train to go to McDonalds and stood on the platform waving me off – to the amusement of the other passengers!'

Jenny's response transformed this encounter from what could have been a soulless, fruitless transaction – to give (or withhold) money, to interact with the old lady in some way or to ignore her altogether – into an interpersonal relationship that impacted positively on the old lady, Jenny and the other train passengers. Jenny's small act was transformational.

This is the personal leadership that is at the heart of the Inverted Pyramid methodology. This is how we have an opportunity in every single interaction to make a real difference in three significant ways:

- for the person we interact with
- for ourselves through the gift that this interaction gives us, and
- through the example, learning or encouragement that we share with others who witness the encounter.

So begging isn't just about money. It can also be an opportunity to build a human connection, no matter how brief. Through our response, we can transform any begging request from an impersonal transactional request for money (or for help or human connection) into an interpersonal encounter.

A handful of pebbles

Just think of what might build from this brief interaction. How does Jenny feel, having responded positively? What is the gift that she has been given from this? How did Jenny change that old lady's day, and what is the story they tell to others? And what about those passengers on the train who have been given a gift that they can respond to (or not)? And here I am sharing Jenny's story with you. One interpersonal moment has transformed a barren transactional landscape.

A transformational response is a gift that we can bring to every single interaction we have – in person, online, via email, text or social media post. We can choose to transform every interaction. Who knows where it will lead? It's all about 'showing up'. How often are we showing up?

By thinking with a transformational mindset and responding in a transformational way, we create the potential to build interpersonal relationships that are the foundation of our Inverted Pyramids. We become an open invitation for collaboration. We become a sharer of skills, experience and expertise. Transformational responses are like throwing handfuls of pebbles into a still pond and watching the ripples growing outwards, overlapping and changing the landscape of who we are together.

Let us now explore each of the three elements in this process:

1. how we can move from TRANSACTIONAL ACTIVITIES
2. through our TRANSFORMATIONAL BEHAVIOUR to
3. build INTERPERSONAL RELATIONSHIPS.

1. Transactional activities

a. Have you space to grow at work?

In the weekly Inverted Pyramid development sessions run by Diversiton, the very first thing we do is to bring people together in groups of six. They have one minute to report back to each other on personal successes and challenges. This is followed by one minute of collective positive feedback, offers of support, suggestions and ideas. And then after 12 minutes, everyone comes to the business part of the meeting.

But in our work meetings, we don't do any of this. The very first thing we focus on is Item 1 on the agenda. We bypass the personal and interpersonal elements and head straight into the transactional process. And there's no space for Dual Responsibility in that process. Wouldn't it be interesting if organisations or businesses took 12 minutes at the start of the meeting to put everybody into groups to do that Dual Responsibility piece, and then come to the 'meeting' with that success and engagement at the forefront of their thinking?

Is it possible to allow space for personal and interpersonal development to come first – and so to provide a platform of positivity, collaboration and motivation as we begin work on the transactional pieces (agenda items)?

I put this question to a senior director recently and his response was, 'Yes, we do have update meetings but these are, as you say, transactional. We bring the company employees together once a year to share developments within the business. But the real interpersonal stuff happens in the bar after the 'work' is finished. When people are freed up from the conference work, they can network with whoever they like. It's at one in the morning that so many new initiatives have been born in our business. What we have to learn to do is to formalise this extracurricular activity into our daily office life, and not just at the bar at our annual conference.'

When Pope Francis talks about creating an Inverted Pyramid and turning the Church upside down, it is not necessarily the organisational structure that he says we should change. It's much more fundamental than that. We still need some formalised structure to get things done. But the way we relate, support each other, work together and build relationships must be very different.

One parishioner, commenting on the Church's synodal process said, 'We really need people sitting down in small groups, including the clergy, so that we can all get to know each other at a personal level. We would love to get past the roles and rules we are given so that we can befriend each other as the ordinary people that we all are.'

And it's the same for other organisations and the way that they seek to build inclusion or community. You can't build inclusion or true community within a structure designed primarily to facilitate transactions. You have to allow the personal and interpersonal connections to happen first.

b. How was your stay?

In the hotel I stayed at recently, check-in was transactional, breakfast service at my table was transactional and check-out was transactional. Personal interaction was kept to a minimum. Nobody ever asked me how I was, is everything okay with my room, the reason for my stay or my plans for my day. There was no smile. The hotel was smart and generally clean, and staff behaved efficiently, but it was all devoid of life. There was no human warmth or personality. When asked how my stay was as I paid the bill, I said just, 'Okay'.

After I left, I had an unexpected call from the manager who was in full complaint-handling mode. When I explained that I wasn't complaining, we began to have a grown-up, collaborative conversation, and he asked me for some concrete examples. He was genuinely shocked to hear about the stains on the carpet in my room and the lamp that needed a new bulb, the 20-minute wait for coffee at breakfast and the absence of a warm greeting on my arrival. I really wasn't trying to give him a list of things to fix – and he got that. We all want to feel looked after in our hotel. We want to know that people care. He thanked me and asked me to come back again as his guest. He wants to do better.

c. What's the problem?

Many of our personal health services, be it a visit to the doctor, optician or dentist, have become medical transactions where they diagnose the 'problem', give us what we need and the job is done. It may be seen as efficient from the healthcare organisation's perspective, but I wonder if there is a greater price being paid in terms of our overall stress, loneliness, mental health or emotional well-being. I'm not blaming the health service for these issues, of course. I'm just wondering whether we have made the transaction so efficient now that we're only focused on one set of symptoms and not connecting with the whole person. Are we trading effectiveness for efficiency? Do we feel like we have been 'dealt with' or 'cared for'?

d. Has our communication with potential clients become transactional?

Transactional marketing is typified by online advertising, list-building and bulk emailing, all in the hope of getting some sales. It's pebbledash selling: if we throw enough stuff out there, in the right general direction, we will apparently be successful.

All the talk is of landing pages, online courses, webinars, videos, ebooks, email sign-up, marketing funnels and, of course, the customer journey. Our transactional marketing treats people as resources to be manipulated or to extract income from. Of course, we hope that we help them. We hope that our service is useful. We hope that they gain something from working with us.

But what about those who see our messaging and don't buy from us? Perhaps they realise that our focus is transactional and not about building interpersonal relationships. They may sense that inclusion is not our priority. They know that real inclusion starts with a conversation. So, what kind of damage are we doing to our core message, brand and overall potential for success?

Social media companies want us to generate thousands of friends, followers and likes. This is the clickbait of transactional marketing. We see lots of activity but very little relationship-building. We have been sucked into thinking that this is how business works on the Internet, how we build relationships worldwide, but it's much easier than this. We don't have to throw valuable time, money and energy into the virtual world. Instead of hoping that all our online 'marketing activity' leads to something, wouldn't it be much easier to reach out to a few people without selling, and start building our Inverted Pyramids?

And imagine what our business would look like if each of our staff did this. They would all be building an amazing, Inverted Pyramid of colleagues keen to work together to build what we really care about.

Years ago, I read that 'people buy people'. Interpersonal relationships require no marketing. We talk to people. We see where they are. We offer to help. We simply work with people who are interested in what we do or how we can help each other. Together, we invest in the relationship. It calls for a different kind of marketing.

It's from this collection of interpersonal relationships that we build a real community. For community is a bottom-up process where we invite others to work with us, where we reach out to help them, share our ideas and journey together. Each of us can build our own Inverted Pyramid, community and piece of inclusion. And imagine what we will achieve when we bring each piece of inclusion together.

We can choose to reach out and work with others or we can try to sell even more stuff. This is at the heart of the personal invitation from Pope Francis: to be transformational in moving from a transactional to an interpersonal way of living. It's a call to put our humanity before stuff.

2. Transformational behaviour

a. It's time to talk to strangers

My wife Pauline has got used to it over the years. I say hello to people in the street. I interview every taxi driver. I'll chat to people when buying clothes to get their reaction and see if the sweater suits me. I am determined in every single situation to go beyond the transaction to build a personal connection. Not taking myself too seriously and accepting that the other person may think I am nuts are key ingredients! However, everybody always responds, even if only with a nervous look. Mostly it's a smile, a laugh and a comment. We've made a personal connection.

b. Working relationships must become personal relationships

If our only relationship with others at work is a transactional one based on roles and responsibilities, this becomes a one-dimensional and restrictive frame of reference. There is nowhere for this to go or to grow because we don't know about each other, what's important to us, what our key skills might be, our experience, people we may have in common and all our other 'lives' that exist outside the workplace. We have turned our working relationships into an inward-looking and potentially limiting series of transactions.

If we could start with getting to know each other first, with camaraderie and friendship, we create a framework that can grow and develop to support not just our job roles, but a myriad of other possibilities.

Fourteen ways to become transformational in our transactions with others:

Our aim is always to engage directly with the person to build an interpersonal connection, rather than simply follow a transactional process.

1. Respond
Don't ignore a request for help or advice: respond to the situation

2. Share what you have
Give of your time, experience, money or resources: help the person to move forward

3. Introduce yourself
I'm Des, I work in the training department; I don't think we've been introduced...

4. Ask for information
Could you please tell me a little bit more about...?
Can I ask you how that would work...?

5. Show genuine interest
I hear that you are involved with... I'd love to know more about...
Can I ask how you manage to...?

6. Be grateful
Thank you so much for the way you explained that. Just one brief question...
Thank you for taking time to go through that with me. Can I just ask about...?

7. Comment on a recent event in the news
Wasn't it sad what happened to that little boy in Aberdeen?
Did you watch any of the coverage on TV about...?

8. Be caring
I know your team has a lot of work on. Are you all OK?
For goodness' sake, let me carry that bag...!

9. Tell them something about yourself
This is the first time I've actually enquired about / bought one of these
I'm going on holiday next week so I need to...

10. Offer to help

I see you're working on... can I lend a hand?

I hear you're planning to... I've been there before so I'm happy to share some thoughts.

11. Ask for help

I'm working on... and I'd really love to pick your brains

Can I ask for your advice on something?

12. Be vulnerable

I'm worried about...

I really don't want to mess this up so could I ask for your advice?

13. Discuss something you have in common

How are you getting on with...?

How do you like working in ....?

14. Ask about life outside of work

What's your plan for the weekend then?

Will you be getting away on holiday this year?

INVERTED PYRAMID EXERCISE

What will we become?

THE GREAT TRANSFORMATION

The great transformation of your life
is about to begin.
You will see things
in a different way.
You will think about things
in a different way.
You will relate to others
in a different way.

And there are no words to describe
this transformation.
For all words limit, and reduce
what you are about to become.

Your transformation has begun.
Hold the seed gently.
Be quiet. Walk slowly.
Give this process a chance
to take root in your busy brain,
and to grow.

For you will never
think the same again.
You will never
act the same again.
You will never
be the same again.

Today you have received
the invitation of all invitations.
Begin to get ready.

Clear the decks.
Be willing to grow.
For everything you do from now on
will speak to you of transformation.

The words you hear
will be of encouragement
for your transformation.
The people you meet
will be the helpers
for your transformation.

And every day will give you
the next stage,
the next piece,
the next step forward
in your transformation.

You have nothing to do but
to be ready,
to be open,
and to say yes each day
to your great transformation.

PERSONAL DEVELOPMENT REFLECTION

1. How can you clear the decks?
2. What might you become?
3. What is the one thing you can do, in this moment, to begin your Great Transformation?

3. Building interpersonal relationships

a. How can we add value to every interaction?

With the Inverted Pyramid approach, Francis is encouraging us to move beyond a transactional view of how we live, how we interact with others, how we buy and sell or work together – to become more conscious and proactive around the humanity within all our interactions, no matter how temporary, casual or embedded these are.

For it is when we listen to others and speak with them that we develop new perspectives, understanding, insights and possibilities. So, look always for the opportunity to smile, say thank you, ask how people are, find out how their day is going and connect at a personal level. Be appreciative of the help that they have just given you. Try to leave people feeling better for having just met or chatted with you.

b. How can we make inclusion a reality in our organisation?

At a recent Inverted Pyramid workshop, senior managers were asked how they were going about making inclusion real in their organisation. Here is an excerpt from the transcript of one response:

'If we are serious about inclusion, we know that our approach will need to follow the principle of Dual Responsibility. We want our staff to know that they don't have to work elsewhere to develop their career. It's those Inverted Pyramids that Des talks about! Inclusion and organisational development are not separate or contradictory. We can be both efficient in how we run our business and effective in our inclusion strategies. We want our staff to grow and develop with each other, and we as managers want to be part of this, not separate from it.'

This is a great example of a company committing to freeing up their people to make the connections that seem most natural and helpful to them personally. Once we bring a group of people together and give them responsibility for how they work and what they do, they quickly build relationships of trust. Then they naturally start to ask, 'Well, can we not do this in a better way?' And then they're in a position to make a positive impact on their roles and responsibilities within the hierarchal structure of the organisation. This is where the two intersect and where the development of collaborative interpersonal relationships actively supports the growth and long-term sustainability of the business.

It's a business development strategy built on engagement, empowerment and collaboration. Because if we've enabled people to build mutually supportive relationships within a corporate environment of trust, then when something comes up that challenges the organisation or certain staff, we can look after each other in this process. We are not trying to defend our position, allocate blame or keep our head down.

Successful entrepreneurs do all of this on instinct. They know that if they look after their staff, then their staff will look after the business. Their small team of people gels first at an interpersonal level, and, from this, drives everything forward. Trust is built into the culture.

c. Free others who are trapped in transactional working

When we receive good service, some people, rather begrudgingly, might say, 'Well, that's their job, isn't it? They are paid to give good service.' However, if we take this attitude then we are accepting that we are both stuck working within the transactional operational framework, with its predetermined way of thinking. It is when we go above the expected, when we step out from the transaction, that we add real value. And then something different is happening...

We see so many people trapped in their daily routine, almost comatose, as they do what they are programmed (or paid) to do. It doesn't matter what our role or position is: we can all become trapped by the transactional nature of the way we are expected to do our jobs or work with others.

And these transactions are typically characterised by a straitjacket of routine, little room for creativity, predictable meetings and no pathway for exploring alternative approaches. By flipping our own personal pyramid and communicating at a human and personal level with those we meet, we can change this. Through our interest in others, we can create new options and a different way forward. We can personally become the drivers and enablers of a kinder and more inclusive world.

We must look to engage, empower and bring people together in new ways, for the current models and approach are simply not enough. Here are a few pointers to note:

- Explain to colleagues the difference between transactional activity and building interpersonal relationships
- Reframe the interaction style between staff and customer as interpersonal, rather than purely a business process
- Train your staff to build relationships first and to follow these through; try role-playing; work through different scenarios; use the behaviours discussed earlier
- Empower your staff to use their initiative and be themselves
- Remain focused on your customer or colleagues; look for opportunities to help and add value
- Build every relationship and explore new ways to work together with staff, customers and everyone you meet.

INVERTED PYRAMID EXERCISE

Are you still leaving caterpillar tracks?

CATERPILLAR TRACKS

I am a caterpillar
among millions of caterpillars.
Some of them talk of breaking free
and living in a different way.

> But I have much to do
> as a caterpillar.
> All talk of freedom and flying
> is for butterflies.

PERSONAL DEVELOPMENT REFLECTION
1. What are the benefits of remaining a caterpillar?
2. When and how are you going to become a butterfly?

d. There is a conversation beyond the transaction

We are all conditioned to stay with the mechanics of the transaction. We answer the query. We make the sale. We get the deal. We deliver the contract. And then we move on.

We leave 99% of the value behind on the table. And this value is in the relationship, the working together and the future potential of what we might do with those individuals, organisations and businesses, and who they are connected to.

Outside of our organisations and workplaces, how many of us chat to the Amazon delivery driver at our door, the older lady on the checkout in the supermarket or the young man in the queue at the bus stop? Do we know how they are, their story, what else they work on or what they would really like to do?

These were my typical candidates when I was writing my book, *Work it Out!*, which explored how we build our career through 'workpieces' such as part-time work, freelancing and the gig economy to earn the money we need to support our loved ones. Each person that I spoke to gave me a new scenario. Each taxi driver was a case study example of what the new world of work meant for them. They were all delighted to share their experience. I was always keen to find out 'what else' the taxi driver did, what their other workpieces were.

I gathered many stories, such as the Syrian doctor trying to learn English, the young guy who imported toys from China (his car boot was full!), the engineer who used to sell and fit solar panels until the Government reduced the funding for households, the entrepreneur thinking about his Next Big Thing, and the guy who lived alone and just needed to get out and meet people. Every taxi ride is a new story. The journey is important, but that's only a transaction. It's the conversation that holds the value and potential.

e. As consumers we must disrupt the transaction

It's easy to see the transactional nature of call centres and online chats. We can readily recognise the way we are conditioned to respond and how the flow of the script/process limits our behaviour. We can, however, gently turn this upside down by injecting our own personality, conversation, attitudes, behaviours and values. Our voice can be heard.

Let's explore how we can inject some personality, humanity and humour into pre-scripted transactions. Make your first statement a positive, upbeat one!

'My name is Anna. For security, can I take your first name?'

'It's Des... and I'm just back from the dentist so my mouth is still a bit frozen. How are you? And where are you working from today, Anna?'

While they are working to resolve the issue, why not find out more about the work they do, the challenges they face, the types of queries (or customers) they get? Be interested in them as a person. Be sympathetic to the transactional nature of the job they are locked into. Ask about the weather, their planned holiday, where they are based, or an event on the news today. What time do you escape today? Any nice plans for the weekend?

Always finish with a really positive sign-off. Something like: 'Thank you so much for sorting that out', 'You've made my day', 'Have a lovely weekend', 'It's been great to chat with you today, take care.'

Those in call centres or dealing with problems online are the same as you and me. You can extend your Inverted Pyramid of Kindness. You can leave them with a smile. You can leave them feeling that they've helped you in some way. You can leave them with a memory of a nice Irish guy (in my case, I hope!) that they spoke with on the phone today.

When we disrupt the transaction and develop an interpersonal connection, we can bring joy to what we are doing. There is warmth, personality, humour and a sense of working together. We are not simply trying to get from A to B and responding to the latest version of the script. There is more going on here. We are creating joy.

f. We are pieces of inclusion

In building our Inverted Pyramid, we are developing pieces of inclusion. Pieces of inclusion can be formed by millions of people across the world, wherever they are, in line with Inverted Pyramid principles of Dual Responsibility, kindness and collaboration. All our pieces of community can come together to build a worldwide community of inclusion.

And so, inclusion isn't something created by companies or implemented by organisations. Inclusion is the relationships that we create to enable, build, grow, look after and cherish each other. We take responsibility for those in our Inverted Pyramid. We look after others. We seek to grow and include others, especially those less fortunate. The mission of the worldwide community of inclusion is for everyone to be part of one big Inverted Pyramid.

CHAPTER 6: Time to harvest

Please take a moment to reflect and capture any initial thoughts, ideas, questions or action points that you wish to note and take forward. You will be able to gather these from each chapter for your personal development Action Plan at the end of the book.

Notes

1 ....

2 ....

3 ....

4 ....

5 ....

CHAPTER 7

Interpersonal working

Here are eight questions on the way we currently work, to see what might need to change or develop for more effective interpersonal working relationships:

1. Should we have more (and different) conversations?

Let's start to think about and play with situations that seek to hold us in a transactional grip. Let's step outside of the expected script. Let's see if we can humanise our interaction with some personal questions. Let's explore how we might change each interaction and create a real conversation.

2. Should we create more space to get to know each other?

Conferences, field trips and team-building sessions are some of the practical ways to build informal links. How many of us have enjoyed seeing a different side of our colleagues through non-work talks? We need to be mindful that working from home, freelancing and hybrid working can reduce the potential for casual conversations.

So, what can we do to help current staff and new starters build these important links? What can we do to establish our personal relationships as the base camp of all activity? How can we build this fabric of understanding so that everything we do, individually and collectively, is connected?

3. Should we change our training sessions?

The typical training course will be clearly laid out with a learning plan. We work systematically through the content and discuss the new approach or learning. The function of much training is related to the transactional machinery for business success.

Within an Inverted Pyramid framework, however, we always begin with the individual. We check in, formally or informally, find out how people are feeling and what's happening, learn about individual successes, identify where help is needed, a future conversation topic or new idea and so on. In other words, each person comes to the training session ready to move themselves along and help to move their colleagues along. It is this space and time for catching up, touching base, putting something out there and asking for help that can provide opportunities to build links, support each other and build something bigger.

So, every update, idea and comment from each person requires a positive response from everyone, with engagement, empathy and enthusiasm as appropriate. It requires further ideas and a next step. We can do this within 10 minutes at the start of any training session. With larger numbers, we do this by splitting people into smaller groups. We start off in small groups to build those links and then come to the wider meeting in a spirit of positivity and support. We have already had our successes before the business of training starts. We have moved forward our own situation and we've helped others. It's our Dual Responsibility that drives and supports everything including collaboration, effective working, innovation and the organisation itself.

4. Should we change our meetings?

Does your manager always run your meetings? Is it usually the same task-driven agenda? Is the focus on reporting, figures and priorities for moving forward?

- Let's think about how we might invert this pyramid and ensure that our meetings are driven by individual connections, links, emerging ideas and developing initiatives
- Let's create a way to enable each person to share what's happening with their Inverted Pyramid – how are we building new connections, partnerships, processes or projects?
- Let's hear about the new connections from outside the business and emerging ideas – how are we building our critical mass of impact?
- Let's explore how we can link all this together so that we are building collective energy for improvement and keeping our business truly people-led
- Let's ensure that we recognise and applaud individual efforts and encourage everyone to continue to grow their Inverted Pyramids.

Tina Corner Stolz and her team of Licensed Peer Advisory Council Moderators at LXCouncil use a different 'Transition Question' at the start of each team meeting. This is unrelated to the agenda and designed to allow individuals to share what is happening for them outside the organisation before getting into the business priorities. Answers to the Transition Question enable individuals to speak, for example, of a recent family issue or a worrying personal situation that would otherwise remain hidden.

LXCouncil also use the FORD method to go beyond the agenda and transactional nature of their meetings and get-togethers with new (and potential) clients. FORD reminds Moderators to ask questions about their Family, Occupation, Recreation and Dreams.

Both the Transition Question and FORD method are structured techniques that require individuals to reach out and connect beyond their job description or tasks – and before the transactional part of that particular business activity.

It is through using techniques such as these that we can explore the potential for building our Inverted Pyramid processes. These, along with many others, encourage us to work together as individuals rather than just work colleagues. They help to build a team atmosphere and level of support, and also to establish personal connections.

Can you think how you might evolve your meetings to become interpersonal development processes in themselves, rather than static reporting sessions? What might a new 'process agenda' look like? How might our meetings change? What should we call these get-togethers? Who's 'in charge' of these sessions? What new outcomes will we hope to see emerge?

5. Should we change our emails?

Are you still sending out those boring, repetitive transactional emails to colleagues and customers? Are people excited to receive one from you? Isn't it time we had some emails that brought life and energy to our interactions, emails that motivate, empower and encourage us at a human level?

Every email we send is another way of building our connections, a way to encourage others, to express our support, to be positive and to offer practical help. Every email should be a launchpad to take our relationship forward. It's an opportunity to update, ask for help, share experience or suggest a new Inverted Pyramid team idea. Every email becomes part of the process of connection, linkage and building something more.

6. Should we change our online greeting?

'When I first met my colleague Dean Minuto from Yescalate on Zoom, he was standing with both arms raised and smiling like he had just won the lottery! He's a world-class presenter. He knows that working online doesn't have to be a limiting interaction. He's injecting energy and joy into our conversation before we even start talking. He's making the first move, inviting me to connect with him at an interpersonal level rather than getting straight into the transaction of the meeting we are about to have.

- So, how would you assess the enthusiasm that others experience when they meet you?
- Do you smile and show the person that you are genuinely pleased to see them?
- Are you helpful, encouraging, motivating and full of energy?
- Is your greeting purely routine before you get into the transaction, or have you both smiled and laughed together?
- Do you ask how they are, about their news or their weekend?

7. Should we change our coffee break?

Please don't sit on your own at your desk eating your sandwich and scrolling through Facebook. Use the opportunity to build interpersonal connections. Catch up with a couple of colleagues and find out what's happening with them at home, with their families, with their new job, with their project, their partner, their sport or their music.

Coffee and lunch breaks are opportunities we have each day to step outside of the transactional business world, build human connections and develop those relationships that are important to us.

8. Should we change our online working?

Online working, especially from home, has enabled us to be much more efficient in the use of our time. We don't have to travel to the office or get distracted by colleagues walking in when we're trying to get some work done.

For many of us, though, this means that we schedule more activities, such as online calls, into our day. Online calendars enable us to carve up our day into 30- or 60-minute time slots and meetings. Even sitting at home, we can find ourselves literally going from one meeting to another.

I've learned to schedule 20 minutes' harvesting time after each meeting, to ensure that I step outside of the transaction and gather up the learning and possibilities that have come from the discussion I've just had.

When we know we intend to harvest from a meeting, it totally changes our perspective from the outset. We move from 'attending a meeting' mode to being keen to explore the full potential of the content, discussion, people and situations that we are engaging with – and how we can take all this forward. The true value is not in the meeting. The true potential and value lies in what we take forward.

And what's more, online tools such as Zoom and Otter enable us to capture the discussion or online meeting as text, live, as the discussion is taking place. We can see the notes being typed out as we speak. This means that any comments made are going straight into our notes, ready to be harvested.

INVERTED PYRAMID EXERCISE

What are the six 'gardening' reminders for inclusion?

PLANTING INVERTED PYRAMIDS

In every day
we can plant an Inverted Pyramid
In every place
we can plant an Inverted Pyramid.

In every conversation
we can plant an Inverted Pyramid.
In every task
we can plant an Inverted Pyramid.

In every moment of silence
we can plant an Inverted Pyramid.
In everything we do
we can plant an Inverted Pyramid.

PERSONAL DEVELOPMENT REFLECTION

1. How can you shift from transactional working to building stronger interpersonal relationships?
2. How can you plant an Inverted Pyramid today?

CHAPTER 7: Time to harvest

Please take a moment to reflect and capture any initial thoughts, ideas, questions or action points that you wish to note and take forward. You will be able to gather these from each chapter for your personal development Action Plan at the end of the book.

Notes

1 ....

2 ....

3 ....

4 ....

5 ....

CHAPTER 8

Inverted Pyramid inclusion skills

In this chapter we will explore examples of positive language and everyday behaviours that help to build inclusion in every interaction. We will also outline the core inclusion skills including the Big Six Power Combos for building effective connections, the Top 14 Inclusion Behaviours and the ALPEN model for interacting with others we already know.

Positive language

1. What we say happens

Those familiar with affirmations will know that we can make real what we think about. Our brain will respond to the messages received. So, if we say *I can't do that* or *This won't work*, that's usually what will happen. It's like pressing the letter **a** on our keyboard and then an **a** appears on our screen.

Try to avoid phrases like *It's impossible* or *That'll never happen*. Change everything to positive language and give your brain the chance to find the solutions you need. Use positive language like *I can, I will, I'm looking forward to this...* Include words such as *opportunity, possibility, options* or *scenarios*.

When faced with challenges or difficulties, try to use phrases that generate positive options for moving forward, such as: *Let's look at this*

- *Can we explore some possibilities?*
- *Let's see if we can find our way through this*
- *Don't worry, we will sort this out*
- *I wonder if we….*
- *Let's create a few options*

2. Get out of your way

When we only think about ourselves, we tend to play the same tape over and over in our head. Sometimes, limiting beliefs or Impostor Syndrome can kick in:

- *I am no good at…*
- *I will never find work in…*
- *I will never lose weight…*
- *I can't get the sort of job I want…*
- *Nobody will buy this…*

However, when we work with others and try to help them, we can find ourselves being more proactive and positive. We can suggest options and ideas that the person may not have thought of:

- *Could you…?*
- *Maybe you and John could link up and see if…?*
- *Why don't you look at…?*
- *Would it be possible to…?*

We shift into an enabling project-helper mode as we learn about others, find out what they are trying to do, see where they are stuck – and suggest ways forward.

3. Become a problem solver

By taking responsibility for others, we free up our brain to explore more, to take on new challenges, to become a problem solver and to build our success together in new ways. All of this in turn unlocks our own thinking and the ideas of others as to how we may resolve our own situation.

Now that we're starting to take responsibility for bringing people together, the situation is no longer just about us. It's about exploring the potential and skills that everyone has. Each of us can start this process today by linking up and finding out more about those we work with in all parts of our lives.

4. Always say yes!

If someone asks for our help, advice or assistance – always say yes! Even if we do not know the answer, we will be able to find someone who does. If it's something completely new to you, then say yes anyway and journey with the person to find the solution.

Every time we say yes to someone and offer to help them we are, in effect, accepting the incredible gifts of a developing relationship and possibility. So:

- Say yes
- Approach the opportunity with a smile and enthusiasm
- Look to deliver the real practical help that others need
- Explore the potential to build upon the relationship and move forward together
- See how you might extend and build upon the work you are doing together

Link to other aspects of the work that you are both interested in, leverage all of this and add even more value.

The alternative to saying yes is to say no. What this does is reduce our capability and capacity. We tell ourselves that we don't want to do things, that we are not capable of doing things and that we do not want to help this person. These are negative messages that limit us in our own thinking, in our own possibilities and in building our Inverted Pyramid. Thoughts such as *What's in this for me?* also reduce the range of possibilities and force our attention inwards.

By reaching outwards, being positive and saying yes, we become the person that people want to engage with. We build relationships and opportunities that sustain our own development and ambitions. We find more people who want to work with us. The reality is that we create our success through other people. Someone asking for our input is an amazing opportunity that we should be thankful for and determined to make the most of.

5. Replace 'I' with 'we'

For those in senior positions in any organisation, there can sometimes be a tendency to give instructions and use authority to get things done. Effective leaders, however, use the word 'we' rather than the word 'I'. Instead of saying 'I want this to happen' or 'I see this as a priority', they re-frame the situation, putting forward scenarios and questions with the word 'we':

- *Can we have a look at how we...*
- *How will we...?*
- *We really need to look at this...*

When we're trying to build new relationships, create additional ways forward or look at new scenarios, the word 'we' becomes incredibly powerful. It helps us to become much more consultative and engaging from the outset.

- *Where do you think we need to start?*
- *What do you see as the biggest challenge for us?*
- *What steps do you think we need to put in place?*
- *What else do we need to do now? What skills and expertise do you think we need?*

111

This involves people in the process and gives them permission to contribute. And once people contribute an idea, it opens the potential for them to take this forward.

We must ensure that those sharing their best ideas are appreciated. It would take us backwards if suggestions were ignored, misinterpreted, stolen by others or failed to explore the possible outcomes.

Beginning collaboration

When someone comes to us with a good idea, we need to respond positively, irrespective of the idea itself. What we have to do is reward and encourage the fact that the individual has taken time to think about a situation, to come up with a solution, and to reach out and present this to us.

The worst thing we can do is say, 'Oh, that won't work' or 'That's not a priority' or 'We have a department to look at that'. Not only do we lose the potential that may exist if we had taken the idea further or explored it, but we also lose that person. For they are unlikely to ever allow their thinking to enter into that creative space again. We have put them back in their box, at the bottom of the traditional hierarchal structure.

If we can reply in a way that says:

- *Thank you, I really appreciate the time you've taken to look at this*
- *I'm excited by your thinking around this*
- *How do you think we could progress this?*
- *Let's get together tomorrow morning.*
- *Let's get a small group of people together to explore this further.*
- *Who do you think we could involve?*
- *What's the first step?*

This positive and engaged response provides validation in five key ways:

1. It validates the process of going to our colleague with an idea and receiving a positive response
2. It validates that the person is appreciated for their expertise and experience, and what they can offer the organisation
3. It validates that the Inverted Pyramid process is alive and growing in our organisation
4. It validates that the person is developing in collaboration with others and through the organisation
5. It provides validation for our colleagues, who can see that the person has been listened to and that there is a process for taking a good idea forward. They are in turn encouraged to think 'What have I got to offer? What can I do? How can I develop my input?'

A positive response from the manager sends out a wave of possibility of participation across that person's team and colleagues, and into the wider organisation. Through this, the individual becomes more, the manager becomes more, the team becomes more and the whole organisation becomes more.

If, however, the person has the door shut in their face, that is a message that goes across the department and the whole organisation. *'It's no use, they don't want to listen. There's no point in suggesting anything. I give up.'*

Everybody in the organisation needs to be trained on how to respond. There are two parts to this response: the first is to acknowledge the approach with gratitude, appreciation, interest and excitement; and the second is to explore how we will take this forward together. The process of engagement begins when the individual reaches out. The process of collaboration begins with a positive response.

Positive messaging

Positive messaging is one of the most important mechanisms for driving positive relationships.

The first of two key elements of this are the messages that we hear from ourselves. This is about the positive language we use. So, the very first thing to learn is how to recondition, reprogram and retrain our brains to give out positive messages that we hear coming from within us. For it is through this that we are able to encourage and invite others to work with us.

The second part of the feedback loop involves the messages that other people give to us. Our position here is really clear. We need to encourage, smile, motivate, applaud, congratulate and be excited about what others are saying or offering. Our response cannot be critical, dismissive or lukewarm. If we disagree with something then we can phrase this in a positive way. We can say '*Perhaps this is one of the things we need to look at*', rather than '*Well, that won't work, will it?*'

Once we bring these two elements of positive message and positive response together, we create a different dynamic. For the world will bombard us with negativity and seek to limit us in all that we do – at home, at work, in relationships, in thinking about our future, in exploring possibilities et cetera.

The Boss with the Broom

My good friend Jimmy Ryan tells a great story about how we can build the everyday behaviours we want to see across our organisations.

'Years ago, in the Dell computer manufacturing facility in Galway, we had a senior manager called Tommy who was responsible for all cleaning and hygiene matters. He didn't actually work for Dell as he was employed by an outside contractor. He was largely based at the plant, though, and people got to know him simply because of his visibility every day.

Tommy always carried a sweeping brush and became generally known as the 'boss with the broom'. He was always pointing out dangers and risks in a positive and helpful way. He was a role model for all of us, taking pride in a clean and safe workplace. Tommy would keep an eye on things during the day and have everything lined up for the cleaning teams that came in after staff left in the evening. And when we had special visitors from corporate head office, Tommy would be leading the charge, reminding us to be on our best game. We would be keen not to let each other down.

Carrying a broom and sweeping up was not 'beneath' Tommy. It was a key part of what everyone was responsible for. For him, this was about showing us all that this was the core behaviour we all needed to have. The manager was setting the mindset. He **was** the mindset. Our priority was keeping the place clean and tidy. It was about a healthy workspace, respect for each other and ensuring we all had a pleasant and safe place to work together. People just had to see Tommy and they knew exactly what he stood for and what we all had to do.'

When you're at work, what is it that you carry to reinforce the key behaviours that you want to see in all of your teams and colleagues? How are you visible and accessible? What would staff and colleagues say that you stand for?

Positive language is for all of us

Positive language is incredibly important. As you read through the next sections on how we can build inclusion in business, local government or education, you may be tempted to think: *We've tried that before* or *That won't work in our organisation* or *I would never be able to do that.* But we can win through if we change our language and look for ways to succeed. We must stop playing the same limiting belief tape over and over again in our heads. We begin by working together to explore the *how*.

Our new Inverted Pyramid Teams can easily be multi-functional and multi-level in their operation. They cut across departmental, geographical and job title boundaries that have traditionally kept people isolated. Let positive language be a mark of appreciation, respect and trust in our organisations.

Everyday behaviours

How many of our induction programmes specify the behaviours and attitudes that are fundamental to working in our organisation? How many organisations have a way of working based on kindness, relationship-building and helping every person that we meet? And if we don't have this, then exactly what business are we in?

Disneyland Paris

I am reminded of the story of when Disney opened their theme park in France. They noticed very quickly that when the public wanted to find a particular ride, where the toilets were or where they could get certain food, it wasn't the customer care staff or the information desk that they asked.

Typically, it was the cleaners customers approached, because those in uniform were seen as less approachable. Recognising this, Disney decided to train everybody as customer care people first and then to add on their specific task – be it catering, cleaning, facilities or management. This went beyond the transactional roles allocated by titles.

I think this perspective is absent in many organisations. We're missing the piece on how we can connect and work with people first, and then bring our technical and service experience to the needs that we find.

Most organisations seem to be doing this the other way around, trying to bolt-on customer care as an afterthought or a training initiative. As a result of this we get comments like, 'That's not our department', 'I need to put you through to somebody else', 'I'll ask someone to get back to you on this', 'You need to put it in writing to …', 'I can give you a form to fill out…', and so the list of non-engagement goes on.

If we try to call, we will very possibly have to wait because we are 10th in the queue, listen to music, respond to largely irrelevant menus, press some buttons, only to be told to visit the website just before we get cut off. Our organisations can become impenetrable castles with the troops safely locked inside, protecting their jobs and failing to address the very reason they exist.

Not only did Disney make everyone a customer service specialist first, but they also identified the key attitudes and behaviours that go with this responsibility. Because they are in the entertainment business, all their employees became actors. As soon as they walked onto the park at the start of their shift, they were on stage and had a role to play. They knew their lines. They knew how to smile and greet people. They knew how to work with people to ensure that the various needs were properly addressed. They literally journeyed with people to the toilets, to the café or to find a missing child. They didn't just end up solving the problem. They ended up building a relationship, reinforcing the values of the brand and providing a world-class customer experience for every single visitor. Who says kindness doesn't pay?

The Big Six power combos for building effective connections

To go beyond the transactional nature of interactions, we can use a range of Inverted Pyramid relationship development skills. Here are the Big Six Power Combos for building effective connections. Mix and match these and create your own…

1. P&T – say please and thank you!

Always say please and thank you! It's not just good manners – it's the foundation block of collaboration. Say thank you to the individuals who help with your recycling, bring your mail or serve you in shops.

2. P&P – be polite and positive!

Be polite and positive, no matter what the situation.

- *I wonder if you can help me with…*
- *That's very kind of you…*
- *I would be grateful if you could point me in the right direction…*
- *I really appreciate your support with this.*

Remember that the other person is stuck in the system of transactions.

3. S&E - smile and be enthusiastic!

Smile and be enthusiastic! Inject energy into your voice!

- *Thank you so much for sorting that out…*
- *That's amazing, great work!*
- *I'm really looking forward to meeting up…*
- *That's fabulous, thank you. You've made my day.*

Learn to smile on the phone. It'll help you to be enthusiastic!

4. C&B – chat and banter!

We can extend our Inverted Pyramid of Kindness to include the lady at the checkout till, or the call centre employee we've been allocated. We can leave them with a smile. We can leave them feeling that they've helped us in some way. We can leave them with the story of the mad Irishman they spoke to today!

Once we recognise the transactional nature of the way that we are trapped and conditioned to perform and behave, we can start to gently turn this upside down by injecting our own personality and our own pieces of conversation.

5. I&S - be interested in others and get their story

Be interested in those you meet, make eye contact, get their story. Talk with the person who serves you coffee or at the checkout till. Ask them how they are, compliment them on the care they took with your coffee or how they helped to sort out items to make your packing easier. Show them that you recognise the skill and effort they made in looking after you, no matter how small or insignificant it may seem.

Recently, for example, I found out that the guy on the checkout was just back to work after a week's break. He'd been off for his father's funeral and to sort out his house and possessions. 'Mind you, it was easy,' he said. 'My Dad was so organised, you know. He had a box with all his papers labelled, his funeral paid for and a set of instructions for me! Priceless, you know.'

'Yes, I do,' I replied.

6. K&I – be kind and take the initiative!

Continually look for opportunities to be proactive, kind and helpful. Give up your seat on the bus or the tube for an older person. And smile. It's a radical idea, I know. Or why not let the other driver in? Wave them through with a smile. Or hold the door open for others.

At the DIY store in New Jersey, my son and I were struggling to load a set of double doors onto the top of his car. The guy parked beside us with a pickup truck didn't wait for us to go and get some help from the staff. He took the initiative instead to see how he could help us sort it out. He loaded the doors onto his truck, tied everything up properly and delivered them to our home. He interrupted the usual transactional arrangement with practical help and kindness. He took the initiative. (I learned as he unloaded the doors that he had just sold his IT business for $20m. This guy just lived for his DIY weekends!)

Our aim is to shift our way of working and living to an interpersonal rather than transactional one – and remember that R>T (the relationship is greater than the transaction).

Always

We mentioned above how we should always say 'Yes' and outlined the incredible benefits that this offers to all of us. Here are five more important 'Always' behaviours:

1. Always encourage people to be themselves

It's okay in our organisation to be unsure, vulnerable, worried about something or struggling in some way. We all carry different things to work, whether it's challenging family relationships, health or something upsetting or worrying that has happened. Let's remember that when we reach out to others, we don't know what's on their mind, what they have left behind at home, what they have to go back to or what they are carrying at this moment. Let's allow everyone to be themselves rather than having to pretend to be something else.

2. Always ask the personal question first

There is always a personal question before a work, task or project question. There is always the personal 'check-in' to see that we are both 'OK' and on the same page. How do you feel when you meet your manager and they say 'Have you finished that report yet?' or 'What do the numbers look like today?' These are old traditional hierarchal control questions. They are not usually the questions that build relationships and encourage people to share and work together.

3. Always look for ways to add value

Once we know about the personal interests of others, what gives them a buzz or what they really want to achieve, we can start to align ourselves in a way that enables us both to grow forward.

4. Always look for ways to help

When we get to know each other properly, we can think about where we might be able to help and support each other. This could be anything: developing a new business idea, babysitting, sorting out a spreadsheet, lending a piece of equipment, helping with a report, doing some gardening or decorating, offering advice, sharing social media strategies, cooking a surprise meal, making a joint video, writing a book together...

5. Always be there

Checking in with others is not just about the practical help we can offer or the opportunities that we might develop together. Often, it is the sense of companionship, the fact that someone is being supportive or a sounding board for our ideas, that really makes a difference. You can change lives with a cup of coffee.

ALPEN - Interacting with others we know

Finally, here is a simple five-part process to apply to conversations with people we already know: Ask, Listen, Positive feedback, Encouragement, Next steps:

1. Ask

The first part of this is to ask – to be genuinely interested in what's happening with the person we are speaking with.

Ask, 'How was your weekend?', 'Any progress with your house project?', 'What are you working on today?', 'How is your little boy?', 'What's happening with your new Inverted Pyramid Team?', 'What's the next step?'

2. Listen

Give the person some space and time to talk. Be genuinely interested in them. Do not start talking about you or your situation. Respond appropriately with concern, excitement or understanding.

Ask follow-up questions where appropriate: 'What are you going to do next?', 'How has this impacted on you?' or 'How do you think this might be resolved?'

3. Positive feedback

The third stage is to be empathetic and enthusiastic, as appropriate. 'It sounds like you've done great with a difficult situation', 'That sounds impressive', 'That's amazing', 'I think that must have been incredibly stressful', 'Well done you.' This is positive reinforcement and recognition for the person to keep going.

4. Encouragement

Along with positive feedback comes encouragement. This is a chance to inject further energy and momentum into the scenario the person is dealing with. We are trying to help the person to build on what they have done or are seeking to achieve. Our encouragement shows that we are genuinely interested in the person.

Every conversation we have gives us the opportunity to plant a golden seed. We can either encourage or not. We can either help or not. We can either show kindness or not. The gift of encouragement enables us to say 'Just keep going at this.' 'Keep it all moving forward.' 'Don't forget to…' 'Let me know what happens.'

5. Next steps

Don't just leave the conversation hanging in mid-air. Ask, 'What can I do to help?' Make some practical suggestions around what you might be able to do. Arrange to check in or follow up. Ask to be kept up to date. Set up a coffee date to catch up.

As a result of the conversation, the person you have spoken with should be in a positive frame of mind. You, in turn, will have another story, another scenario and another relationship to move forward with.

CHAPTER 8: Time to harvest

Please take a moment to reflect and capture any initial thoughts, ideas, questions or action points that you wish to note and take forward. You will be able to gather these from each chapter for your personal development Action Plan at the end of the book.

Notes

1 ....

2 ....

3 ....

4 ....

5 ....

CHAPTER 9

Getting to know each other

We learn so much about ourselves when we find out more about others.

In this chapter we will look at how we can uncover and utilise our personal assets to build inclusion. We will do this by going through the set of eight practical steps that we use in our Inverted Pyramid workshops. You will be able to apply these techniques immediately to your workplace or groups.

Step 1: Personal interviews

This is the very first exercise we do, literally within five minutes from the start.

We ask individuals to sit with somebody they don't know, and we display on screen five questions similar to those below. Their task is to 'interview' each other and find out the answers to the questions. You can add to or change these questions as you wish:

- One thing you enjoy or are good at
- Something you can make
- Key passion / interest
- Something you could help others with
- One thing you would like to see happen in the future

They only have one minute each to do this – and so inevitably the whole atmosphere explodes with chat and laughter! People relax with each other as they focus on getting the five questions answered in the short time allocated.

We update them on how long they have left, and then tell them to switch over after one minute. Some will not get the task finished! But that doesn't matter, of course. It is the frantic search for answers, the mad creativity and the encouragement to think of something that makes this exercise so effective.

When the interviews are finished, we ask each person to introduce the other to the rest of the table by saying just one thing about them. For example, we find out that Peter is fantastic at making scrambled eggs, Jenny loves her Japanese garden, Gordon runs a Men's Shed in his town, Gwen speaks six languages, Heather has an aromatherapy business, Saaeda is studying part-time for a law degree and Andy restores vintage toys.

Step 2: Invert the Pyramid

When we ask the group why we did this exercise, they usually reply, 'It's an ice-breaker!' or 'To give us a chance to meet each other' or 'Finding out about each other.'

And when we ask them what they noticed about the questions, they generally reply that they are all positive. This is a key feature of beginning the Inverted Pyramid process. It focuses on our strengths, what we like to do and what we're good at. For these are the spaces that offer us the greatest potential for growth.

The whole context of the training shifts people, in the first ten minutes, from a mass of listening individuals to teams of people working together in a joyful spirit of collaboration, possibility and discovery.

We then explain the concept of the Inverted Pyramid. Individuals can see how at the start of the session they probably mentally placed the trainer at the top of the Pyramid, with all of them sitting passively at the bottom. We show them that what we're doing now is inverting this Pyramid so that they start to 'move upwards' to build their connections and ideas with others.

The initial exercise works effectively online as well, using breakout rooms for the initial interviews followed by group introductions. It is an exercise that can be run by any trainer, manager or team leader. It helps to get people out of their work boxes and enables them to begin to build relationships around topics that are personal to them.

When working in-house with businesses and organisations, this introduction process establishes relationships at a human level rather than simply at a business, task or operational level. We begin to see that there is more to each person than their job title as a Sales Assistant or a Customer Care Manager. This personal awareness process enables us to begin the very early stages of exploring possibilities for our individual Inverted Pyramids.

And as we grow and develop these relationships, we can start to see possibilities for linkages. For example, people link up around a common interest or complementary skills. We may uncover that somebody is an empathetic listener or incredibly effective at getting things done. Perhaps we will meet a situation where these skills are just what is needed.

Step 3: What do you really want to do?

We encourage people from the outset, as they embark on this new Inverted Pyramid journey, to think about the question, *What would I really like to do?* This provides the key to the direction we should take. You can join in with the workshop at this stage. Step back from your current role, or situation, for a couple of minutes and ask yourself: What would I really like to do, achieve, create or make?

- How can I encourage others and work with them to build my Inverted Pyramid?
- What would I like to see happen in my community, business, workplace or in the world?
- What does success mean in two years' time? Be brave and imagine exactly what it looks like
- What will happen in all areas of my life? Be ambitious and write down all that you want to see happen
- How can I share my skills, experience and knowledge in new and more creative ways?
- What's my key message as I reach out to others to build my Inverted Pyramid?
- What legacy am I creating?
- How can I work with others to make the world a kinder, fairer or better place?

These are the kinds of questions that help us to clarify our direction and what we should be doing.

Our key starting question always has to be *'What do I really want to do?'* If you don't know the answer, don't worry! It will become clear over time as you start to build your Inverted Pyramid and journey forward with others. Simply concentrate on reaching out to others and building new links to share your key skills, what you enjoy, what you are passionate about, and so on.

INVERTED PYRAMID EXERCISE

Is this a leap year?

LEAP YEAR

The core personal development question is
What am I really capable of?
The response isn't about
business, work or money.

It's about who we are
and looking beyond our perceived limitations.
It's about growing into our capacity
even if we cannot perceive it fully.

This is the search for something
we never thought we would look at,
even though deep down
we know we have the potential.

This is the leapfrog.
It's not linear, cumulative or predictable.
It's about us leaving our lily pad
and just going.

PERSONAL DEVELOPMENT REFLECTION

1. What are you really capable of?
2. What have you never thought you could do?
3. What might your new lily pad look like?

Step 4: Remember to mix it up!

We mix people together in all our Inverted Pyramid training sessions so that they have a chance to link up with people in different sectors, industries and departments, backgrounds, age groups and experience. We need people to share different perspectives, to understand the situation that others are facing and to see where they might learn and grow together.

The Inverted Pyramid offers us and our organisation a similar opportunity. You can introduce the methodology by bringing people together from different locations, roles and levels within the organisation. It's time to get people out of their silos! Not only will you be building an understanding of what an Inverted Pyramid process is and how it works, you will also be developing relationships and understanding that will strengthen the creative fabric of your organisation.

Step 5: Personal asset management

How do we capture and leverage all that is unique about us?

Diversity is about identifying and celebrating the whole of what we are. It is capturing that which is unique in each person. It is recognising this and then leveraging the skills, experience, knowledge or expertise to benefit us in some way. Diversity is nature's way of ensuring that we have all we need to look after everyone and ensure that everybody is well. Diversity is the global soup of inclusion.

Here are some key areas that can help us begin harvesting what we have to offer to others and the process. Think about what you can bring to others as you journey together. Make sure you capture all your ideas in your journal.

- **Skills**
  What skills do I have that could help me and others on the journey of Synodality? What am I good at? What do others say I'm good at? Where do I feel I could make a positive contribution?

- **Experience**
  What experience do I have? What have I achieved? What have been my successes? What have I learned at different stages in my life? What's important to me? Where do I find happiness?

- **Qualifications**
  What qualifications do I have? Qualifications are not just pieces of paper! What could I teach others to do? What am I able to teach others about?

- **Things I like to do or work on**
  How might things I like to do (at work, at home or with others) help colleagues on their journey? What do I enjoy working on? What gives me a buzz?

- **Areas I'm really interested in**
  What would I like to learn more about? Could I find other people who share this passion or interest? Could we journey together?

- **Ambition for the future**
  How can my ambition for the future give me ideas that could help myself and others on the journey? What is my ambition for the future? What is my vision for building a community of love? What exactly do I want to see happen in my life? What will I be doing two years from now?

Step 6: The pieces of working together

Now we can put people into small groups of four or five and ask them to share some of the words they've written down. They begin to find out what they have in common and where they might be able to move forward together. This provides ammunition for collaboration on creating quality initiatives.

The task in the next group exercise is to come up with the craziest, most ambitious, wacky business idea that they can! The purpose of this is to free people from their conditioned thinking. It's to get them to look at and play with the ideas of others, think about the skills and experience in the group and see how they can put things together in different ways. Again, this is all about fun interactions, creatively and joyfully exploring ideas together. *What if…? Could we…? What about…?*

And it only gets better when each group feeds back their idea to all other groups. Now we have 50–200 people sharing ideas together, based upon their skills, experience and key interests. And some amazing business ideas!

Step 7: Our Pick 'n' Mix

We often tend to think about career development in a cumulative way. In other words, we ask ourselves, *What will I do next?* or *How do I proceed from here?* We treat our starting point as if it is now. But this is not the case. You have spent your life building your knowledge, skills, contacts, experience and expertise. This is your personalised Pick 'n' Mix – your bespoke bag of sweets. All the different sweets represent your knowledge, skills, contacts, experience and expertise.

You have this bag of goodies ready to use at any time! We can harvest in so many areas of our lives – our work, relationships, projects, successes or times when we overcame difficulties, made things happen. There are many more options available to us.

One way that we can harvest from our Pick 'n' Mix is to ask ourselves lots of questions:

- *What jobs have I had in the past? Is any of that experience relevant now?*
- *What do I know a lot about?*
- *What work have I really enjoyed?*
- *What was I doing 2, 5, 7 or 15 years ago?*
- *What was the work that gave me the greatest joy?*
- *Who did I really enjoy working with?*
- *What documents are on my computer? Could I use this information in a new way to help others?*
- *Where did I help others most?*

Harvesting allows us the time to revisit, repackage, rediscover, reorganise, re-present everything that we've learnt – to gather up all the gems, insights and opportunities that are available to us. Harvesting allows us to sort out the good stuff and reflect on our past in a totally positive and productive way.

Step 8: Harvesting is a daily activity

Our harvesting process is not only about the past, it's about today. It's about capturing the value in what we do and in our experience as we go through each day.

Questions which can help us to pull out this information include:

- *Who have I just spoken with?*
- *Where was the big surprise today?*
- *Who did I meet?*
- *What crazy idea did I have today?*
- *What did I read today that got me thinking?*
- *What is my priority action point from that session?*

We can often be too busy doing things (or going from activity to activity) rather than cherishing and bringing to fruition the value of what we have already been given – and are constantly being given in every single day.

Try to recognise valuable moments as they happen and pause briefly to capture these – on your phone, in your notebook or on your laptop. You can always write up the idea more fully later, but don't lose the significance or impact of that learning or experience. Be mindful of these moments and always grateful for what you are being given. It is this growing sense of appreciation and thankfulness that in turn builds our awareness of the potential of what can be harvested and leveraged.

Capture ideas on your phone when you are out and about. Use the microphone button to record notes wherever you are and email them to yourself. Create your harvested files and folders on your computer or laptop. Start to collect all the experience, reports, ideas, stories together in relevant folders for your new Inverted Pyramid ideas and projects.

Become someone who harvests every day, as they go along...

INVERTED PYRAMID EXERCISE

What makes you unique?

UNIQUENESS

Uniqueness is another word for diversity. So please allow me to encourage you to capture and explore every moment, opportunity and wonderful event of your journey.

Go where your heart takes you. Have moments and days filled with new thoughts and experiences. Get off the worldly commute and see the countryside. Go without your satnav.

Every moment can hold something amazing, for it is a doorway to understanding. Do not settle for more but for insight, perspective and personal truth.

Create your own crazy life journey. Make it up as you go along. Enjoy every minute, especially failures, disappointments, illness and fatigue, for these can teach us so much about who we truly are.

Share your successes with humility and use these to encourage others. Fire them up with joy and enthusiasm. Hold out your hand and offer to help. Surprise others with a call. For the more you reach out, the more you learn about yourself.

We build our own truth from the building blocks we have been given: our DNA, health, parents, culture, schooling, religious upbringing, gifts and talents and much more.

This is the key purpose of our lives: to be a unique structure, a unique creation and a unique offering of love in the world. It doesn't matter how we do this, for each journey is of its own.

Our task is to learn and enjoy being fully ourselves in this life. For life is meant to be a process of joy. If we can understand this, we will see beyond the difficulties, suffering, pain and death that we must endure. This is the quest.

No one perspective, teaching or personal development book will get you there. Life is an ongoing personal development process. Only you can know what is going on within you and what makes real sense. There is, in my experience, no quick fix or instant download.

Our worldly attachment to power, position, money, instant satisfaction, ego, vanity and self-centredness all work against this complete understanding of who we are. And yet, these are so often part of the daily reality of our lives.

But there can and will be moments of light, glimpses of understanding and instances where we see things differently. These are the stepping-stones for uncovering our path.

Every life, with its glamour or failures, successes or poverty, holds its own unique, beautiful and infinitely precious journey of understanding. This is the wonder of life, for we are born with nothing and we die with nothing. The only thing in between is our journey of understanding.

Help everyone to have the courage to step outside of the norm, to take time for themselves, to be different, to listen and to offer ideas and perspectives that most of this world would find strange, crazy or unrealistic. Let us all be an inspiration of difference and acceptance. Let us all go with the flow and see where it takes us.

The beliefs of another are no threat to you. The traditions and practices of your neighbour should be the greatest joy, especially if you disagree with them or 'just don't get it'. For we should all celebrate not just our uniqueness but our ability to be different in a world that drives conformity, control and standardisation.

We need creativity, innovation, compassion and new perspectives. We need alternative ways of dealing with the new challenges the world is facing. Let us all be champions of uniqueness. Encourage others to 'have a go', say what they really think, question values and create better ways of living.

We are all protected under an umbrella of uniqueness which cannot be troubled, overthrown or destroyed. It is not confined to this world but is there forever, cherishing each of us, as together we build an eternity of love.

PERSONAL DEVELOPMENT REFLECTION

1. In what ways are you unique?
2. Describe your outlook or philosophy on life.
3. What are the key messages you will pass onto all of our children?
4. How can your uniqueness help to build an Inverted Pyramid?

CHAPTER 9: Time to harvest

Please take a moment to reflect and capture any initial thoughts, ideas, questions or action points that you wish to note and take forward. You will be able to gather these from each chapter for your personal development Action Plan at the end of the book.

Notes

1 ....

2 ....

3 ....

4 ....

5 ....

CHAPTER 10

How to build your personal Inverted Pyramid community

This chapter encourages us to connect with others, explore ideas and build our first Inverted Pyramid team. By collaborating and working together, we build community from the bottom up. Community starts with each one of us. This chapter gives us fifteen guiding points and reminders to help us build our personal Inverted Pyramid community.

Community

Here are some key perspectives of community to get us started:

- Community is an outcome of building inclusion. When we work through our Inverted Pyramid process and link with others, we begin to build community. Community is not something out there as a separate entity. Community is where we are. We are the heart of the Inverted Pyramid community.
- Community is the fabric of relationships that links and holds all our different Inverted Pyramid pieces together. It's the common values, aspirations and objectives that unite all of us. Community is bigger than us and bigger than all the work that we do.
- The logical extension of our Inverted Pyramid is that everybody in the world is part of our personal community.

Let's look at the fifteen guiding points and reminders:

1. Build community with the Inverted Pyramid

Fifty years ago, the idea of community was very much about where we lived and who our neighbours were. We got to know each other through our daily personal contact and interactions. Kids played together and neighbours helped each other out. Our front doors didn't need to be locked, for we kept an eye out for each other. And we could often pop in for sugar or a drop of milk if we went short. Work was largely what we did to earn money, but community was where we lived with each other.

This balance has, of course, changed over the last 50 years. There are fewer local area-based communities now. Many of us have our milk and sugar delivered if we run short.

We now build our own communities around a mixture of the people we work with, those we socialise with and family. We reach out to support and help those who are important to us. The Internet has added an online component to our personal efforts to build our community, and in many ways has replaced the local neighbourhood connections that we used to have. Rather than popping next door, we now chat to people online. We are sometimes more likely to send a text than walk over and talk to that person.

The transition to taking greater personal responsibility for building our community has been further heightened in recent years as we work more from home. Hybrid working, where we save time by not going in and out of the office while juggling a range of workpieces, emphasises this development. The business world is keen to tap into this loss of area-based community by trying to establish greater connections and a sense of community in the workplace. Diversity and inclusion can be part of this approach. For some, it's for commercial reasons and equality legislation, but for others it's about adding new layers of connection and recognition for staff.

Many businesses and organisations are encouraging people to link up, support each other, give back and pay it forward. They are trying to create a kinder and more collaborative business that is directly relevant to the needs of the people who work within them. They are looking to help build Inverted Pyramid communities.

2. Work with those who take us forward

The way that we link up and connect with other people is through our Inverted Pyramid Teams. These consist of the people that we choose to collaborate with and support.

The purpose of our work is to use our skills, knowledge and experience to help build an inclusive worldwide community in whatever way is meaningful to us, whether by reaching out to others, helping those in need, developing our spirituality, addressing priorities in our local area, being kind to those who are stuck, looking after those who are poor and so on.

And as we have seen, we can be in multiple Inverted Pyramid Teams, talking with different sets of people and working on different projects and initiatives that we enjoy. We start by connecting with those we work with and develop joint activity from there. It's all about getting to know each other, building relationships, developing trust and focusing on what really matters for us.

3. Work with just a few people

The Inverted Pyramid offers a different model to the traditional social media model of building 'friends', 'connections' and 'email lists', with perhaps many people we do not even know. We are encouraged to get lots of people to 'like' us and what we say. But the process rarely goes beyond that one click.

This somewhat tired and commercially driven model operates on the basis of having lots of people in our networks. The bigger our network, the more targets the social media business can offer advertisers. It's all about others paying to try to sell products and services to our 'friends'.

Our Inverted Pyramid Team approach is more real. It focuses on a small number of people that we really want to work with. It's about building relationships to help us and those who work with us, as we grow together to build our piece of a worldwide community of support.

INVERTED PYRAMID EXERCISE

Who is it that you turn to?

THE DEPENDABILITY QUESTION

When it all goes wrong,
when you're struggling,
when you desperately need practical help or advice,
who is it that you turn to?
Who is your real friend?
Who can you really depend upon?

Close personal relationships
are at the heart of community.
It is these relationships that bind us together,
to share what we are
and to be there for each other
as we journey together.

PERSONAL DEVELOPMENT REFLECTION

1. Who is your best friend?
2. How are you supporting each other?
3. How might you begin to build an Inverted Pyramid together?

4. Build your first Inverted Pyramid Team

Can you identify the two or three people you'd like to begin to talk with about the Inverted Pyramid? Who would you like to share this book with? Have you a project that you'd love to suggest that others could help you with? Have you thought of someone you can help and support?

Those who work with you will bring their own ideas, experience and connections. Your Inverted Pyramid Team can grow quickly and begin to create further Inverted Pyramid Teams as the network that you started grows upwards.

5. Imagine you are creating an upside down family tree!

The growth of our Inverted Pyramid Team is like an Inverted Pyramid family tree. You begin with your colleagues and close connections. They, in turn, may create other Inverted Pyramid Teams of their own with their colleagues and close connections, as well as working with you. It's like an upside down family tree!

The wonderful thing about all of this is that we can encourage and help others to build Inverted Pyramid Teams in different sectors, across different parts of the community, for different age groups, in different areas of the world. As we reach outwards, our Inverted Pyramid Team will look like the trunk of a tree, with branches reaching out and supporting other branches. All this positive work can only happen because of us.

6. Aim to make an impact

When we reach out to others to suggest something better, we are looking at the potential to create a new workpiece, one that is rooted deep within us. As our Inverted Pyramid Teams are linked to us, they represent who we are, gradually uncovering the contribution we can make.

We become much more focused on the way we work and those we are trying to help, addressing key needs, making an impact, looking for opportunities for growth and extending the reach of the organisation. Inverted Pyramid Teams add value at so many levels.

INVERTED PYRAMID EXERCISE

Are you a team player?

INVERTED PYRAMID TEAMS

An Inverted Pyramid Team
is a group of people
who work together
for their common purpose.
They all share the same goal
and work to ensure that
they all arrive together.

PERSONAL DEVELOPMENT REFLECTION

1. Who is in your first Inverted Pyramid Team?
2. What is the focus of your collaboration?
3. What impact would you like to imagine?

7. Show up!

Woody Allen had a great saying: '*90% of success is just showing up.*' If we're not there, it can't happen. If we don't make the effort and go to that event, meet that person, have a chat, send that email, make that phone call, follow up that enquiry, get on the train, how can we be open to inspiration and opportunity?

We also need other people, for it is through and with other people that we get things done. We need the companionship, friendship, support and encouragement of others. So, if we don't show up, how will we make those links?

On our Inverted Pyramid workshops, we encourage people to have health and well-being workpieces. These include getting regular exercise, looking after our diet and getting out into the fresh air. Showing up is as much about journeying together as it is the destination.

And one final part of this. Sitting alone in the park, enjoying the quietness of an empty church or strolling by the beach are other ways of showing up. For showing up is not just about going somewhere or being with others. It's about showing up for ourselves and building our understanding of what is truly important for us.

8. Create new and better connections

Community comes from the word *commune*, which is a collective or group of people. It means that we come together to share what we have in common: the air we breathe, the food we eat and the world we live in.

The potential for our Inverted Pyramid communities is to create more and better connections so that we become much more effective in the way we work together and look after each other. The opportunity is there to look at how we can work together to create a kinder and more inclusive world.

9. Get to know your colleagues

If people do not know each other well, then how can we build community? For we won't have an understanding of a person's situation or background and the key challenges that are facing them.

The reality is that most people only know their colleagues at a business level within the context of their workplace, except perhaps for two or three close colleagues. We need to actively encourage people to meet up. There must be a driver for this, a purpose (motivation) to building a community. So why exactly are we trying to build a community?

This comes back to purpose and our big vision for our community. If it's simply to instil a fuzzy feeling around the organisation, then we can organise awards, sponsorships or charity fundraising instead. All of these are great and will encourage and motivate employees, but they may also keep them firmly rooted within a traditional hierarchal structure.

A true community is one that links people together in a way that enables them to reach out. It expands, extends and stretches the organisation in ways that individually, we could never dream of. Our vision of community is what will attract people to work with us. It is the glue that will bind people together, the fabric that will underpin a new hybrid way of working as the traditional organisational ties and controls are loosened.

10. Define your community

If we define our community as our employees, this can easily become just another work network designed to make the business more effective.

If we define our community as our employees and our customers, it is simply a customer service network designed to improve the customer experience.

The point here is that it's not up to us to define our community within the Inverted Pyramid process. The community is created through the empowerment process that we and all of our colleagues are part of.

If we frame our community within or around our organisation structure, we simply strengthen that hierarchal position. We can, of course, create a wonderful support framework for our staff. Just look at what Cadbury, the chocolate maker, did in Bournville back in 1879. They brought the employees and their families together by creating a model village (with no alcohol) to provide low-density housing and to promote the Quaker lifestyle. They didn't have the Internet. They addressed practical issues such as housing and healthcare for their employees and their families. They were so much more than chocolate makers.

So, what are we so much more than? What are we going to dramatically improve? What big issue are we going to address – in our community, in the world? Are we going to bring all our people together in a true community, rather than isolated within an outdated employment structure?

11. Community is not owned

Community is not a framework owned by the business or organisation. If businesses try to make it 'their community' then it simply becomes about corporate development and organisational growth or individual ego, vanity and power.

Instead of building our community within our organisation structure, we must enable and empower our staff to come together and identify the needs and priorities in their lives, the things that they want to impact upon and the changes they want to see happen in our world. We do not have to manage this process, for it is their community that we are helping to build. And in doing this, we will encourage the building of Inverted Pyramid teams within, across and outside of our business. The key connection will be the people who work with us, who will now bring us into other areas. They will uncover insights, benefits and perspectives that can literally change the world.

So we cannot build an Inverted Pyramid Community within our business. The way that we build community is by enabling our employees to link together and to develop their Inverted Pyramids. And when this takes them beyond the normal work they do, into a new territory that has nothing to do with our business, then we are winning. What they are doing is helping to reshape the business as an Inverted Pyramid which addresses the needs of those who work there, and which is not only in touch with what is important to employees but is also a champion and an advocate of making it happen.

The first rule of any Chief Executive, business owner or senior management team is to begin to build their own Inverted Pyramid by reaching out at all levels within the organisation and beyond. In effect, they are the role model. They are giving permission. Their efforts to build an Inverted Pyramid community will empower others.

12. Describe your community

I asked a group of Senior Managers, who are all working on building Inverted Pyramids in their organisations, to explain in a sentence or two what they saw as community. Here are some of their responses:

- *Our Inverted Pyramid community has turned into an inclusive, ever-expanding, outward-looking, proactive team that looks after each other, respects individual interests, reaches out first, and works on the basis of abundance rather than scarcity.*
- *We are building a team by consciously looking after the people who work with us. We don't look for employees any more – we look for partners. We believe that the total is greater than the sum of the parts.*
- *We work on the principles of kindness and compassion for each other. Our core behaviours look to pay it forward, give back, and to share our experience and knowledge freely.*

- *Organisational measures such as income, growth, profit and key performance indicators (KPIs) are simply by-products of our effective Inverted Pyramid community of kindness.*
- *Our business exists to meet the needs of those who work with us and all those we serve. We have become, in effect, a community business.*

13. A structure is not a community

It's easy to assume that a company is a community made up of employees or customers. It's easy to assume that a neighbourhood is a community made up of the residents.

But simply being linked together in some structure or location does not necessarily mean that we are a community.

You see, for us to achieve Inverted Pyramid community status, we need to have a shared vision and a common purpose. Simply being linked in a transactional way does not achieve this, which is why so many businesses fail in trying to build community. They have a business structure but they do not have the overall driving purpose, values and agreed behaviours which unite people through a common goal.

It is therefore essential that we understand that the Inverted Pyramid community is different to our organisational structure. The community thrives by building linkages outwards and upwards, and by loosening the confines of the traditional organisational reporting boundaries.

14. Collaboration builds community

We all need to work. It doesn't matter what the job or activity is – cleaner, carer, part-time shop assistant. What is important is that we all have the opportunity to interact with others and contribute. This is what builds community. This is what underpins individual well-being.

Collaboration doesn't just happen by bringing people together and asking them to talk or sort out something. Collaboration happens when we meet in the same place. This is an interpersonal linking, where two or more people come together with the intent of producing more than they may have anticipated. It is this entity which holds potential far beyond the initial task that we envisaged, because it is built around who we are, rather than what we are planning to do. To treat collaboration purely as a management task misses 99% of the potential for impact, change and moving forward together.

The whole is greater than the sum of the parts. The whole is different to the sum of the parts. For this new entity that we create extends who we are. It leverages what we are about. These are the direct, real and significant fruits of collaboration.

INVERTED PYRAMID EXERCISE

What is collaborative working?

COLLABORATIVE WORKING

Let's sort it out.
Let's get going.
Let's not wait for others.
Let's join together.
Let's start the ball rolling.

This is our task.
This is our piece.
This is our love.
This is what we are about.
And this is who we are.

Let's press the button.
Let's change things.
Let's lend a hand.
Let's share what we know.
Let's give what we have.

This is our task.
This is our piece.
This is our love.
This is what we are about.
And this is who we are.

PERSONAL DEVELOPMENT REFLECTION

1. What is your piece?
2. Who are you working with?
2. What are you going to sort out?

15. Networking is not community

The Inverted Pyramid family framework is very different to old-fashioned networking.

In typical networking arrangements, people meet up and see how they can build their network or find new customers. In many networking groups, the members are simply trying to sell to each other. They are working as individuals to try and make their mark in the network, effectively competing with every other person trying to do the same. It's no surprise that many traditional networks fail to deliver, except for the people at the top.

INVERTED PYRAMID EXERCISE

Is it a fixed menu today?

OUTSIDE CATERING

The boss and employee relationship
is deeply flawed.
It is not a true construct
for it restricts both parties.

We can only bring a fixed menu
to the job table,
providing the same meals every day
in every workplace.

We all leave behind
kitchens full of food,
unused equipment
and recipe books unopened.

PERSONAL DEVELOPMENT REFLECTION
1. List all of the skills, experience, interests and knowledge that you
   leave at home when you go to work.
2. What new 'recipe' might you create today?
3. What job would you really like to have?
4. How will you build your 'outside catering' business?

CHAPTER 10: Time to harvest

Please take a moment to reflect and capture any initial thoughts, ideas, questions or action points that you wish to note and take forward. You will be able to gather these from each chapter for your personal development Action Plan at the end of the book.

Notes

1 ....

2 ....

3 ....

4 ....

5 ....

CHAPTER 11

How can we increase participation in our Inverted Pyramid community?

This is one of the questions I get asked most often!

There are lots of tips for building community on the Internet: quizzes, membership schemes, email newsletters, competitions, online events, online training and much more. Unfortunately, most of these will have little long-term sustainable impact and may indeed be seen as irrelevant or just as more 'work' to do. Essentially, they fail to grasp the fundamental nature of what community is and how it works.

If you are serious about building a thriving, vibrant, effective and sustainable community, this chapter details 17 key recommendations (along with interactive questions) to help you and your team.

1. HAVE A CLEAR PURPOSE

The community must have a clear and separate purpose from your organisation or business. If it doesn't, it's just another set of organisational activities and things to do. This is largely why many online communities trapped within a hierarchal structure have little, or only casual, interaction. They are seen as a top-down senior management initiative.

- What is the purpose of your community?

- Is your community important? Is it vital? Is it going to make a real difference in the world?

2. KEEP COMMUNITY SEPARATE

It is important to distinguish between the organisation and the community. The organisation has a financial structure, essentially revolving around income and expenditure, that leads to profit or delivering the required services. The community is all about people and enabling them to grow, collaborate and contribute in new ways.

Interacting solely within the structure of the business means that staff will not necessarily feel part of something special or different, but simply workers in the business.

- Does your community have a distinct and separate identity?

3. ENCOURAGE FLUID RELATIONSHIPS

A business is typically a structure in which we work within our own specific roles and responsibilities. A community, however, is all about our individual relationships with other people, and these are not fixed as they are inside an organisational structure or culture. The measure of a successful community is its ability to enable and support the development of individual relationships in line with the bigger vision. Community relationships are fluid, enabling people to link up with others, form small groups and build teams to support projects. Communities are dynamic and ever-changing as relationships grow and develop, new people join and new projects are created.

- How does your community encourage and enable people to link up together to work on activities separate to the business?

4. LOOK AFTER THE HEALTH OF YOUR COMMUNITY

All communities need their own operational framework. There must be clearly set out methods of engagement, means of discussion, opportunities to support each other, a framework for driving all activities forward and mechanisms for looking after the overall health of the community.

- Where and how do the members of your community get together to discuss their priorities, plans and projects?
- How does your organisation support community activities?

5. ENABLE EXPERT GROUPS (SHARING EXPERIENCE, KNOWLEDGE AND EXPERTISE)

It is essential to encourage and empower individuals to share their knowledge, information and expertise with others. On a typical six-week Inverted Pyramid programme, individuals will be sharing their expertise and working with others who would like to know more about a particular topic. All colleagues on the programme are welcome to join in any of these sessions.

It is important to note that this is not a centralised activity. Interest is sparked in these and many other potential areas. These expert Zoom groups grow out of individuals chatting together and identifying that the topic would be of interest to them.

A typical list of Inverted Pyramid Expert Zoom Groups might include topics like these:

- Getting used to Zoom
- Writing and publishing your first e-book
- Personal innovation and creativity
- Meditation
- Three-day juice cleanse
- Bullet journaling – the difference between busy and productive
- ASD and neurodiversity
- Compassion fatigue (for carers and others)
- Passive income group
- How to Instagram

- How to do a Facebook Live video
- All you need to know about Excel
- Guided relaxation
- The weekly gardening team
- Start your own business series
- Introducing young people to the Inverted Pyramid methodology
- Job group – CVs/Resumes, job applications and volunteering
- Income generation for community and voluntary organisations
- Setting up your website
- Getting work done with Fiverr

These are all new groups created by Inverted Pyramid colleagues to support others within their group and across all the groups. They are an excellent way of developing presentation and project management skills, effective online working and, of course, relationship-building outside and beyond the initial core structure.

Look at the above list and imagine you are part of that initial training group.

- Which groups would you like to attend?
- What expertise do you have that you could share?
- Could you start an expert group to help others in your community?

6. LEVERAGE ADDITIONAL VALUE FROM COLLEAGUES

The community must bring added value for individuals that isn't currently available within the organisation. There's little incentive if it's simply just to 'link up more effectively' or to 'keep up-to-date'.

With a wide range of expert groups and inputs, individuals have numerous ways of connecting with others, developing skills and building initiatives that are meaningful to them.

- What is the 'added value' that your community offers to individuals?

7. HAVE A DISTINCT COMMUNITY IDENTITY

If you see community as distinct from your core business, then we must address its identity.

- What is the name of your community?
- Do you have a strapline or logo?
- How do you promote your brand?
- What are your values?

8. GIVE YOUR COMMUNITY A SEPARATE VOICE FROM THE OUTSET

Think about how your community can have a voice.

- Who is your community speaking to?
- What are your key messages?
- What is the public face of your community?

9. BE A PARTNER – NOT A MANAGER

Strong communities can grow quickly and build their base by working with their stakeholders.

It is a 'work with them' (partnership) approach rather than a 'do it to them' (management) approach.

- Are all of your managers seen as partners (equal players) in your community?
- Are your managers active contributors?

10. MOTIVATE, ENCOURAGE AND INCENTIVISE

We are all busy: busy at work, busy with our families, busy with all the stuff of life. So, we need to be clear that this is worth devoting precious time to.

- What's the big incentive for people to join the community?
- What will they achieve, create or contribute to?
- What is the big win that you are all working for?

11. BE A PLACE OF PEER SUPPORT

We might be better off thinking about our community as one big peer group. Each of us has our own challenges around work, family, health, giving back, personal issues, career development, relationships, feeling stuck and so on. Our community could be the place for us to access the help that each of us needs, and a place to share our knowledge and experience.

- Has your community got clear rules of working?
- Is your community a confidential and safe space for all staff colleagues?
- Is it a place of trust and trusting relationships?

12. MEASURE AND SHARE YOUR IMPACT

Communities exist for a purpose. And this purpose seeks to produce certain outcomes or results. These are specific, measurable and urgent tasks to be achieved. There are relevant plans to be implemented. The work of community is urgent because it is directly related to our personal priorities, needs and ambitions. Community priorities are not secondary to the business. Community is of a different order of magnitude to the business.

- How are you making the world a better place?
- How are you building new models of collaboration, giving back and adding value?

- How are you leveraging the skills, talents, expertise and experience of every single person for maximum community impact?

13. MAKE AND LEAVE A LEGACY

Businesses grow, go bust, get taken over, are sold or die a slow death. There is often little left behind. However, this is not true with communities. Individual relationships still exist. Inverted Pyramid projects grow and develop. Lives around the world are changed forever. Communities are driven by everyone looking after each other, and therefore expand upwards and outwards as their normal operating framework.

- What is the enduring value of your community?
- What are the relationships being created and developed that go beyond the life of the roles that people have in the business?
- What is the legacy that your community is creating as it grows?

14. DESCRIBE YOUR COMMUNITY STRUCTURE AND HOW IT WORKS

The community structure, as we know, is not the same as the organisational structure. A community infrastructure is organised, managed and operates in its own 'space'. Of course, the two structures overlap but the important point is that they are two separate structures.

- What kind of structure does your community have?
- How does your community structure support and help colleagues?

15. YOU ARE NOT AN ONLINE COMMUNITY

Communities are about personal relationships rather than an online presence. Apps and websites are very limited in their ability to truly capture some of the messages, key points or successes of what is happening. It is the fabric of activity that is happening above and beyond an online presence that is the true nature of community.

In reality, there is no such thing as an online community. Rather than say we have an online community, it is better to say that our community has a presence online. This in turn means that our community activity is not constrained to the limitations of an app, website or online meetings. Communities thrive when people link up with each other in multiple ways.

- How does your community develop and grow way beyond your online activity?
- How are you encouraging the development of interpersonal relationships?

16. BUILD A PARTNERSHIP APPROACH FOR ALL

Business owners, CEOs and senior managers sometimes think they will lose something if people link up in a way that isn't directly connected to the business.

Nothing could be further from the truth. For it is only through the gifts of connection, sharing and collaboration that new value is created. This has the potential to enable employees to achieve more and become more. And that, in turn, creates something more than the owner or CEO could ever have imagined.

- As a business owner, CEO or senior manager, are you able to adopt a peer group approach of equal collaboration for everyone – or are you still making the decisions about the community, what it is and how it works?

And remember, once we start to link up with others across the organisation, we begin to build community. This is the essential difference between operating within a traditional hierarchal structure and within an Inverted Pyramid process.

The traditional hierarchal framework drives us to complete tasks that have already been specified. The Inverted Pyramid process encourages each of us to build relationships across the organisation to help achieve our collective purpose. The structure and the process must move forward together with each informing the other. They are not in conflict!

Our Inverted Pyramid community becomes our engine of inclusion.

17. DESCRIBE YOUR COMMUNITY

I asked a group of senior managers who are all working on building Inverted Pyramids in their organisations to explain, in a sentence (or two!), how they see and describe their community to others. Here is a selection of their responses:

What is your Inverted Pyramid Community?

- *It's the functioning framework of possibilities and initiatives that flows directly from our mission of collaboration and inclusion to help those most in need. Our community is only limited by individual imagination, determination and mutual support.*

- *We provide Inverted Pyramid training and ongoing support for all staff. We encourage each person to build and be part of Inverted Pyramids across our organisation.*

- *Our Inverted Pyramid Community is driven by the seventeen Sustainable Development Goals of the United Nations and Agenda 2030. Individually and collectively, we are working with others to build a better world.*

- *We work on the principles of kindness and compassion for each other. Our core behaviours are based on the principles of paying it forward, giving back, and sharing our experience and knowledge freely. We have an annual awards programme to recognise 'exceptional individual kindness and amazing Inverted Pyramid initiatives'.*

162

- *The success of our Inverted Pyramid community is measured by the range of initiatives that extend our reach to provide help and support to others.*

- *Our Inverted Pyramid of Inclusion is becoming embedded across our organisation. For example, every job specification has IPI priority behaviours and a set of tasks, every meeting features 10 minutes of IPI success updates from staff as a constant reminder and encouragement to support one another, and a percentage of our income is allocated to staff IPI initiatives on a monthly basis. We are determined to make a real difference.*

- *We recognise that organisational measures such as income, growth and profit are simply by-products of our effective and growing Inverted Pyramid community of kindness. We have a kindness policy and specific kindness behaviours that inform and guide our way of working. This is the cornerstone of our induction process and ongoing staff development process.*

CHAPTER 11: Time to harvest

Please take a moment to reflect and capture any initial thoughts, ideas, questions or action points that you wish to note and take forward. What are your main reflections from Section Two?

Notes

1 ....

2 ....

3 ....

4 ....

5 ....

SECTION 3

The Inverted Pyramid in all our Workplaces

What are the challenges and opportunities of Inclusion that different sectors are facing? Section Three invites us to explore the application of the Inverted Pyramid methodology in our various workplaces with businesses and organisations, charities, education, public sector bodies and government agencies.

Each chapter contains a series of 'snapshots' to help us gain an understanding of the inclusion challenges faced in different sectors.

Although the section is divided into five broad categories much of the learning and many of the recommendations apply to numerous sectors. Please read through all chapters to gain a good understanding of the potential for your organisation and priorities. You will find elements in other sectors that may be directly relevant to you.

CHAPTER 12

The Inverted Pyramid in businesses and organisations

This chapter is all about organisation realignment and transformation. It asks some hard questions, such as: 'How do we enable "bottom-up" activities and individual empowerment to happen in a hierarchal organisation?' and 'How do we actually make the Inverted Pyramid work at a practical level in our businesses and organisations?'

What is the purpose of our Inverted Pyramid?

What would be the purpose of building an Inverted Pyramid community through our business? What is the big vision? What are we passionate about? How can we make things better? Who would we really like to help? What would we like to see differently in our world? How might we leverage each other's skills and experience in a different way, for a bigger impact? These are central questions for all staff, because if we are not here to make the world a better place, then what are we here for?

Many businesses do not have a vision beyond the balance sheet simply because that's been enough over the years or that's the model that they've been told they must follow. That may have been okay at some point in history, but will it be enough to sustain us given the pace of change and challenges in our interdependent and uncertain world?

If we choose not to have a vision beyond profit, then what do we have to offer our staff? Will it be enough to excite people? Will it be enough to entice the best talent to work with us? Will it be enough to encourage people to give much more of themselves and to go beyond the old norm of working for money? Will it be enough to build daily excitement and enthusiasm in every part of our organisation? And will it be enough for our customers and clients? For they too are part of our new Inverted Pyramid communities.

And this offers us another way forward. For those people we work with may have a better sense of what we can or should do. They may be closer to the customer. So, reach out and engage with your colleagues at all levels. And remember that the strategy flowing from our purpose can be multifaceted. We don't have to concentrate on one thing alone, just as we don't have to have only one job. Our business too can have multiple Inverted Pyramid Teams, just like each of us.

Organisation design and transformation – how do we enable 'bottom-up' activities in a hierarchal organisation?

Developing an Inverted Pyramid infrastructure is not about creating or imposing a new management system. It's about empowering individuals to be responsible for the Inverted Pyramid initiatives that they create and are involved with. And this must take account of the practicalities of the organisation, for one informs and supports the other.

There is no ready-made template that we can apply when we are seeking to build an inclusive Inverted Pyramid organisation, for we are in essence changing the way that people in the organisation relate to and work with each other. We are in the early stages of building Inverted Pyramid inclusion organisations and it is likely that many different models and journeys will evolve. And this is the way it should be, because this is an individually driven process – not a top-down management template that we are seeking to impose upon individuals.

We need to ensure that we are building a fabric that supports global collaboration. For if we are not enabling our people to reach out beyond the business or organisation then we are simply reinforcing a traditional management hierarchy of internal authority and control.

1. The fusing of Inverted Pyramid activities with organisational priorities

It's of little use expecting people to do their current job in the same way and yet also build Inverted Pyramid relationships. It cannot be something that is squeezed in when we have some time. Inverted Pyramid activities have to be at the heart of our work. These activities of reaching out, building new linkages and tackling priority issues have to be the focus.

So this requires restructuring of time and priorities, resulting in more effective use of time addressing bigger issues with a greater return for everyone. Again, if we believe we will lose out by reducing our focus on current activities, this might be a sign that we are still thinking in terms of the traditional hierarchal control structure.

The reality of home working and hybrid working shows us that people generally do not abuse the additional freedom. The vast majority of people have treated this new Inverted Pyramid relationship with greater respect and a higher level of personal responsibility. This is important because the suggestion that the Inverted Pyramid means that managers 'lose control' is not the case. It's the opposite. Inverted Pyramid organisations have a stronger internal fabric of collaborative working that is not dependent upon telling people what they can or can't do.

Honesty, integrity and personal effectiveness are all boosted by the fact that people have greater control of their time and work structure, and therefore are much more likely to take responsibility for themselves and their outputs. We have to communicate very clearly what our organisation is seeking to do, and how each person is important in enabling us to turn the traditional organisational hierarchy upside down, by linking up and working on what really matters.

2. Safeguarding

We must avoid any contradiction between the 'normal way' of doing things and the new projects. This typically can manifest as not having enough time to do 'both roles', current managers not 'freeing up' staff as required or 'prioritising old routines'.

If there is not clear and consistent leadership from the top of the organisation and managers are not fully on board, then the efforts of staff can be frustrated. Experience shows that the weight of traditional work pressures and operational requirements can quickly swamp new behaviours.

On the flip side, we can reward the efforts of these individuals and work groups. The organisation can promote case studies as role models which will help to embed the approach.

Realigning the management ecosystem requires a range of interventions at different levels and processes throughout the organisation. These are important to protect, nourish, encourage and promote the emerging initiatives as well as our colleagues' well-being.

Inclusion is not a 'nice to have'. It is a foundation stone of our sharing economy. An inclusive organisational mindset can drive success, individual engagement, staff and customer loyalty and brand value – and so enable the organisation to fulfil its potential at all levels within society.

3. Becoming Inverted Pyramid guardians

Traditional business structures offer a top-down system of control to try to manage people and processes. The Inverted Pyramid transfers that control to the individuals, who then take responsibility not only for looking after themselves but also for supporting all others.

Within the Inverted Pyramid, individuals become the guardians of the organisation, promoting its values and making real its purpose. They become champions of all that we are and do, reaching out from within the organisation. As part of the Inverted Pyramid of Inclusion, all individuals have the same status, recognition and respect, irrespective of their role or remuneration.

With a top-down system of control, the traditional hierarchal management structure does not promote flair, innovation, creativity or personal ownership in every role. The Inverted Pyramid has these built-in as part of its operating system.

4. Moving towards a self-managed organisation

I believe that we can have the best of the old and the new business worlds. We can have our organisational structures but without a traditional authority system which tends to limit people. We can transfer that control to each individual so that they can take ownership for linking with others, creating new relationships and driving everyone forward in a way that contributes to what is most important.

So in other words, we keep the organisational structure in terms of reporting numbers and outcomes because this is the functional measurement of the success of the business. The Inverted Pyramid way of working between individuals and across all parts of the business can only serve to complement, support and enhance all that we do through the expanding network of personal linkages. All of this individually driven activity becomes the real engine of our purpose and our business.

Essentially, we are retaining the conventional organisation structure while breaking the linkage with hierarchal personal power based on position. We no longer need to check up on people or try to catch them out. We 'transfer' the responsibility equally to all individuals. The power is no longer in the structure. Responsibility now rests with each person using their right to initiate grown up conversations about practical issues and challenges as they arise. This is what we mean by empowerment.

Organisation structure then simply becomes a methodology for enabling the work to be done and operational results to be captured.

We see the change when we introduce the Inverted Pyramid into our traditional hierarchal structure, and the subtle shift of power results in the creation of new work teams as individuals reach outwards and upwards and create their new connections. We therefore enhance and develop the strength of the business from the bottom up.

We have to invite and seek to include everyone so that they feel motivated and able to play a full and equal part in the process of building inclusion. The shift from top-down managerial control to enabling each individual to take ownership for linking with others, creating new relationships and driving everybody forward, reshapes and contributes to our collective purpose as a team and organisation.

5. Having the bigger discussion with colleagues

Many companies already operate in a positive collaborative style, although they may explain it slightly differently. We want to generate lots of ideas, and to encourage everyone to come up with new ways to improve things. We are looking for creativity, innovation, crazy thinking, impossible ideas, random suggestions, well-thought-out plans, and better ways of working from each individual. At the same time, we are managing one overall business process which is informed by the outcome of these initiatives. In other words, we work with multiple ideas and initiatives that all work (on an ongoing and consistent basis) to inform one process.

To build an Inverted Pyramid organisation, we need to reset and calibrate the purpose of the organisation. It is much more than profit, share price or sales. It's actually about doing all of this in a way that includes and empowers all of the people to be fully themselves in a way that connects us all to a bigger world out there.

Our bigger objective and purpose are beyond profit share price and sales. It's about the contribution that we make to others. We see our organisation in a bigger way, both internally within individuals and externally in terms of what we are all connected to. So the Inverted Pyramid organisation is ultimately about redefining the purpose and operation of business in a way that works for and supports everyone.

6. Unleashing personal creativity and innovation

When I started my first training business, one of the very first rules I said to everybody who joined was that if they could see something that could be improved, they wouldn't need to ask for permission. They had an implicit responsibility to take the action needed.

This can work in a young organisation or in a business with a flat structure. But what about in a larger organisation with multiple management levels and more complex or connected initiatives involving more people? What we do here is maintain the same personal responsibility process but extend this to take account of the complexity of the organisation. In an Inverted Pyramid, if you have a good idea, you become the key part of the team that takes it forward. We are then all empowered to make things better for everyone. We get out of our boxes and our silos. We look for the best people in the organisation to help us take this forward.

The person who proposes the solution becomes part of the work team which takes that idea forward. They become part of the implementation. Now this doesn't mean that they would have 'control' over others or become responsible for 'managing' the initiative. They would, though, be essential to the process because it was their idea, their initiative and they are the key driver in progressing it.

Many people don't come up with good ideas in traditional hierarchal organisations because they sense that nobody will listen to them or take their ideas seriously, or the suggestion will get lost on their manager's desk and never go any further, or somebody else will take credit for it.

Sometimes we may get some feedback along the lines of 'Let me look at it' but never hear anything more. While the intention may be good, the process for progressing ideas between levels and across departments is not there. Individuals are trapped in their boxes and whole departments are trapped in their silos, doing the tasks they have always done.

7. Getting it wrong is positive

Not all ideas will work. Many of the suggestions and ideas that individuals bring forward around new initiatives or to improve existing processes may not be feasible or practical when examined in greater detail. This is a normal part of creativity. Some ideas will work, and some will not.

The real success is in the fact that we had an idea and also the opportunity within our organisation to move it forward in some way, through discussion and collaboration with others. More than this, however, we have had the opportunity to build linkages with other people and to strengthen relationships across our organisation. We have got to know other people better in terms of their skills, role within the organisation, personality and what drives them. From this we can see how future ideas and initiatives have a stronger platform from which to grow. There is no such thing as a bad idea.

Unfortunately, in many traditional hierarchal structures, ideas from those at the bottom never see the light of day. People give up contributing ideas because 'nothing ever changes' or 'no one ever listens' or 'it's not the right time' or 'we've tried that before'. All real decision-making rests with the managers.

The Inverted Pyramid process, on the other hand, provides us with a framework that expects and encourages everyone to bring forward their suggestions and their ideas around how these could be developed. We're not passing this idea up the line in the hope that it might be acted upon. We are moving with it.

We might develop our initial discussion and bring in further experience or expertise. We might do a trial run, test a new approach, set up a task group, undertake a feasibility study, have a wider consultation, do some research or pilot a different process.

And this is not about getting it right all the time. This is about creating a culture which encourages every team member to look for opportunities. Because if we don't try new things, then where is the new learning going to come from?

Years ago, we talked about Continuous Improvement, Quality Circles, Lean Manufacturing, Total Quality Management (TQM), Just-In-Time, Process Mapping and many others, but these all had one thing in common: they were geared towards improving our production and efficiency within the hierarchal structure. Inverted Pyramid thinking takes us beyond tinkering and tweaking with one established process to a scenario in which we create totally new processes, systems and approaches, driven by each individual.

Not every idea will continue to develop and grow, but our relationships will. What we create between each other will be a platform for future discussions. And often, one idea will lead to a better idea. Getting it wrong and learning together is a positive. It strengthens our interpersonal relationships.

8. Stepping outside our box

We need to establish an ethos and way of working in our organisations whereby everybody is able and encouraged to talk to others. Our expectation is that we know and can talk to people at all levels and in all departments. Our culture has to be about encouraging the linking up of individual members in new ways. Everyone should have access to and be able to speak to each other on a first-name basis. This reminds me of the first business that I worked in, where the managers were all referred to by their titles: Mr, Mrs or Miss. This kept the workers reporting to them firmly in their place, at the bottom of the hierarchal structure. Many organisations still have glass ceilings.

What we're saying here is that the Inverted Pyramid process offers a framework and platform for people to link up in a needs-driven way which is not constrained or confined by traditional reporting mechanisms, seniority or status. We still have the organisation structure, but now we add a fluidity around interaction, engagement and inclusion. We are creating the conditions for bringing together people inside hierarchal organisations who wouldn't usually be brought together.

9. Leapfrogging

Leapfrogging is the process of accessing all parts of our organisation in order to make new contacts. This is not just a random 'Let's talk to anyone' process. It's a way of seeking to connect with people who may be able to help us to progress an initiative, who may have expertise in a particular area, who may be able to advise us or link us up with someone internally or externally that we should talk to.

We need to encourage leapfrogging, to get people out of their boxes, to encourage them to take forward their ideas, to look for new solutions, to address gaps that are not being met, and to explore new and better ways of doing what should be done.

INVERTED PYRAMID EXERCISE

Is this a leap year?

LEAP YEAR

The core personal development question is
'What am I really capable of?'
The response isn't about
business, work or money.

It's about who we are
and looking beyond our perceived limitations.
It's about growing into our capacity
even if we cannot see it fully.

This is the search for something
we never thought we would look at,
even though deep down
we knew we had the potential.

This is the leapfrog.
It's not linear, cumulative or predictable.
It's about us leaving our lily pad
and just going.

PERSONAL DEVELOPMENT REFLECTION

1. What are you really capable of?
2. What have you never thought you could do?
3. What does your new lily pad look like?

10. Freestyle Management

When we think about our current business structures, we realise how constrained we have become in the way that we work and think and organise ourselves. We limit ourselves to working within boxes rather than looking at where the big steps are, where the real jumps can be made and where the important points of leverage and contribution may be in terms of all of our colleagues. Because we're so consumed by tasks day after day, we miss what's happening beyond this. It's as if we are stuck on our phones using the same social media app and scrolling through everything that we already know.

Matrix management tries to build links across, as well as up and down, the organisation. It seeks to encourage people to work across and between departments. The key challenge with matrix management is essentially that it is seen as a more complex form of organisational control, and we end up having to ask 'Who is in charge of this?' or 'Who are you reporting to on that?'.

Matrix management therefore has the potential to create additional work tasks and/or to confuse employees as it can seem as though they have another totally new role now, complete with an additional set of priorities.

Freestyle management, on the other hand, is about individuals as self-managers working behind, alongside and in front of others in alternative ways with a variety of projects and priorities. We identify specialist coaches and mentors for this new arrangement, who can help individuals to work though practical priorities and challenges in a collaborative spirit.

Initially, the Inverted Pyramid projects can be seen as separate from the day-to-day activities of the organisation, but in time they will help to expand and develop it. The initiatives that people create will gradually influence the organisation culture and so reshape it, making it more outward-looking and inclusive. Nothing changes until we enable, encourage and support staff to do the things that matter to them.

11. Let's include all managers

If we don't prepare and support managers properly for this new activity, then it is likely that some element of misunderstanding or potential conflict will arise. The line manager may see that somebody in their team is spending time on work 'outside' the department or tasks that are not directly connected to their 'role'. The team member and the manager both need to have a context to show how that workpiece supports the whole organisation.

I remember some years ago developing an Inverted Pyramid pilot initiative within an organisation. We had around 200 people all working in various Inverted Pyramid Teams from across all departments and at different operational levels to drive the organisation forward. Teams were coming up with imaginative new initiatives, addressing needs, looking at how to deliver better value and developing better ways of working.

However, because one or two line managers or department heads were not directly involved in the pilot, all they could see was their staff 'going off' and spending time on what they perceived as non-critical

179

activities. It wasn't surprising then that staff productivity in relation to their traditional roles was perceived as less than expected. The organisation had failed to bring all staff into the process. The managers did not have a sense of a greater commitment, a wider view and a different way of working.

12. Senior management thinking

When our organisation embarks on the Inverted Pyramid process, we are beginning an endeavour that will grow and develop organically, in its own way.

We will naturally still be part of the overall process, but it can also grow alongside us as well as without us. Unlike most other parts of the business that we may manage and control, the Inverted Pyramid process, in its way, manages and leads us.

Control of our employees is replaced by trust in our colleagues as they build a new way of working. It's a bit like assembling a large machine where there is no plan or set of instructions – just an ambitious dream to build something special. With the Inverted Pyramid process, we are bringing the pieces together to see what people can create and build with their imagination and commitment.

Management, then, is not about instructions or telling people what to do. Management is about encouraging others to do what they are keen to do and travelling with them.

Here's an excerpt from an email sent by a Senior Manager to all her staff which demonstrates how she was seeking to encourage and empower them:

'*You and our colleagues know our organisation well. You know what we could do to make a bigger impact. You have ideas for how our organisation could reach out and work with other groups and bodies. You can see opportunities for serving customers and the public in better ways. You know where many situations could be improved. You know the things we could do so much better.*

'You know what you would do if you were asked for your opinion or if you were invited to lead on a project. I'm looking forward to working with you on the ideas you have, especially those that you thought nobody would want to hear about. Let's start with...'

13. Working with the business

Our corporate culture has to be one in which our new Inverted Pyramid Teams can naturally emerge out of the creation of individual projects and initiatives we want to take forward and explore. For while these initiatives are built through the organisation, they are actually rooted in individuals.

Our creativity and innovation are unleashed from our understanding of the workplace and the overall context of what our organisation is seeking to do. We see ourselves as working together with the business rather than working for the business.

I asked a group on a recent workshop what they liked about the Inverted Pyramid approach that their organisation had adopted, and here are some of the responses:

- *It invites us to extend the work that we do and build critical mass in key areas that really matter.*
- *It offers the opportunity for our organisation to reach out into the world and contribute in some way to the current challenges we are all facing.*
- *This workshop has shown us how to create a personal, bespoke framework for building our career in line with our priorities, and utilising all our skills, passions, interests and experience together.*
- *The Inverted Pyramid approach is the way that we will work in the future. We are impressed by its focus on how we can utilise our skills and experience to create and deliver what we most care about.*
- *We see this as a framework for individual empowerment and personal responsibility. We finally have a clear approach to developing a real attitude of inclusion in our organisation.*

14. Looking beyond our transactional approach to work

Inclusion happens when we have seamless borders between traditional hierarchal structures and Inverted Pyramid processes.

People can journey to be fully themselves at work, at home, with others and in all that they do. Hierarchal structures confine and limit us. Inverted Pyramid processes encourage us, motivate us and help us to grow. Once we are part of the Inverted Pyramid approach, we build Inverted Pyramids everywhere! We grow outwards in everything we do!

The challenge for our organisational structures, workplaces and businesses, therefore, is to embrace the potential of inclusion. The Inverted Pyramid process offers a way that enables people to add real value to their role, to become fully motivated colleagues and to bring a new and valuable dimension to their contribution.

We must encourage active participation with Inverted Pyramid processes, groups and initiatives. This should happen within the business, outside the business and between Inverted Pyramid initiatives.

In other words, a huge opportunity for growth and expansion emerges when the organisation frees itself of its one solitary traditional hierarchal structure, to encourage and empower staff to 'leapfrog' and grow, to link with others to build new frameworks and so add real value to the business.

Instead of the fixed organisational structure, where growth is limited by predictable economic factors and top-down control, we now have an engine of human creativity and motivation that is in touch with and working to address all of the real issues facing us.

We can no longer talk about inclusion within the workplace without talking about the Inverted Pyramid. For by excluding Inverted Pyramid processes, we are simply limiting people to operate within the confines of their existing team, their specific tasks and their job description.

CEOs, Managers, HR personnel and other key players across all departments can become 'guides', 'servant leaders' and 'enablers' in helping all their staff to learn about this new approach. Let's start with our senior team to see how they can get their heads around the potential of this new way of thinking.

The last 25 years have shown us that we cannot build equality through legislation. Organisational diversity and equality models seem only to categorise, divide people and emphasise our differences, rather than bringing us together.

If we are serious about inclusion, then we need to shift from legalistic and organisational approaches to ones which are based around the way that individuals work with others. The Inverted Pyramid, with its ethos of sharing, respect, caring for one another, contribution and positivity, offers the freedom upon which we build inclusion.

CHAPTER 12: Time to harvest

Please take a moment to reflect and capture any initial thoughts, ideas, questions or action points that you wish to note and take forward. You will be able to gather these from each chapter for your personal development Action Plan at the end of the book.

Notes

1 ....

2 ....

3 ....

4 ....

5 ....

CHAPTER 13

The Inverted Pyramid in government

Many governments have priorities around the redistribution of wealth, levelling up, closing the gap between rich and poor or building a society with greater opportunities for everyone.

This chapter explores the key messages and lessons from the Inverted Pyramid methodology and asks 'How can governments and local authorities engage and empower individuals to embrace a different way of working, and so build inclusion and equality of opportunity for all?'

Inverted Pyramid initiatives in local communities

As we saw earlier, the Social Inclusion and Communities Unit at the Department of Rural and Community Development in Ireland, along with Tipperary County Council, supported a three-year pilot by Diversiton in 2017 to boost individual economic development, improve collaborative working and build inclusion across County Tipperary. This was to test the effectiveness of the *Work it Out!* Inverted Pyramid methodology in supporting local people in areas of deprivation and low economic activity.

How *Work it Out!* informed the Inverted Pyramid methodology

The *Work it Out!* approach was a needs-driven method for delivering real, substantive and sustainable change for individuals. *Work it Out!* supports the design of new ways of working which are delivered and made real through its collective coaching methodology.

Work it Out! is driven by the principles of inclusion, empowerment and responsibility for others. The commitment to building individual strengths, positivity, kindness and collaboration were at the heart of what became the Inverted Pyramid methodology. These pilots supported personal economic growth, the development of local enterprise cultures, inclusion and integration, individual work and career support, community cohesion, social enterprise and more. The approach has delivered sustained outcomes for individuals in finding meaningful work and designing alternative career models, looking after each other and helping to achieve what is important to them and their families.

More than this, though, the Inverted Pyramid is a highly effective inclusion and empowerment tool to support the priorities of organisations, government agencies and local councils. We work collaboratively to build innovative, bottom-up and effective networks of all sizes and types.

The Inverted Pyramid methodology offers new ways to bring people together to leverage their collective experience and expertise – whether in tackling poverty and disadvantage, harnessing potential, promoting inclusion, improving profitability or driving economic growth.

What are the key recommendations and points of learning for governments?

We have learned much from 5 years of pilots and thousands of collaborations to date. The main points are summarised below:

Key Point 1: Stop categorising and segregating people

The two guiding principles here are *self-selection* and *inclusion* rather than segregation. For example, we wouldn't want to train a group of people with disabilities as just one homogenous group. We would mix them with an assortment of people with diverse backgrounds and circumstances, as we are mixed in everyday life.

Workshops should be open to all. We don't separate out all of the people who are 'poor' or 'unemployed' and work with them in isolation. We engage on an open basis so that there are linkages, perspectives and indeed role models outside of the area or demographic we are seeking to support.

Key Point 2: Have an asset-based personal development approach to individual development

The concept of asset-based personal development can be explained as our personal Pick 'n' Mix of skills, experience, knowledge, relationships, contacts and resources we collect as we go through life.

So often when we are stuck, we think, *What shall I do next?* But our future workpieces do not have to start from our last job or where we are now. We can use any skills, experiences, interests, hobbies we have accrued at any time throughout our life to create new workpieces.

The Inverted Pyramid calls on us to utilise our strengths and interests. It is not an approach based on what we cannot do. It seeks to build upon people's strengths and interests. We think about who we can help. We learn with the help of others, to explore and play with possibilities and ideas. We become creative and outward-looking. *What if ...?*

Key Point 3: Help individuals to harvest

The concept of *harvesting* ideas from our Pick 'n' Mix is central to personal development. We've learnt amazing things. We've met wonderful people. We've survived life. Now is the time to use all of this experience! There are many options available to all of us.

The way that we *harvest* ideas from our Pick 'n' Mix is to ask ourselves lots of QUESTIONS.

- *What jobs have I had in the past? Are any of these relevant now?*
- *What documents are on my computer? Could I use this information in a new way to help others?*
- *What do I know a lot about?*
- *What work have I really enjoyed?*
- *What was I doing 2, 5, 7 or 15 years ago?*
- *What am I really interested in developing?*
- *How could I help others?*
- *How does all of this help me to do what I really want to do?*

Working in an asset-based way enables people to become better connected with each other and encourages a spirit of cooperation, mutual support and caring, so that people can be in control of their lives. As confidence and self-esteem grow in individuals and neighbours, trust, support and community cohesion are built. An asset-based approach recognises that individuals and communities can move from being consumers of services to designers and providers of services.

Key Point 4: Don't limit your offerings

The old categorisation of unemployed or self-employed or employed is no longer sufficient if we are to address real needs and encourage people to grow. Here are some of the ways individuals at our Inverted

Pyramid courses have defined their current situation. People can easily identify themselves in two or more of the following categories:

- *Unemployed*
- *Under-employed*
- *Employed*
- *Freelance*
- *Self-employed*
- *Teacher / tutor*
- *Studying at home / career development*
- *Retired*
- *Writer / author / creator*
- *Entrepreneur / looking to start a business*
- *Coach / mentor*
- *Student*
- *Parent*
- *Carer*
- *Working from home*
- *Consultant*

The way that people see themselves nowadays is not necessarily in mutually exclusive categories. Initiatives therefore need to address not only the new world of work but also people's views of their situation and where they want to be, and then respond appropriately to their needs.

There is clearly a need for a more relevant approach which recognises the way people work and engage with each other economically in the jigsaw of work.

Key Point 5: Recognise why training programmes have limited impact on poverty

Most training or government initiatives provide skills development and/or information perceived as necessary to address a particular situation. These programmes generally work because the individual and social context that they are 'adding onto' or 'linking in with' is capable of absorbing this new element, integrating it, owning it and working with it. The programme adds value in some way.

But in addressing income poverty, isolation, migration, addiction, detention, sectarianism, racism, cultural issues, poor self-esteem, personal history and so on, this is usually not enough. The people that we are dealing with are 'stuck' in some way. These individuals recognise that their current situation makes them feel trapped or ineffective or a bit lost.

Skills development and/or information will not bring about the sustained changes in attitudes and behaviour that will help people to change their lives for the better. Simply giving these people more information or suggesting a different way of doing things or developing their skills doesn't work. It's like rain on a windowpane: the raindrops just slip off and evaporate, leaving the window much as it was before the intervention.

The idea that we can go along and 'do something to people' or 'train them in something' in isolation is usually ineffective. Training programmes are therefore limited because this is not about training – or indeed a programme. People need to be committed to living in a different way, supporting each other and able to sustain this week in, week out to ensure that benefits are realised. Typically, government programmes do not seek to deliver this.

This is about developing a different way of working together. It's about people thinking and behaving differently. It's about creating a different process that enables people to be successful.

Key Point 6: Respond to what people want to do, not what you decide for them

What do you really want to do? The Inverted Pyramid is an alternative to devoting all your time to one job or working just to pay the rent, so often to the exclusion of other needs and priorities.

The Inverted Pyramid approach helps people to build their future from a series of individual 'pieces' of work, to put these together with the support of others, and then move in the direction of what they really want to do.

Key Point 7: Why it's partners, not participants for policy makers and trainers

This is all about empowerment and ownership. As long as the trainer 'owns' the situation, nothing can really change. The trainer is the one who has the power and control. We have to flip this from the outset. That means people must take control of the process. We do this with the Inverted Pyramid and Dual Responsibility.

From day one, all participants are partners in making the process work for everyone. If something needs to be done during the process – something arranged, an activity set up or whatever – the group sorts it. There is no trainer or administrator to sort it. Partners look after arranging meetings, catering, recruitment, promotion and communication. It has to be their process.

Key Point 8: Give everyone a sustainability skillset and the opportunity to learn and use it

We know that individuals thrive in a supportive environment based on three key factors:

- A positive attitude: no negative language, encouragement of others
- A clear set of values: kindness, looking after others, reaching out, and
- A framework of supportive behaviours: working together, sharing skills and expertise and collaboration.

Key Point 9: Dual Responsibility means we all have to work differently with others

Dual Responsibility means we are responsible for making the most of the opportunity given to us. It also requires us to look after every other person in the group.

This allows our thinking to become outward-looking rather than inward. We are tired of chasing our own situation around in our heads. We look to solve problems and create options for others. We become consultants. We become creative problem solvers. We build our confidence. We develop our presentation skills.

Key Point 10: Generate work possibilities and income ideas with every person

To help people boost their income, we have to be able to show them exactly how to do this – and help them to make it happen.

Unfortunately, however, many government agencies and training organisations are not skilled, experienced or comfortable in helping people to generate income streams. They know little beyond the tired old job application route that typically leaves people demotivated, disheartened and sometimes desperate.

On the Inverted Pyramid process, for example, we show how every person can segment their core skill or experience (everybody has at least one!) into 20 different income streams – and then we work together to deliver on the easiest ones:

'Don't just describe yourself as a gardener. Start to think about how you can segment your gardening into landscape gardening, grass-cutting, hanging baskets, power spraying, window boxes et cetera. Against each of these areas you can have a range of products and services to help to monetise your skill. In other words, get paid for all you do. So, for example, in hanging baskets we can have an e-book and video course describing how to make a hanging basket. We can sell hanging basket kits. We can make bespoke

hanging baskets. We can run a craft class in making your own hanging baskets and so much more.'

Once individuals have this skillset, they have it for life. They can pass it onto their partners and children. This is work and income education and, as every parent on the programme says, this should be taught in schools.

Key Point 11: Teach success behaviours

- Focus on what's important; don't waste your time surfing the net / watching TV / reading papers
- Collaboration – it's your role to reach out and motivate others
- Ask for help; don't be stuck
- Always say YES! You'll find a way
- The night before, note the two things you want to achieve tomorrow
- Say your Affirmations or Positive Statements every morning
- Be determined – create and stick to your To-Do list
- Stay happy – change your mood; don't listen to negative inputs
- Get out of bed determined to get your priorities done
- Do not open your emails first thing
- Be successful before 10am
- Do something every day

Key Point 12: A COMPrehensive methodology for tackling poverty for policy makers

So how do we effect real change at a grassroots level? We build small pockets of collaboration, with confident, outward-looking, mutually supportive and personally driven people. We add to this and strengthen it.

These four spaces (COMP) provide the basis for the development of networks, products, services, income, enterprise and independence:

- **CONFIDENCE:** Confidence comes from a sense of empowerment and belief that is supported and made real with and through others
- **OUTWARD-LOOKING:** Outward-looking means people go beyond the physical limitations of local community, their present situation and their life map to date
- **MUTUALLY SUPPORTIVE:** A mutually supportive environment with others enables people to develop a different perspective – one they have confidence in, are comfortable with, can be successful in and can grow with
- **PERSONALLY DRIVEN:** Building upon success, interests, passions and being forward-looking – all in line with what that person really wants to do; a commitment to doing things differently, to being accountable to colleagues, to focusing every day on their new priorities and to looking after each other, not just themselves.

In this way, we are creating a platform for development and change, not just telling people what they need to do and expecting them to do it. We are giving them the tools and techniques that we know will underpin their success – but ultimately, what they do, how they do it, when they do something and who they do this with is totally up to them.

This is about developing frameworks, supportive networks, new relationships – from day one – with laughter, energy, fun, encouragement and 100% positivity. We must work to build new outward-looking, supportive relationships capable of dealing with personal, financial and day-to-day challenges as they arise.

So, if you are creating programmes around unemployment and anti-poverty, school-leavers, economic or community development and business start-up, our experience suggests that unless you are building upon a COMP approach, the chance of achieving and sustaining grassroots change is minimal.

Key Point 13: Build local infrastructure in the design and delivery of initiatives

Many government programmes run year after year, repeating a similar process with different people. There is often little built upon from an infrastructure perspective. People finish the programme and move on. Government departments and agencies seem to annually reinvent the wheel.

With the Inverted Pyramid approach, individuals in the first tranche of training become the drivers and champions bringing the next group on board, helping to develop the next range of initiatives. We are building a community that extends upwards, capitalising on the strengths, links and expertise of all its members. The Inverted Pyramid community starts with that one intake and builds long-term sustainable relationships as new connections are added.

Key Point 14: Evaluate individual economic activity

As part of the development of the Inverted Pyramid process and working with thousands of individuals, Jimmy Ryan and I devised and implemented an evidenced-based approach to assessing and evaluating each person's ability and activity in terms of generating income and improving their overall economic situation.

The Ryan and McCabe *Individual Development and Economic Activity* (IDEA) is based on 13 key journey points evaluated through an ongoing assessment process which is based upon practical outcomes and verifiable deliverables. It also provides a clear measure of the distance travelled by each individual on their income generating journey. It looks like this:

1. Made a commitment to attending the process regularly over the last 6 weeks (min. 3 weeks)
2. Contributed to group discussions and shared my ideas and suggestions with others

3. Built confidence by presenting to others in small/main group sessions
4. Developed new relationships/friendships and so extended my network
5. Created a personal project to develop and promote my service, products or ideas
6. Clarified what I really want to do – and defined a clear direction for my career and income development strategy
7. Worked collaboratively with others to develop an income generating project or initiative
8. Became clear about my personal strengths and could identify a range of possible products and services that I could potentially create and offer
9. Researched and tested my ideas and so identified at least two realistic and achievable products and services that I could create and deliver
10. Produced at least one of the following – an e-book, leaflet, website, new CV or Facebook page to promote my products or expertise
11. Generated income locally – e.g. through part-time work, freelance work or a product or service
12. Generated income online – e.g. on eBay, Amazon or from a website
13. Now have two or more income generating initiatives (workpieces) in place – e.g. a part-time job, freelance work, web sales, local service, online products etc.

CHAPTER 13: Time to harvest

Please take a moment to reflect and capture any initial thoughts, ideas, questions or action points that you wish to note and take forward. You will be able to gather these from each chapter for your personal development Action Plan at the end of the book.

Notes

1 ....

2 ....

3 ....

4 ....

5 ....

CHAPTER 14

The Inverted Pyramid in local councils

In this chapter we look at some of the specific challenges faced by local councils in seeking to build inclusion.

How can we build real links?

Many organisations struggle to build inclusion because they are trying to embed new behaviours on top of the task-based roles that people already have. These task-based roles already have systems and procedures that go directly against working with people. We're trying to get people to do their job first, and then say, '*Now we want you to do these other things as well*' and it doesn't fit. It's not consistent. It's not seen as our essential way of working.

One senior manager from a local council said recently, after reflecting on the Inverted Pyramid approach:

'*Our primary responsibility is to adjudicate, to say what can and can't be done, to accept or reject ideas or proposals, to enforce rules and to ensure compliance. We are separate from the actual process of making things better. We are the administrators of the policies, procedures, rule books and regulations. Our staff must deliver services in line with these. We therefore must remain separate from the people we serve. Our job is not about connecting with or even helping people, although this is always a nice outcome.*

'You can see how the administration of the rules and regulations has become an end in itself. Instead of using all the customer-facing opportunities that we have to build relationships, we effectively shut the door, every time. We are not interested in building relationships. Our role is to provide services in line with the rules we've been given.

'I personally think that supporting our community starts with every one of our employees building a relationship with those we serve, but our council doesn't value, measure or reward this. Indeed, we get criticised because it is not our role to discuss or get involved in these things.'

Contracting out services

One of the key challenges of tendering work to service providers is that it introduces a third party (a buffer) and so separates the local authority from its end user, the customer. Most businesses, ironically, are trying to get closer to their customers!

Within some local authorities, for example, we often see a range of disjointed contractors delivering isolated pockets of services and support. Most of those tendering organisations do not work with local authority staff on a collaborative basis. What's worse is that many organisations are not seeking to create a sustainable infrastructure when they tender out chunks of their work.

Often there is little shared learning from previous contracts or efforts made to maintain and build upon relationships created by other contractors. Many of the service providers will not be enabled to link up with each other to provide joined-up working. There are not many annual get-togethers for service providers to harvest best practice, share learning and suggest better ways of working.

Indeed, there is likely to be a regular relearning every time a new tendering situation takes place, and the winner must get to know procedures and clients from scratch. The current approach to tendering seems to continually reinvent the wheel, drive fragmentation rather than collaboration, and ensure that the potential for the development of real community relationships (between council staff, providers and residents) does not develop or grow. In short, we repeat the transaction contract by contract, rather than develop and build relationships with customers. The local council ensures that all three parties stay securely in their own boxes.

Instead of individuals collaborating, we end up with a plethora of traditional hierarchal structures all separately doing their own transactional activities. The focus is on budgets, spending and satisfying accountancy procedures for claims. There is no common vision driving and linking a shared endeavour. There is little focus on capturing and measuring real improvements for individuals and their families such as income, well-being or opportunities.

How often do service providers meet with council staff and the public to discuss local priority needs, gaps in provision and opportunities? Where is the working together, collaboration and trust being built? This is not about consultation! This is about working together in an open, transparent and non-defensive way. How often does a tender or bid come out and local people ask incredulously 'Who dreamt this up?' or say 'This is a waste of time' or 'We tried all this before and it didn't work'?

If we are serious about inclusion, we have to include people in the design, development and implementation of all that involves or impacts on them. But this is not enough. We need an Inverted Pyramid mindset so that we can enable our communities to build their own Inverted Pyramids. They must not remain subjects of our actions but become partners with us.

Provision of local community grants

There are three important questions that we can all work through together:

1. Can we offer real engagement rather than be administrators or funders?

Being the administrators of grants creates a transaction that strictly limits any interpersonal relationships with those that councils are seeking to serve. Many staff do not have regular meetings to develop relationships, understand priorities, discuss potential initiatives and work collectively on a way forward. The approach often seems to be that initiatives are decided and budgets allocated behind closed doors – without the involvement of communities. And so, if staff do venture out to people, they are doing so in a managerial, control and authority capacity. For the staff hold the purse strings and can decide who gets help and who doesn't.

2. Can we work alongside others rather than just process transactions?

If we are serious about inclusion then we have to work for the people that we seek to serve. We have to turn our triangle upside down. We need a different collaborative model of engagement rather than an authoritarian one.

3. Can we build organisational learning and community capacity rather than reinvent the wheel every year?

We continue to reinvent the transactions every year with new projects and new providers. The people that we are seeking to serve must go through everything again and hope that we make a little more progress this time around. But in many cases, it's like going to the doctor with no patient records, and it's a new doctor every time, who only has 10 minutes to see you.

And we don't connect those intermediary delivery bodies together so that they can build a collective impact. We don't even work with them, never mind those we seek to serve in our community.

This whole approach is largely ineffective in developing real community relationships, creating local capital, building cumulative knowledge and encouraging collaboration. Its separatist, top-down allocation of resources and delivery of projects actively works against building inclusion. It looks like an inefficient waste of time, money, resources. More than this, however, it reinforces a continuing loss of opportunity, potential and indeed hope for those we should be serving. We can do much better.

Building inclusive growth

A local authority has decided to appoint two Transformation Directors. Reporting directly to the Chief Executive, their role is to bring together all departments in line with two key strategic aims: one around the green economy and sustainability, and the other around inclusive growth.

Inclusive growth is essentially about levelling up, the redistribution of wealth and looking after those less fortunate in our local communities.

I was speaking with the Transformation Director for Inclusive Growth, who was explaining to me how difficult it was to get people to take action. He had put in place a matrix management-type framework where he was bringing people together across the council, as opposed to them just working in their departments or teams. His aim was to encourage people to break out of their silos and work collaboratively.

The difficulty, he explained, was the inability of people to see the opportunity, to take responsibility or to act. This cultural reluctance could not be broken down, irrespective of the encouragement he gave. His question for me was very simple: '*How can I build greater activity to drive our inclusive growth priorities?*'

For many staff, this was just added another layer of management, bureaucracy and confusion about priorities. As one employee said, *'They're asking us to develop initiatives but don't tell us how. Who do we work with? What exactly are we allowed to say and do? Do we have a budget? What happens if this is in someone else's area or department? What happens if I talk to the wrong person or suggest something that is somebody else's responsibility? It's all so confusing. On top of this, I have a job to do. And now they are looking for me to do more.'*

For many councils, building inclusive growth remains a project or a bolt-on initiative. It is still not their core purpose. They lack a big vision around which senior management, all departments and people (inside and outside the organisation) can work collectively.

Staff remain safely stuck in their silos doing their tasks, consumed by their transactional responsibilities. *'Building inclusive growth is really just another management fad or the latest buzz word... it will pass.'* But for some who understand the Inverted Pyramid principles, seeds are beginning to grow.

Building inclusive growth isn't so much about developing new initiatives. It is effectively about developing our staff and helping them to learn to work in a new way. It's about making our values and behaviours visible and transparent. It's about each of us holding each other to account and recognising each other for our successes. Many of the organisations struggling to make inclusion a reality don't have a big vision around what this actually looks like for staff and customers. They fail to recognise that their current systems and processes actively work against inclusion. This is because activities are transaction-based, rather than building interpersonal relationships first. Staff are measured on how well they manage transactions, and not on how well they build relationships with clients, customers or people in the community.

Instead of maintaining barriers that exclude and complicate things, we have to connect with those we are here to serve. We have to create ways of making it easier for our staff to help people.

What this means is that we are now talking about redefining what we do every day and how we do it. Because ultimately, by changing the way we work, we make it a lot easier to achieve what we're trying to achieve. When we become explicit in our values and in our daily behaviours, there's no way our outcomes will not be in line with what we want.

So, tell me, what is the big vision for your organisation? Are you treating inclusion as an HR-led task or building inclusive growth as a bolt-on initiative? Are the public genuine collaborative partners in what you do? What are the daily behaviours that you want to see from every member of staff? Are these behaviours transaction-focused or are they about building interpersonal relationships at all levels? Do all staff know what they are expected to do to build relationships? How will you train and develop all staff to bring about the transformation necessary for inclusive growth?

We can change all of this

Could we encourage our training and service providers to come together and share best practice and learning on an ongoing basis? Could we link up groups within our area and indeed across other areas to develop new linkages and joint initiatives? Could our staff work across departments, with other councils, funders and agencies to help build a joined-up response? And why not bring together providers, communities and staff in new ways to tackle urgent priorities that affect us all?

Local councils can take the lead in this transformation from now. We need to start by training all staff, service providers and those in our communities about the Inverted Pyramid methodology. How else can we come together and work together in a new way? Inclusion cannot happen if we just tell people to work differently!

Let's train and empower our staff so that they can begin to engage and equip people to build new arrangements from where we all are now.

A local authority case study

I was fortunate to work with an English local council for a 2-year period (2014–16) to pilot and explore the development and implementation of an Inverted Pyramid strategy. Here is an extract from a note from one of the departmental managers:

'*Our aim was to deliver corporate objectives through personal development and inclusive working amongst staff and our community. Our vision was that all staff can innovate to create a culture of collaboration, kindness, positivity and so reach out to and work with local people.*

'*The Inverted Pyramid process was launched in Autumn 2014 as a catalyst for staff to have the space to think about the approach and skills we needed to develop to make what we do every day better. Inverted Pyramid project ideas began to germinate to improve services, deliver value for money and make our region a better place to live, work and visit for everyone.*

'*The Inverted Pyramid teams quickly grew into an assertive, confident, strategic thinking bunch who enjoy challenging processes, networking to facilitate change and presenting the results. We talked about our work as Inverted Pyramid Small Initiatives because each one of us can contribute something. Each of us can improve something locally every day.*

'*Significant achievements in the early months included:*

- *Ongoing passive income ideas for the council's local advertising project*
- *Tuesday evening running club – improving well-being and building links between staff and local people*
- *Linking tenant services energy with environmental health energy*

- *Updating the induction process to build interpersonal links for new starters into every council department from day one*
- *Abandoned vehicles project for schools and colleges*
- *The pop-up museum: a staff/community engagement initiative on a sheltered housing scheme*
- *FUNdamentals of work experience: staff in various departments working with local colleges, training providers and school leavers to create new opportunities, events and resources for young people aged 17–24*
- *Income/business potential of vermin control services and products*
- *Affiliate marketing opportunities on the council website for generating income*
- *Community led tourism initiatives: heritage tours, old railway line walkway and spiritual tourism*
- *Dramatically reducing waste through community engagement and collaboration*
- *Reviewing the impact of welfare reforms and identifying ways to help individuals and families*
- *Reducing conflict in the council as a workplace through the development of a new mediation service*
- *Developing a range of joint health and well-being initiatives for staff and individuals in communities*
- *Translating corporate values into everyday behaviours that all staff work to.*

'Following these initial successes, the delivery of the Inverted Pyramid process quickly shifted in two major ways:

1. From training to project management

'Group members quickly took responsibility for the ongoing day-to-day development of the process. A fledgling Empowerment Group made up of people from across the Council coordinated all activities. This is significant as it moved the initiative from a training/facilitation process to an organisational improvement resource owned across the Council with a *bottom-up, mutually supportive framework. The group took responsibility for managing the Inverted Pyramid process. Exciting!*

2. From HR to the corporate team

'The Inverted Pyramid quickly shifted from an HR initiative to a valuable new way of working and thinking for the corporate team, who reviewed its effectiveness, outcomes and impact on a monthly basis. An annual community event was held each December to recognise key individuals, share success stories, promote initiatives and reinforce the key values and behaviours of the Inverted Pyramid way of working.

'Lastly, from a personal point of view, the Inverted Pyramid is a gentle creature. It took us a little time to build critical mass and confidence across all levels of the council. When the critical mass was reached, this way of working became the new norm. Our priority is always to nourish and look after one another and to make sure that we do not go back to our old transactional way of working in silos.'

INVERTED PYRAMID EXERCISE

Will we stick together?

COMMUNITY COHESION

A new community will emerge.
A new type of community
will emerge and grow
offering help and hope.

A new definition of community
will emerge and grow
changing the why and the how
and serving all.

For community is not an organisation
or a structure.
Community is not based in a place
or even in a virtual space.

Community rests in each of us
enabling us
to reach outwards
and to work with all others.

PERSONAL DEVELOPMENT REFLECTION

1. How can you build a new type of personal community?
2. What will you work on?
3. Who will you offer 'help and hope' to?

`

CHAPTER 14: Time to harvest

Please take a moment to reflect and capture any initial thoughts, ideas, questions or action points that you wish to note and take forward. You will be able to gather these from each chapter for your personal development Action Plan at the end of the book.

Notes

1 ....

2 ....

3 ....

4 ....

5 ....

CHAPTER 15

The Inverted Pyramid in the charity and voluntary sector

Can we build our Inverted Pyramids from the day-to-day work that we do and change lives from where we are? In this chapter we explore the concept of the inclusive charity model. Instead of depending on intermediary organisations as the main delivery method of aid and support, we ask, '*How might we and our organisations make a direct impact on those who need our help?*'

Inclusion outputs

Each day, 25,000 people, including more than 10,000 children, die from hunger and related causes.

Global warming is making famine more likely. If extreme poverty is not high on our list of inclusion objectives, then how will we ever change anything? If inclusion is simply a training initiative within our organisations, then what is going to change for those who really need our help?

We can be proactive and reach outwards. We can build some links through charities we respect and trust. We can do our own research to find out what is happening. We can link with local organisations near and far. We can look for practical ways to use our skills and expertise. This isn't only about fundraising. It's about connecting us, our colleagues and perhaps our organisation to prioritise inclusion in a real way. It's about making a real difference in the lives of others. It's about our organisation being an amazing place to work because of the impact that we have.

Could you build an Inverted Pyramid project targeted at those who have no one to help them?

The personal disconnect

Businesses exist to make money and increase shareholder value. Public bodies are there to serve the particular needs of their local communities. Individuals work to look after their families and to build their futures. We all sit in our respective boxes, looking inwards, focused on our priorities.

We can feel so helpless when we see the latest news and the many tragic stories of famine or war. Many people do make a donation or give a regular financial contribution and share what they have. Others can see this as just more 'news' or put the images to one side, knowing that our governments and aid agencies are doing what they can. We are detached from what's happening for we do not have a personal connection with the child suffering on the screen, or the families who have lost everything.

In our world of poverty, starvation and increasing migration, where is our personal day-to-day response? Where is our direct connection to those in desperate need? Is Dual Responsibility, our Social Meitheal or Platinum Rule only for those in our workplace or local community? This is an uncomfortable and challenging conversation for many of us.

But the Inverted Pyramid methodology gives us a way to impact personally on the global issues that affect us. It enables us to get out of our boxes (our transactional job roles and day-to-day living) and begin discussions that can shape the way we connect with and help others.

We do not know where these discussions can lead until we have them, but it is the fact that we are having them that matters. This is what can begin to influence those in our community, those we work with and the policies of our governments. When we look outwards and make our move to build our personal Inverted Pyramid, we begin to reshape who we are, build new connections and change the inward-looking cultures of where we work and live.

Connecting us together

In his book, *Let us Dream*, Pope Francis says:

'This is a moment to dream big, to rethink our priorities – what we value, what we want, what we seek – and to commit to act in our daily life on what we have dreamed of. Let us dare to dream. God asks us to dare to create something new.'.[vii]

Francis is calling on us to create a new politics that works with the marginalised to ensure that we all have the basic necessities and can contribute to the key decisions that shape our lives.

The 2030 Agenda for Sustainable Development (see Appendix 1) adopted by all United Nations Member States in 2015, provides a shared blueprint for peace and prosperity for people and the planet, now and into the future. There are 17 Sustainable Development Goals (SDGs), which are an urgent call for action by all countries in a global partnership. They recognise that ending poverty and other deprivations must go hand-in-hand with strategies that improve health and education, reduce inequality, and spur economic growth – all while tackling climate change and working to preserve our oceans and forests. It's a framework to link all Inverted Pyramids together and to focus our efforts on agreed global priorities.

Five priorities for measuring the effectiveness of our inclusion initiatives

In line with the 2030 Agenda for Sustainable Development, how can we respond to the five priorities of *people, planet, prosperity, peace* and *global partnership*?

The Inverted Pyramid methodology gives each one of us an opportunity to engage directly on these issues, to focus our initiatives on one of the 17 SDGs and to make a measurable difference. The Social Development Goals Global Database (https://unstats.un.org/-sdgs/dataportal) gives us access to data on more than 210 SDG indicators for countries across the globe. We can check by indicator, country, region or time period.

We can change the world for the better

'When I was a young man, I wanted to change the world. I found it was difficult to change the world, so I tried to change my nation. When I found I couldn't change the nation, I began to focus on my town. I couldn't change the town and as an older man, I tried to change my family.

Now, as an old man, I realize the only thing I can change is myself, and suddenly I realize that if long ago I had changed myself, I could have made an impact on my family. My family and I could have made an impact on our town. Their impact could have changed the nation and I could indeed have changed the world.'

Unknown monk, c.12th century

Charity is not just about the donation of goods or services – that is simply a transaction. Charity is about how we express our love for all others in all of the work that we do. It's about how we work together and journey together.

Francis talks of the 'preferential option for the poor' meaning that 'we need always to keep in mind how any decision we make might impact the poor. But it also means we need to put the poor at the centre of our thinking.

'The poor are not the objects of our good intentions but the subjects of change. We do not just act for the poor but with them.'.[viii]

The inclusive charity model

For many organisations and entrepreneurs, the idea of supporting those in need often comes down to holding a fundraising event, ongoing sponsorship or perhaps making a donation.

There is typically a separation between the income raised and the person benefiting on the ground because of the charity or organisation standing between the two. There is effectively little connection between the donor and the beneficiary. We don't see personally how a person has benefited or how we've helped to improve things. And we haven't developed a personal relationship or learnt very much about the person.

The inclusive charity model is another way for us to journey together, in which a business, organisation or individuals link directly with those in need of help. We can make a clear and tangible impact on the lives of others and see at a personal level what is happening.

This joined-up and collaborative approach helps us to build relationships, develop understanding and create a platform for greater inclusion. The inclusive charity model offers a much more satisfying way to work with others, help them to improve things, learn from them and see the outcomes. The traditional charity model typically offers little engagement and indeed little learning or personal feedback for us.

A personal gift

The inclusive charity model is not something new. There are frequent stories of people coming together to fundraise and then going directly to the people in need. Look at the help and resources that many ordinary people delivered by taking clothes, food and medical supplies to people in Ukraine in vans and ambulances when the Russian army destroyed their homes. These people weren't just going to deliver aid. They were going to help in whatever way they could. Many of them brought their own nursing and medical skills.

The inclusive charity model is not simply about extending the transaction so that we see the aid reaching the person in need. The real value is in the personal connection made throughout this process. For this connection defines the sharing of resources and help, as a personal act of compassion, a gift from one person to another and a human connection that goes beyond the practicalities of the situation.

Black Babies

When we were at primary school we used to bring in sixpence every Friday for the Black Babies charity. The money was used by Christian Missionaries who were some of the pioneers of outreach to help those most in need in our world.

The poverty of Africa was remote then, but the impulse to connect to fellow human beings we did not know was a logical, natural and important thing to do. It had a spiritual dimension in that we were linking our wealth with others' needs. We trusted in redressing the imbalance in some small way, and so it was connected to God's work.

When we queued up to give our sixpence to the teacher, we were acting as a school community. When we reminded our mums at 8:40am that we needed sixpence for the Black Babies, we linked home into that as well. The frantic scavenging in the bottom of the purse for an elusive coin and *'You're always leaving it till you're going out the door'* come fondly to mind.

We brought the magazine, with its stories and activities, back from the priests with a sense that we were contributing to something important. It was a fantastic model, connecting families, schools, teachers, and informing the young of the realities and their responsibilities for others that we share the planet with.

I think that we lost out when we stopped giving to this charity. Besides the small financial cost, it was a regular reminder to think and to give, even if we were talking about last night's football. The poor and starving were, in reality, kept somewhere at the front of our minds with our weekly contributions.

A lot has changed over the last 50 years. Countries are closer, yet over 10,000 children die needlessly every day – that's one child every 8 seconds.

The needs are apparent, stark and brutal. The Internet, instant communications and greater personal wealth should also have ramped up our personal capability to respond. Yet we don't seem to have moved far in our thinking or approach.

We don't seem to have the continuous engagement of activities like the Black Babies charity initiative. We seem to rely on big events like Live Aid, Red Nose Day or Children in Need – which are all tremendous. It is interesting, though, that we have to be cajoled and entertained by celebrities and presenters to contribute.

Perhaps there is still a sense of helplessness – that we as individuals can do so little. We rely on politicians and political leaders to act to redress the imbalance, yet they have so many other priorities to deal with.

Our individual ongoing actions and contributions can make a difference. As we know from the Black Babies project, it is not just the sixpence. It's the linking, the conversations and the ongoing commitment that really count.

The Inverted Pyramid of Inclusion offers us an overall global framework upon which to build our individual initiatives. These are no longer fragmented isolated events and activities but part of an ongoing, ever-expanding umbrella of compassion and kindness in action.

Dual Responsibility is greater than corporate social responsibility

Corporate social responsibility (CSR) is the practice whereby a company seeks to play a positive role in the community and wider society. It's a way of giving back or paying it forward.

Imagine if we could link our CSR efforts into our wider Inverted Pyramid initiatives, with our work and contribution being spearheaded and led by staff rather than by the corporate team. Just think how we could build links in other parts of the world, explore and capture the learning that is coming through, create case studies, share models of best practice, engage the whole business and so continue to build our global community of Inverted Pyramid initiatives.

Business and the inclusive charity model

I am reminded of an initiative I was fortunate to be involved with when there was widespread publicity about *'irrecuperable'* babies and young children living in shocking conditions in orphanages in Romania back in 1990.

The Training and Business Group (TBG) utilised its client base of 400 companies, its training expertise and its desire to do something for the children, and created a Team Challenge competition where individual organisations could put forward teams of four people to compete against other companies.

Everyone knew that this was a fundraising challenge to support the children of Romania, and the entrance fee was £200 per team. So here was a traditional profit-making training company reaching out beyond its remit to create a bigger version of itself and offering that to its current client base.

Each team got instructions at the same time and had 14 days to complete the task. The aim of the Challenge was to raise as much money as they could for the orphanages. However, from a competition perspective, the figure they stated they would raise at the outset was the one that counted as their final result in the competition, if they achieved it.

If their team effort didn't achieve this, then their entry was void. If they got more than this figure, they would be recognised only for the initial figure given. The aim was to encourage organisations to create new linkages, build their teams, show their creativity and deliver the projected result on time.

Organisations used their in-house expertise especially in the areas of project management, staff and customer links, marketing, promotion, advertising and more. The organisations taking part were able to offer their staff an additional personal development and team-building opportunity that sat outside of their traditional business operation.

Individual staff were building their Inverted Pyramids across their organisation, reaching outwards into their communities and client bases, and seeking to connect what they do with the needs of children thousands of miles away. It was also an opportunity for many international companies to reflect in practical terms on the values of their brand and what these mean in the wider world. Over 200 teams entered and £250,000 was raised within 14 days.

But this was more than a one-off event. There was a shared vision at the senior management level that TBG could do more. Neil Thorogood, Cynthia Bostock and Pauline McCabe worked to create a separate charity to manage delivery of the help directly to children in the orphanages. There were no medical skills within this business, so new links were developed between the health services and independent health experts in Scotland and England and the Romanian government's Department of Health.

Fundraising continued for three years to support the project's ongoing delivery on the ground and to ensure that the new learning approaches and standards were being consistently implemented and maintained. The operational challenge was to ensure that the new learning and work practices would be embedded and continued long after the project was finished.

Countless business opportunities

Every one of us can look at the news in the world on our phones or TVs and feel helpless. But what if we asked: *'Is there anything we could do here? How could we utilise the technical experience and expertise that we have? How can we use the logistics experience and infrastructure that we have? How can we utilise our IT know-how? How could we offer an opportunity for our clients and customers to work with us to address this important need?'* All it takes is for us to ask the questions with colleagues and engage our creativity. For this is how we give ourselves an opportunity to build our Inverted Pyramids from within our business.

If we do not do this, we simply remain a traditional, inward-looking hierarchal structure which is operating solely to the financial interest of shareholders. There is a bigger benefit for all of us.

Direct connections

Reaching out to those in need does not necessarily have to involve a fundraising component. We can utilise what we already do to support those in need.

As a licensing specialist I was fortunate recently to meet Sally, a food scientist working in Saudi Arabia as a trainer for a major international consultancy. Sally's brief was to provide technical training on the preparation and production of food products for women entrepreneurs in Saudi Arabia wanting to start up their own food businesses. Funding was not an issue as wealthy Saudi families were happy to fund the training courses.

But Sally's heart was really in Kenya, with women also trying to set up their food businesses. A typical charitable response would probably have been for Sally to use her income from the Saudi training and then to offer the training for free to the Kenyan women who could not afford it.

Sally and her consultancy colleagues took a different approach. They brought together the two sets of women from Saudi Arabia and Kenya for the training. All the women were treated as equals. It didn't matter if some paid and some did not.

The additional benefits were immense! Both sets of women learned from each other. Both sets of women were able to find new market opportunities. They all developed new personal relationships. They gained a deeper understanding of the linkages between food and culture, and the potential for growth possibilities in the wider world.

Furthermore, they were able to develop a range of joint ventures, alliances and partnering initiatives. They became role models for women working together and collaborating at a global level.

Sally had created her own Inverted Pyramid – not just delivering training and moving onto the next assignment but by building relationships across her group, encouraging them and enabling them to move forward to discuss new ideas and possibilities.

Becoming more

TBG and Sally are two examples of individuals and organisations reaching out beyond what they were immediately involved with. I know of many more wonderful people who are, for example, leveraging their property business to support projects in Ghana, using their event management skills to fund schools in Madagascar or partnering with their local hospice. Because of their passion, desire and commitment, as individuals and teams, they create an initiative that goes beyond the traditional shape of what they do, and use this as a platform to journey (with skills, knowledge and experience) in a different environment, in the service of those who need help. This all leads to new learning for everyone as their Inverted Pyramids grow way beyond the business or organisation structure. This is how we can create community, build inclusion, have a direct impact on those who need our help and literally change lives.

CHAPTER 15: Time to harvest

Please take a moment to reflect and capture any initial thoughts, ideas, questions or action points that you wish to note and take forward. You will be able to gather these from each chapter for your personal development Action Plan at the end of the book.

Notes

1 ....

2 ....

3 ....

4 ....

5 ....

CHAPTER 16

The Inverted Pyramid in education

What are the key implications and opportunities from the Inverted Pyramid methodology for education? How can education become a driving force for inclusion? In this chapter we ask '*How can we reset our approach to education and work to ensure that all our children and young people help each other to reach their potential?*'

Feedback ratings

Our 20th century model of education which we still use was based around a competitive approach.

It's easy to see why academic results have become the benchmark for choosing schools for our children. We don't look at the happiness of students, their overall well-being and the contribution of the school in building a world of inclusion.

There is, sadly, no rating scheme in place whereby students can have their say about how the school performed on aspects of kindness, support, encouragement, practical help or teaching quality, and give assessments on each of the teachers. Our children do not have an opportunity to talk about their experience or to offer ongoing feedback, and neither do they have a forum for suggestions, recommendations, or concerns. Why would we choose schools without knowing what current and former pupils think about all of the issues that really matter to our young people? Look at the trouble we go to when picking a hotel or holiday.

We, as parents and educators, need to find a way to give our young people a greater opportunity to build their Inverted Pyramids and to develop their careers in line with their aspirations, skills and interests. We can help them to break free from the rigid curriculum and classroom-based learning that in many cases simply demotivates and demoralises those who are never likely to be in the top 10%. And what message are we giving to the other 90%? It certainly doesn't look like an education of inclusion and collaboration at the moment.

One hundred percent

We build confidence in young people by recognising who they are as equals, not by placing them in a league table or order of merit. When we rank people in order, we imply that they are somehow less than they should be. They are failing to meet the standard. But there's only one person who can ever be the best. So where does that leave the rest of us? It is an education system based on elitism, and one that creates a growing army of disenfranchised and dispirited young people.

The model is not that we must all do our best and support each other. The model is that we must be the best at the expense of others. Education teaches us that life is a competition that starts in the classroom.

This value of success is taught in school as we learn to judge and measure ourselves against one another. Our whole system of learning is to drive us towards being better than others and then to take these values beyond the classroom. *'Look at how much more we have than others.' 'Look at how much more we earn.' 'Look at the size of our house and the colour of our new car.'* Education for competition turns into materialism. Materialism tells us that success is about getting as much as we can, holding on to what we have and making sure that others do not get what is ours.

This emphasis on competition and materialism diverts us from recognising ourselves as citizens of the world to recruiting us as consumers. We all need to have more and better stuff. We are told that buying more stuff can make us happier, richer, slimmer, better-looking, more successful or important or whatever. And the marketing machine works well. Look at the stuff that we are continually presented with online.

We have separated humanity from the natural world and put in its place a system of economics and markets, of protectionism and self-interest, of individual wealth rather than kind communities.

Are we really surprised that this approach might lead to some young people forming gangs as they look for recognition and acceptance? Or that drugs and self-harm may just be one outcome of the consistent messages that we give, that our young people do not measure up to our outdated model of so-called education standards and worldly success? As parents, teachers, grandparents and friends, we can change this. We can have a different message.

The real value comes from peer acceptance within an Inverted Pyramid, and so we must encourage young people to work together. We can find ways of bringing them together in groups, to build successful projects, to be able to make their mark and to see how they can make a real difference in the lives of others and in our world. This is what builds confidence and self-esteem, and creates a caring and supportive can-do culture.

The Inverted Pyramid offers an invitation to all of us because of who we are, and not because of exam results or qualifications. We have a responsibility for building an education system that supports all of our young people, rather than demoralising 90% and leaving them to struggle through life in the search for something meaningful. Ending up in any job that is offered or becoming part of the rat race simply to pay the bills seems to be the 'success framework' that we promote.

You see, if we work together and look after each other, we can all do the work we are meant to do. We can uncover, explore and develop the skills, abilities and talents that each of us has been blessed with. Where is our passion? What gives us a buzz? What brings us joy? What makes us laugh? These are the questions that give us an indication as to the direction of our strengths and abilities. And it is by working with and supporting each other that we can develop all that we are intended to be.

The traditional hierarchy of a class structure, with the teacher at the top and all the pupils underneath, needs to be inverted. Our teachers must be enabling our students to link in new ways to learn skills and build experiences. We need to facilitate the development of an inclusive education infrastructure for our modern world.

INVERTED PYRAMID EXERCISE

What is the purpose of education?

BE YOUR BEST SELF

Our education system seeks
to produce and reward
the best achievers.
It's geared to promoting the top ten percent.

We drive our kids to be
top of the class, the best.
Not the best they can be,
but the best compared to others.

But not everyone can be in the top ten per cent.
It's a false best.
It's an exclusive best.
It's not the best they can be.

Measuring the wrong things

We need to treat seriously the mental well-being of our young people. We need to address the isolation of online working and detached education. We need to provide real relationships that go beyond online 'friends', abuse, bullying and the continued and relentless bombardment of unrealistic and impossible standards such as body image, fame and success that the world throws at young minds.

Isn't it time that we changed all of this? We can shift our education system from being one of judgement, measurement and comparison to one that is interpersonal, friendly, supportive and kind. Our education system can be an Inverted Pyramid that is rooted in the priorities of the world that we live in today and we see on our TV screens. We can encourage young people to come together, address local issues and global needs in tangible ways and help to build a better world.

Flipping your education pyramid

Are you ready to teach the Inverted Pyramid methodology in your class or school? Are you ready to help your young people to link with all others in a new way? There is much to be done.

Our education system promotes values that tell us we're all separate and that we must compete with each other. We have to be better than the others. We have to be the best. Our parents reinforce this at home by asking, '*What marks did you get?*' or '*Who came top of the class?*'

Working together in an Inverted Pyramid promotes an alternative value system of kindness and caring for each other. Education can become about showing us that we are all connected and that we all need each other. And if we help each other to do well then everybody succeeds. We want everyone to be the very best version of themselves, from now. Our education must tell us that we are already winners rather than that we are not good enough. We are all stars. Education must help each of us to sparkle in the world.

Collaborative education

Collaborative education invites all of us to be partners in the ongoing development of young people and also of ourselves. Collaborative education includes all aspects of personal development, such as individual creativity, sports, sustainability for our planet, healthy eating, well-being, income generation, relationship-building, personal projects, music, gaming, interpersonal skills, starting a business, global events, personal care, volunteering, project management, confidence and public speaking, tackling poverty, arts, drama, team-working, kindness, local community initiatives, home finance, fair trade, leadership, website development, etc. There is a whole new fabric of activities and connections to be created here!

So, can we encourage and help our young people to work together more, to take greater ownership of their future and become changemakers? Can we enable them to be the architects and partners of an education process that includes and promotes all students?

We can all support a collaborative education process in a direct hands-on way. We can share our ideas, workplaces, projects and experience with young people. This is about active engagement and participation by all of us and seeing young people as partners not subjects in this process.

Individuals within businesses, community groups, public sector bodies and charities all have key roles to play here. Teachers and parents can be the lynchpins at the heart of this new collaboration to ensure that we are meeting the needs of all children.

Older people and recent graduates can share their wisdom and experience. They can help to explore areas of interest, crazy ideas and the dreams of youth. They can support those who are struggling. This is intergenerational learning with a local, national and international focus. It's about our role in life and our place in the world.

Our school-based education system needs to become a collaborative, joined-up, community-based, personal development and support framework for young people. We need to move from 19th century schoolrooms to 21st century engagement and empowerment. Collaborative education is a process where everyone can participate, work in teams, contribute and share their skills, online and in person, to help our next generation.

We have universities, schools and colleges that are largely empty of students after 4pm each day. We have schools that are largely empty at weekends and school holidays. Surely we can better use these resources to support the complete personal development of our young people?

We have the buildings. We have the students. We have the expertise. We have the technology. We have the time. Collaborative education with the Inverted Pyramid methodology can bring it all, and all of us, together.

So, what role might you play in collaborative education if you were asked? And how can you begin to play your part from now?

You are amazing!

Our whole education system has to move. The years of students sitting absorbing information are long gone. We now need to help build confidence, develop strong communication and presentation skills, and enable young people to develop their interests, whatever these may be. Working with others, they will find their way together.

We can create a new type of education that is built around a tapestry of opportunities for our young people to reach out and work together. We must plant Golden Seeds and tell all students (again and again) that they are unique and amazing. We have to stop giving children scores (again and again) that tell them they are not good enough. Is this really the best message that our education system can offer to our young people to carry into adulthood?

We have to offer a new canvas of possibility and collaboration rather than one of limitation and isolation. We have to create a servant mentality and be vulnerable to change rather than seeking to protect our positions of 'expertise' and 'authority'.

INVERTED PYRAMID EXERCISE

What is lifelong learning?

TEACHER TRAINING

The student must become
an extension of the teacher,
and not just one who copies.

In other words,
the student must grow with the teacher,
so that the student can become the teacher.
And the teacher is then the student.

In this way, our role is continuously shifting.
For we are all both teacher
and student,
at the same time.

Let us quickly move beyond
the outdated teacher-pupil concept.
For our teachers are here to empower us
so that they can learn.

Let us move from teachers to enablers
for we are all learners.
It's just that we have different
roles within each project.

PERSONAL DEVELOPMENT REFLECTION
1. Write down when you were last a teacher – and a student.
2. Who could you teach? What would you teach?
3. What would you need to learn?

Training and developing young people

The Inverted Pyramid of Inclusion offers a new model for engagement, participation and collaboration within our education systems. The intersection of home life, project work, online collaboration, local relationships and joint learning can become our new hybrid classroom.

The key challenge for education is to bring the fun back. It is to empower students to take control so that they enjoy every moment of what they do because they see that they are building themselves and making a difference. We have to move beyond education being pure drudgery and a task that society and parents impose upon young people and they, in turn, on themselves.

The reality now is that we do not need to know everything. We do not have to store everything in our heads anymore. We can access the Internet to find out how to do things. We can link up with people on their phones and communicate.

The real strength, the real skill and the real ability we need is simply one of encouragement for us to go and then go again and never give up on our dreams of who we are to become. Our big task in education is to encourage everyone that we meet every day to keep going and make it happen.

INVERTED PYRAMID EXERCISE

Shall we play together?

ISABELLA'S INVITATION

'Can I run and play, Grandad?'
Isabella asked excitedly
when we reached the playground.
'Yes, of course,' I replied.

Isabella ran up to a little boy about her age
and said with a smile,
'Shall we play together?'
'OK!' replied the little boy.

'Let's go on this,' said Isabella,
but he was already ahead of her.
'Come on, can you do this?'
he shouted with encouragement.

All I heard after this was
laughter as they ran
around the playground.
I watched the process unfold.

Within 10 minutes,
three more children
had somehow joined in,
and we were now into Hide and Seek.

The bigger children looked after the little ones,
helping, encouraging, and protecting
as they all interacted seamlessly
at multiple levels.

And of course, everybody got their turn.
If a four-year-old can build an
Inverted Pyramid within ten minutes,
then what are we waiting for?

PERSONAL DEVELOPMENT REFLECTION
1. In the above piece, can you see the various stages of building an Inverted Pyramid? Where is Isabella's decision to start, her invitation to others, the acceptance, the encouragement, the working together, the sharing of common interests, the joy of interaction, the building of the team and Dual Responsibility?
2. What do you take from Isabella's example?

Turning the education pyramid upside down

Our approach to education must become one of Dual Responsibility. It is not only about each of us doing well individually, but also for us to help others to do well. Our rule has to be to help each other to find, build and develop what we're good at and what we enjoy, so that we can grow and be happy.

We all have to find our place in the world. Teenage years are difficult, especially when we are told to follow some pre-determined plan set out by schools and parents. What if young people could do it their way? What if we let them manage their own education? What if they were encouraged to really make a difference every day in our world? What would their education system look like?

Skills audit

We have gone long past the years of teaching knowledge and information. The core skills in demand now are clearly people skills including team-building, project management, innovation and creativity, problem-solving, planning and organisational skills, and customer relations. Several recent employer surveys have identified that over half of employers who recruited directly from school felt that young people were poorly prepared for work.

If we as parents are going to continue to outsource the education of our children to others, let's make it one of feedback that encompasses well-being and happiness. We need one that develops key skills, that empowers and encourages all of our children to build their Inverted Pyramids, to reach out and to work well together. We need one that continually recognises and indeed promotes the successes of our young people.

We need to flip the hierarchal pyramid of education from being teacher-centred, qualification-driven and subject-controlled to empowering each of our young people to reach out, develop links, build new relationships, address key needs and build the skills and indeed relationships that can last a lifetime.

Powerplay

Our determination to hold onto power and control is directly proportional to our inability to build inclusion.

Indeed, one of the main things that our education system teaches us is to work apart from others, in isolation. We learn from day one to be competitive at the expense of those who are closest to us, often in the same class or at the same desk.

If we're lucky, some of us will leave school with a piece of paper that states our exam successes which will apparently give credibility to our potential to be better than others. We can only wonder if a failure in an exam is actually the mark of our greatest success, our refusal (or inability) to compete and our determination not to be categorised as successful by these standards.

How can we measure something that we're not even teaching at the moment? And how can our education system value our young people when it rewards the outcomes of behaviours that can marginalise and demotivate them, leaving so many branded as, or feeling like, failures?

A ten-point education checklist for everybody

So, what exactly should we do?

1. Set out our values of collaboration, kindness, looking after everyone and working together
2. Explain how the Inverted Pyramid of inclusion works; show students what this means for former hierarchal classroom teaching
3. Provide a framework that encourages individuals to work together all the time
4. Stop teaching subjects and encourage students to work on issues and topics that are important to them
5. Encourage students to explore and find out more about the world we live in; let's encourage our students to make a real difference to those who need our support or who are struggling
6. Get students to present to each other on topics of interest and their own research around them

7. Help young people to build their Inverted Pyramid projects and initiatives from where they are now – support and encourage them
8. Let's create champions of every single person and cherish their uniqueness
9. Let's all celebrate each day in our classrooms: the successes, the ideas, the questions, the individual contributions and the continued working together of each student as they each strive to build a kinder and better world for everyone
10. Start now!

We can start to build this framework from today. Especially for the students who have already 'failed' and are simply going through the motions, we can offer a positive framework to engage them and an opportunity for us all to build from the ground up.

Let's start with learning around the Inverted Pyramid, collaboration, working together and Dual Responsibility from now on. So many of our courses and lessons have space for introducing real world topics and situations, for example citizenship classes, pastoral care initiatives, geography, social skills, religion, business skills, politics and economics.

Parents and teachers can redefine and reposition their role as empowering friends rather than as an education standards police force. For we are all learners and teachers. But more so, we are all learners and teachers working together.

Of course, learning about Maths, English, Languages, Science etc. are all important but there is a higher-level curriculum that is relevant equally to everybody. It's one of interpersonal relationships, of collaboration, of being able to work together and look after our world for all of us.

It is through the development of Inverted Pyramid projects and initiatives that young people learn project management skills, communication skills, confidence, creativity, out-of-the-box thinking, presentation skills, research skills, problem-solving, dealing with difficult situations and awkward colleagues, struggling with things that aren't working, working to deadlines, etc. They build their confidence, creativity and resilience in real-time scenarios and situations.

And these are the skills that employers are increasingly demanding.

Towards a new school curriculum

There's a new school curriculum based on need, rather than subjects. It is one that empowers children and students to use their skills to the full and to become agents of change.

It addresses eight key questions:

- How can everyone in the world have food today?
- How can everyone in the world have a home today?
- How can everyone in the world be safe today?
- How can everyone in the world look after our planet today?
- How can everyone in the world work together today?
- How can everyone in the world use their skills to help others today?
- How can everyone in the world be kind today?
- How will each of us change the world today?

The new school curriculum applies to adults also. Which question will you work on today?

INVERTED PYRAMID EXERCISE

What is a friendly takeover?

TAKEOVER

It's that point in life
when the younger generation
take over the reins.

It's a specific incident or situation
where they step up
to assist us or sort something out.

And we think,
This is it.
This is the moment of takeover.

And we smile
with gratitude for their help
and for them.

INVERTED PYRAMID EXERCISE
1. What do you think this specific incident or situation might be?
2. What will our younger generation help us with?

New space for peacebuilding – a case study

Pope Francis says that he wants to develop the ancient process of Synodality '...*as a service to a humanity that is so often locked in paralyzed disagreements.*' He explains that the goal of Synodality, or walking together, is '...*to recognize, honour, and reconcile differences... where the best of each can be retained... What matters most is that harmony that enables us to move forward together on the same path, even with all our shades of difference. This synodal approach is something our world now needs badly… we need processes that allow differences to be expressed… [so] that we can walk together without needing to destroy anyone.'* [ix]

Growing up in Northern Ireland

When I grew up in Northern Ireland, people were either 'Catholic' or 'Protestant'. You were assigned to one of these two competing tribes from birth, irrespective of your belief or non-belief. The two churches had divided up the spoils. We went to different churches on Sunday. We went to different schools. We had different sports. We had different newspapers which gave us our version of the news. The churches certainly didn't work together in a collaborative way to look after all God's people. Quite the opposite. They made sure that we had little opportunity to journey together.

At an individual level, humanity did break through and despite the institutional chains, many wonderful people gave years of service (and some, literally, their lives) to reaching out across barricades, borders and all sorts of barriers to try to build a different future.

A new generation is coming through now, and hopefully a new 'middle ground' will slowly find a place. But it's a space that has still not been embraced by the old Christian traditions which continue to prop up a political system of division and separation, while trying to hold onto dwindling and increasingly disenfranchised congregations.

Moving beyond difference

Sometimes our differences seem so entrenched and have been around for so long that our way of thinking is fixed, and we can see no way of working together. Our attitudes, habits and actions have been well conditioned and honed over generations. We hold tightly to that which divides us; we accept this as 'normal' or 'truth', and we are unable to go beyond this.

But it doesn't have to be this way. We can broaden our perspective. We can change the way we are with each other. We can work better, together. Our priority must always be to journey towards what unites us, rather than to stand still in the false comfort of what divides us.

Coming together can drive us apart

I am reminded of a project that I was fortunate to be involved with during the 'Troubles'. It was started some 20 years ago by a small peacebuilding charity called The Training Trust in the search for peace and reconciliation for a divided Northern Ireland.

Working with the support of US Senator George Mitchell's Northern Ireland Fund for Reconciliation, Trinity College Dublin and the Irish Government, Pauline McCabe and Lisa Rose and her colleagues brought primary school children of all different traditions together to see whether they could create a different way of working together. The children were aged 9–11 years.

The traditional approach with reconciliation work until then had been to bring people together to learn more about each other's differences, in the hope that this would translate into different attitudes and behaviours. Although there was usually some communication, there was typically little real engagement or opportunity for building relationships. Children were seen as subjects, rather than partners in the process. It was easy to see why any new learning was quickly 'repositioned' when the young people returned to their families and local communities. Unfortunately, many well-meaning projects simply helped to reinforce sectarian attitudes and behaviour.

When we bring opposing perspectives together, whether in politics, religion or in the workplace, it is of little use to focus on difference. For one side is trying to hold onto what they believe is right and the other side is trying to gain what they believe they are entitled to. There is no 'space' when we argue over difference. In Northern Ireland, political leaders and religious leaders were all holding tight to their traditional positions and, indeed, still are. Many are still stuck.

Journeying together

So the idea of The Training Trust in 2003 was to try to create some 'new space' which was not framed around difference but which encouraged relationship-building and journeying together. The new space that Pauline and Lisa chose was to work with children in Namibia. The idea was to link the Northern Ireland children from different schools (state, Catholic and integrated) with their economically poorer counterparts in Namibia.

It was a low-tech project that ran over six months. Each month, the two sets of children from schools in Northern Ireland and Namibia got together and produced a range of stories, drawings and paintings around a particular topic. Blue boxes arriving between Africa and Northern Ireland (courtesy of DHL who kindly sponsored the project), were excitedly anticipated. All the children opened their boxes on the same day.

When the children in Northern Ireland were creating their pieces around 'my family' or 'my weekend' or 'my school' or 'my home' they were very sensitive to the needs of the children that they were sending material to. They knew that in Namibia, these young boys and girls were walking two miles to and from school with one little bottle of water.

So, when they were drawing the pictures and chatting, they were not talking about political differences in Northern Ireland, or their cultural heritage or the strengths of their religious tradition.

They were asking each other *'Should we tell them about our Games console, our Nike trainers or our mobile phones?'* The conversation and relationships built up among our children went way beyond any differences that their local society was seeking to impose on them.

They were building global relationships with different sets of friends. They were journeying together, learning together, creating together, and being as one with other less fortunate children. The seeds of building an inclusive worldwide community, for me, rested with those children.

New space and the Inverted Pyramid

We can take this concept of finding new space and apply it to our Inverted Pyramid. It is of little use just being in the pyramid if we have no purpose. We need to be clear where we are going. We are not just working together to discuss our differences or the status quo, for that takes us backwards. We are working together to build our piece of an inclusive worldwide community.

But for this process to grow and not be squashed by politicians or clergy or corporate culture, we all need to work together in new ways that are not conditioned or controlled by generations of negative thinking and self-interest.

At the outset of the project, we brought children together from different communities and backgrounds. We wanted to know what was important for them in learning to work together, in building a future without bombs and fear.

We took them to a hotel and mixed them up on round tables. Many had never been to a hotel or indeed outside of their community before. Many had never met people who were different. But they drew on their flip chart pages in the centre of their tables. They wrote the words that they dared not speak out loud. And they drew pictures that showed exactly what they felt.

The reality, however, was that when children and young people went back to their families and communities, these collaborative behaviours failed to take root. There was no process to take this forward or to build relationships. There was no journey. Government agencies refused to fund the work and there was no interest in rolling out or mainstreaming the project.

How does new space work?

Research findings graphically illustrated how little room for manoeuvre exists in the traditional Catholic v Protestant model. New space that is both non-threatening and capable of withstanding distortion or misunderstanding is therefore essential.

If we are to be effective peacebuilders, we have to come together with others in a different 'space' – one, in this case, that looks beyond the sectarian framework of Northern Ireland.

This new space must offer meaningful, creative and challenging opportunities. 'Shared activity' is then possible when we move forward, meet and work with others on an issue, challenge or opportunity arising in this new space. Humanitarian needs in Africa and the Third World provide an array of new space opportunities for young people to work together. There are many needs and opportunities to explore within the Sustainable Development Goals.

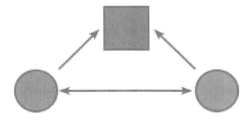

In this context we can address issues of concern/opportunity for mutual benefit and for the benefit of others. It is as a result of working jointly on this new activity that the process of reconciliation can begin.

The Training Trust believes that peacebuilder projects have the potential to provide young people with opportunities for reconciliation through their work with other young people in Africa and the Third World. This is potentially reconciliation in action – a new space, a new time and genuine shared activity which young people can initiate and own. They can be peacebuilders.

With these tools, new skills, confidence and successes, young people can learn to enjoy what they have in common with Hindus, with people with disabilities, with the unemployed, with Catholics, with the English, etc. Their political, social or economic history may be different – Nationalist or Unionist, middle class or working class, well off or poor, prisoner or victim – but this definition becomes secondary to the 'real person' they have worked with on the project.

Kofi Annan, then Secretary General of the United Nations, wrote to the Trustees at the time:

'I am delighted to send my warmest greetings to the young people who have come together in the Training Trust to work in concert to improve the lives of young people in other countries, many of whom live in extreme poverty and other dire circumstances.

'Growing up in Northern Ireland, you have witnessed how intolerance in its various forms continues to ignite social tensions and cause enormous suffering, including through armed conflict. It is particularly disheartening to see the persistence of such hatred and division at a time when the world faces so many challenges – such as climate change, AIDS and terrorism – that can only be addressed if people and countries work as partners.

'There are few things that serve to unify people so much as the pursuit of a common goal. By coming together in this way, both Protestants and Catholics in Northern Ireland can help others to build better lives in other parts of the world even as you enrich your own lives and repair your own society.

'While this is clearly a task for people of all ages, it is especially important for young people to rise above the lines that divide and build meaningful relationships with your peers, since this can prevent destructive prejudices from being passed on to future generations.

'It takes strength of character to try to overcome the stereotypes and biases that often pervade our societies. You are showing real courage, and I commend you for it. Let us continue our common struggle against intolerance in all its forms and build a world that allows all human beings to accept, respect and live in peace with one another.'ˣ

New space for us

With conflict and difficult situations in our own lives and workplaces, it is easy to get caught up in the details and try to resolve them along the lines of what divides or separates us. We continue to think within the parameters of our role, our situation or our organisation.

New space reminds us that we can look outwards beyond our situation, our roles and our organisation. For the opportunity for us to come together and work together does not exist in the definition of the problem but in the wider (and perhaps more significant or more important) opportunities for collaboration.

But these initiatives cannot simply be one-off projects that showcase new models and approaches. The real challenge is to enable each of these activities, projects and initiatives to develop and expand upwards and outwards. We have to 'let it go' so that it can become viable in its own right. We have to see this new way of working all around us. Only then will our new approach be able to offer an alternative and a real choice for others to see that there is a viable and better way forward. Only then will it become embedded.

If the custodians of power in politics, business, education or religion are determined to keep everything as it is, then it is clear that innovative projects and initiatives will be seen as temporary, funding will cease and so nothing will really change. For those in charge are always unlikely to do something new, especially if it reduces their power and impacts on their personal credibility, income, ego or position.

This is why the Inverted Pyramid can offer us a sustainable and viable model of positive change. It's an approach that builds from the ground upwards, one person at a time linking with others, creating an initiative, joining their initiatives together, and building a critical mass of inclusion. The Inverted Pyramid does not ask for permission.

INVERTED PYRAMID EXERCISE

Are we Peacebuilders?

PEACEBUILDERS

52 years on
from the start of the Troubles,
we still send our children
to separate schools,
to learn division.

52 years on
from the start of the Troubles,
we still align our lives
to different churches,
to promote exclusion.

52 years on
from the start of the Troubles,
we still send our politicians
to lead our tribe,
to represent us.

52 years on
from the start of the Troubles,
we send our children's children
out on the streets,
to celebrate our success.

INVERTED PYRAMID EXERCISE

1. What can each of us do to break the exclusive and top-down mould of schooling, Church and politics and begin to build a different way of living together?
2. What conversations can we have with others?
3. In what new ways can we bring our children and young people together?

CHAPTER 16: Time to harvest

Please take a moment to reflect and capture any initial thoughts, ideas, questions or action points that you wish to note and take forward. What are your main reflections from Section Three?

Notes

1 ....

2 ....

3 ....

4 ....

5 ....

CASE STUDY: Future Church and Pope Francis

With our understanding of the Inverted Pyramid methodology in different sectors, we can now look at what Pope Francis is doing. Section Four offers us a ringside seat in a 'live' case study as Francis tries to turn the Catholic Church upside down. It's not going to plan. What should he do next?

CHAPTER 17

How can we go beyond our religious differences?

This section features a real 'live' case study following the development of Pope Francis's plans to turn the Catholic Church upside down by implementing an Inverted Pyramid approach. As you read through the next few chapters, there are three main questions to address:

- First, think about what you would do and how you would respond if this scenario was happening in your organisation, business or community
- Secondly, be specific about the advice that you would give to Francis, the bishops, the clergy and the people they are seeking to serve in local communities
- And thirdly, what would you say to those outside the Church who are interested in building inclusion? How might we respond in a positive way to add a different kind of leverage and a greater critical mass to take this journey forward in ways not yet imagined?

The old Church and the new Church

Francis's view of an Inverted Pyramid Church emphasises that not only are we all together (clergy and people) in the Church but that we all have equal parts to play. There is no hierarchy in the Church of

Francis. What is more, this is a Church of all, with no exceptions. It is a Church of inclusion where everyone is welcome. It is a Church of love.

This calls for a fundamental shift in attitude by all of us, whether Catholic or not. We can no longer wait for the bishops or the Church to sort out our world of exclusion. We can no longer blame 'religion' and then do nothing ourselves. We cannot criticise the present arrangements if we are not part of the change now for a better world. It was Gandhi who said that we should *be the change we want to see in the world*.

The old hierarchal Catholic Church has much to answer for, but the emerging inclusion-driven Inverted Pyramid Church has much to do here and now, if we are to look after everyone. For the Inverted Pyramid Church is each of us and we are fully accountable for what we do, create and build.

The spirit of love does not sit in Rome as the 'CEO' for the Catholic Church. The spirit lives through each of us, whoever we are, as friend and helper, with gifts and graces to share every day.

So, when we speak of the Church, Francis is asking us to separate out the old institutional hierarchy (effectively an organisational structure) from the individually led Inverted Pyramid Church (our interpersonal development process with each other). For so many people, the hierarchal Church as an institution has lost credibility and relevance. The Inverted Pyramid Church is each one of us and what we do together. This is reborn through us every single day.

Synodality

Synodality is the development of our interpersonal Inverted Pyramid Church, and is where we journey with each other every day, in all aspects of our lives. Synodality does not belong to the hierarchal institutional Church or to the bishops. Synodality is a gift we can share with everyone else (irrespective of religion, belief or non-belief), for we all can journey together and help each other.

Our process of building our Inverted Pyramid is one of journeying from where we are now. It is a process that holds our real everyday experiences and challenges in all aspects of our lives. Our career choices, money worries, relationship issues, health matters and present concerns are all the fabric of Synodality. These are the everyday 'windows' that help us to see the concerns of others and to look at how we might help and support them. It is by knowing others that we create opportunities to help, and so to journey together.

INVERTED PYRAMID EXERCISE

Are we okay?

TRANSACTIONAL ANALYSIS

It's okay to be religious.
It's okay not to be religious.
It's okay to be spiritual, but not religious.

It's okay to believe in God.
It's okay not to believe in God.
It's okay not to be sure about God.

You see, '*I'm okay, you're okay*'
means that we are all okay.
We can be together, in our own way.

PERSONAL DEVELOPMENT REFLECTION

1. How do you see others who have different views about religion or God?
2. Are you open to friendly chats with others to explore our different understandings – or do you just ignore these topics?
3. How can you help others to be 'okay'?

The true path

When religious institutions say they have the 'truth' and they are the 'right way', they seem to imply (explicitly or implicitly) that what other religions believe is not the truth or the right way. Religious institutions can therefore take an exclusive position in relation to other beliefs and non-beliefs.

However, if religious institutions or those with any belief were to say that we are all journeying or searching together, then perhaps we could create some 'new space' to move forward in a spirit of collaboration.

The Golden Rule calls on us to look after our neighbour and treat them as we would like them to treat us. The focus of many religions – to maintain a position of exclusive religious difference, rather than working together to help others who are desperately in need – seems to be at odds with this core principle.

This is a clear example of why we need to invert the institutional pyramids of all hierarchal religions. Otherwise, we get caught within the old structure which excludes other beliefs and ensures that we are unable to reach out in a spirit of collaboration to help those most in need. We stay focused on sorting out our declining attendances, defending our theological barricades and missing the point of why we are here.

By building our personal Inverted Pyramids we all as individuals can change this, irrespective of our belief or non-belief.

A divided Christian Church

The visible structures of Christianity can be characterised by a plethora of Churches and approaches all claiming to be 'right' as they split theological hairs. Over the centuries, formalisation of differing Christian Churches with robust organisational structures has created seemingly unbreakable walls between their traditions. Christian Churches outwardly acknowledge each other but do not work together on what really matters. There are prayers for Christian unity every year, but no one changes their position. The institutional Christian Churches are the opposite of the idea of everyone journeying together. We should not be surprised, therefore, that Christianity is seen as irrelevant by so many.

We have to be open and fully take on board what is really happening, and has happened, in the Church. The actions of some clergy in various countries have brought untold pain, suffering and cruelty to so many, especially to the youngest and most vulnerable.

This is exactly why the Church needs individuals to take the lead and act. It seems to be that the institutional ship of the Church is incapable of turning itself around. However, there are millions of small boats ready to be launched. Francis sees this and has opened the harbour gates. He is inviting us to set sail together, and to bring others with us.

Interfaith

Learning about other faiths and beliefs can be an important part of getting to know one another.

With an interfaith approach, we come with our boxes of belief to meet each other. Our faith traditions form the platform upon which we get to know one another. It's about learning and respecting each other's differences. But it's not inclusion. The conversations are rooted in holding firm to our own beliefs first.

The inclusive Inverted Pyramid approach is very different. It means that we can meet each other and journey as individuals rather than as representatives of any tradition. It's an interpersonal collaboration. There is no underlying sense of holding firm or needing to defend, just a human call to love one another.

Meeting and getting to know people is at the heart of the Inverted Pyramid approach. We just need to be aware that Interfaith dialogue on its own can promote the bonds of difference and keep us inward-looking, rather than asking how we can help to meet the real needs of others.

Taking away the barriers

Can we engage with those of all faiths and none, and journey together? This may challenge some of us to venture out of our comfort zone, but Synodality places the responsibility for the first move with us. So, what can we do to begin to move this forward?

There is a great piece in the *Acts of the Apostles* (Acts 15:7-21) where Paul and Peter disagree as to whether Pagans need to be circumcised to become part of the new Christian Church. Peter, representing the traditionalists, thought that this should be a requirement, but thankfully Paul won!

As Paul said, let's not put any barriers, unnecessary obstacles or preconditions in the way of people joining us. And as Pope Francis now says, let us build a community which is fully inclusive and open to all. We can reach out to everyone with a message of kindness, collaboration and compassion. Let us remove any barriers in our own thinking that may stop others from journeying with us.

Interpersonal Christianity

There are no rules to be satisfied here, beyond wanting to look after each other so that we can become fully who we are intended to be. We must place no barriers in the way of people coming together and working together.

Let us not look for excuses not to act. Let us not drag up the past and say that we've always done it this way. Let us not worry about who we might offend as we reach out to others in need. Let us not be concerned about what others might think of us if we talk with those of other beliefs, use the 'God' or 'love' words, or embrace those who are different.

Christians, Muslims, Hindus, Sikhs, Jews, Baha'is, Humanists, Buddhists, Agnostics, Atheists and everyone else, including those in business, those in work and those not working, are all invited to journey together with Francis. We must all reach out, especially to those we see as different and would not normally include in our circles, or pyramids. Those of any belief and no belief must be part of our future. The Inverted Pyramid belongs to all of us. How can we build an inclusive worldwide community if we leave some people out?

The new visible signs of Pope Francis's Interpersonal Christianity will be characterised by multi-ethnic, multicultural, multi-belief Inverted Pyramid teams which open themselves to everyone, are fully inclusive, are directly connected to the needs of local people and global issues and are joined up as a worldwide community of inclusion. God is love, love is what we are, and it doesn't need to be any more complicated than that.

Francis has provided an invitation to an 'open door' Christianity which welcomes everyone and sees each individual as essential in building a worldwide community of love.

But one man cannot deliver this on his own! Francis is literally fighting centuries of institution-building, rule-creation, outdated systems, fierce internal politics and direct opposition, archaic processes and a culture of exclusion, complacency and superiority – and that's just within his own organisation. His personal Inverted Pyramid calls on each of us to journey with him as individuals. So how do we respond? Will we join him and, at the same time, begin to free ourselves?

Religion may be dying – thank God

This 79-year-old priest greets me in surprise when I pop in to check out the local Church. Not many people come to this Church for Saturday morning Mass.

I explain I'm new to Sheffield and he sits down to chat with me. He outlines some of the challenges of small congregations: too many Masses, an underused Church, a continually shifting student population and the growing percentage of elderly priests. If it wasn't for African and Indian priests, he says, the Catholic faith would struggle across the UK.

'They ask me when I'm going to retire', he says, *'but what happens if I go? There is no one to replace me. All the priests are covering two, three or even four parishes. And community worship doesn't exist in the way that it used to. People are more fluid. They come and go for university, work or whatever. Community and Church are no longer one – they have both changed dramatically. The response to this has been piecemeal and disjointed by the Church. I find the same stories in Ireland and I find the same stories across many of the western Christian Churches.*

'Religious churchgoing is increasingly becoming a minority activity. It has become separated from the main thrust of our lives where it used to be when I was younger. The connection with God through religion is gradually being eroded. Evangelical initiatives, new Church planting [the development of a new Church congregation] *and online ministry all seek to address the need for traditional Christian Church activity, but they are really just playing at the edges.'*

The main method for building some type of understanding of *What is life all about?* is now increasingly through our own personal spirituality, however we describe or experience this.

So, I think that religion in its present form is dying. The institutionalisation of God has had its day. The era of our predecessors trying to turn God into an organisation is thankfully coming to an end.

258

Many religions have sought to claim their territory through a doctrine of difference rather than promotion of love. They have been uncompromising and determined not to work together. It takes generosity, humility and perseverance to start working together.

This is an opportunity (especially for young people) to create and build relationships based on love rather than outdated models of division and doctrine. We need initiatives and projects that address the most fundamental of human needs, especially food, our environment, housing, safety, contribution, companionship – and all of this needs to be made real in and through love.

We are all part of the great love. That is who we are. Life is about utilising our skills, interests and all the gifts that we've been given to promote, share and develop that love.

CHAPTER 17: Time to harvest

Please take a moment to reflect and capture any initial thoughts, ideas, questions or action points that you wish to note and take forward. You will be able to gather these from each chapter for your personal development Action Plan at the end of the book.

Notes

1 ....

2 ....

3 ....

4 ....

5 ....

CHAPTER 18

What should the bishops do next?

The response from many bishops to their global Consultation shows that the initial process has not worked out as they had hoped. The idea seemed to be a good one, but what it has thrown up is a whole list of things that need to be addressed or sorted. These ideas, priorities, recommendations and indeed demands are now back with the bishops! This was certainly not their intention. It's hard to see how they can produce a response to address all the points raised.

The bishops were supposed to be empowering local people to take responsibility but unfortunately, they created a process designed to ensure that this did not happen. Many bishops are asking themselves, and each other, 'What do we do now?'. Let's see if we can offer some ideas and suggestions in this chapter.

Learning from the Consultation Phase

A notetaker from one of the local Consultation sessions said to me, 'One piece of feedback I would give the bishops is that the synodal process was effectively providing a forum to "have a go" at the Church. Many people had a rant at what the bishops should be doing.'

Another said, 'I think that the preparation of the process was not in line with Pope Francis's intention as I understood it. The bishops needed to *position it more as people meeting together, and not the bishops giving us a task to do. The focus should have been about what we wanted to do and were going to do – not a requirement to produce a long list of things that we were sending to the bishop to act upon. It just seemed like an unrealistic wish list given where the Church is at the moment.*

'*It seems that the Consultation Phase was a missed opportunity. Even calling it a Consultation is the wrong framing. It should have been a collaboration with people to encourage them to take forward their ideas.*'

Another attendee said, '*Those of us sitting there as notetakers were powerless. We couldn't respond to the people who were being negative. It wasn't our brief. It wasn't our role to open up the discussion. In other words, there needed to be a facilitation of the process, not simply a recordkeeping. And we needed to train good facilitators to do this and give them the authority to encourage people to put forward ideas, agree the next steps and then to take responsibility for making it happen. The bishops need to allow and encourage people to act. A good facilitator will create a positive framework for everybody to have their say and to find a way to move forward.*'

Walls or bridges

One young priest said to me, 'bishops and clergy have to go beyond seeing people as confrontational or negative towards the Church when they provide positive critique or suggestions for improving things. We have to move from a defensive position where we hide behind our walls of history, clerical structures and status, to one of genuine collaboration where we have the confidence to journey with others and build bridges to places we've never been'.

And from the Consultation Process itself, 'We have to stop leaving the organising and decision-making to bishops and others and recognise that we are the shapers of what happens to our Church. We as individuals have to accept responsibility for the ongoing process of Synodality'.

For all of us, there must be a willingness to begin again better as we continue each day to journey together.

We are not 'a listening Church'

There were some people who came to Consultation events with stories about how the Church has caused them pain or distress. In some instances, this was the first time that someone in a Church context was prepared to listen to them.

We should welcome these interventions, not only because they can begin a process to help the person concerned, but also to allow us to show ourselves as people who listen. Let us not be afraid to engage with those who are apathetic, negative or disillusioned with the Church. We must have the humility to welcome criticism and critique, and to learn from it.

When we talk about Church, we think of the institutional organisation. We do not think of our next-door neighbour. We must dramatically shift this perspective. So, instead of talking about a listening Church, we need to speak about ourselves as *people who listen*. We need to personalise our relationship, for each one of us is the Church. Our Church is an interpersonal, not an organisational one, belonging to each person. This understanding and shift in position is at the heart of Francis's Inverted Pyramid.

Questions for the Synod of Bishops to address now

- When do we give ownership to local parishes and dioceses?
- How do we give ownership to local parishes and dioceses?

- What is stopping us reframing the complete synodal process as one of inclusion, participation and personal responsibility?
- How can we build trust in the process?

The confidence of bishops

The key priority is to get Synodality moving at a local level everywhere, and to build momentum and confidence in the process. bishops must act now. They can encourage new arrangements, welcome individual actions and promote the Inverted Pyramid approach. They can work with business, government and education in new ways with clear leadership and purpose. As one person said to me recently, they have to be brave. They must have confidence and they have to trust people.

But there is much low-hanging fruit. The Consultations showed that there are so many people keen to engage and work on this if only they were asked or allowed to. Many people, however, don't think there is any point in trying, given the attitude of the Church. The bishops need to get out a message of collaboration, cooperation and personal ownership – quickly.

A different set of relationships

Many bishops and priests have been their own boss for many years and some don't take kindly to other people suggesting that things could be done in a better way. The Inverted Pyramid will be a significant challenge for many of them. Indeed, there may be uneasiness around creating new relationships. Some may see this as challenging the balance of power that already exists within the Church, offering less control, and so it may be better to just stick with what we have. Better the devil you know, so to speak.

The bishops will need to think about power in a different way – *with people* rather than *over people*. But it also means people taking responsibility for being part of this new arrangement. So, there are two sides to this evolving relationship.

Individual bishops and priests will respond in their own way. So, it is possible that this may not be one centralised, coordinated process but rather the explosion of a myriad of small processes, where different individuals, groups and organisations build their own Synodality process locally.

Power and separation

In forming a more equitable and inclusive relationship between the institutional players of Church and the public, we have the dual challenges of power and separation. Power is characterised by a hierarchy imposed upon the public. Separation sees both the clergy and the public operating in different environments – rarely connecting or intersecting in any meaningful relationship. How many people meet their local priest for a coffee or chat with the bishop on first-name terms?

So, we are not talking about the development of the Church, but rather the journey that we must all take. What we're talking about is how we journey together. Everybody has to move in this process if we are serious about inclusion. Because otherwise it doesn't work.

All this can lead to very different types of project initiatives and coordinating arrangements at a local level. Maybe it's a flatter arrangement, something more cellular or circular, like a cooperative or a network of initiatives. It's certainly not going back to the old local hierarchy managed by the bishops sitting together in Rome.

The bishops' confession

The bishops have to start by realising that the process has gone astray. The design and implementation (so far) have not been faithful to the Inverted Pyramid principles set out by Francis.

This admission is a sign of learning and humility. For it is through this recognition that bishops can open up the potential for genuine collaboration and a new beginning. This admission of getting the process wrong in itself changes the balance of power. The individual bishops' acknowledgement creates the potential to flip thousands of local individual Inverted Pyramids into action. It is this sign of vulnerability and empowerment that creates the space for others locally to respond.

With this acknowledgement of getting the initial process wrong comes a request for help and support, for people to take responsibility, to own their piece of the process and to start again, better. It's an invitation to all sectors of society and not just 'the faithful' to embrace an Inverted Pyramid process and promote inclusion for everyone. This is a personal call to action by each bishop at a local level. We are all called to build our Inverted Pyramid from the bottom up, and bishops are no different from anybody else. Jesus did it with his disciples.

The call to bishops is to urgently 'give' the process of Synodality to every person, and to encourage people to build their own Inverted Pyramids. For as long as the process is owned by the religious authorities, it is destined to remain detached and irrelevant to the very people it should be seeking to help. The invitation is for bishops to begin their own journey of Synodality, to reach outwards with a new confidence and remit to promote the Inverted Pyramid of Inclusion to governments, businesses and every part of society. And we can help them to do this.

'… the purpose of this Synod is not to produce more documents. Rather, it is intended to inspire people to dream about the Church we are called to be,

to make people's hopes flourish, to stimulate trust, to bind up wounds, to weave new and deeper relationships, to learn from one another, to build bridges, to enlighten minds, warm hearts, and restore strength to our hands for our common mission.' (PD, 32)* xi

And what about priests?

Many priests have become isolated and insular. Instead of being at the heart of their faith community, they have been left to try to protect themselves against a sense of apathy and negativity towards the Church.

Priests are part of a dysfunctional structure, for they are not responsible to their bishop. Priests report to Rom*e – but who wants a manager you never see or speak to? The bishop tries to manage his priests as best he can. In many cases, there is little camaraderie or support.

Priests are often stuck in their own bunkers and there can be little fellowship, sense of collaboration or active community among priests. There is no collective voice, no continuing professional development process.

It is no surprise, then, that many priests did not attend the Synod Consultation Process in their area. Perhaps they could see that this would be another occasion when they would be unable to defend what cannot be defended.

Of course, we need a new model of priesthood. But we also need to look after, train and work with those who are doing their best as the foot soldiers of an army trapped within the castle walls.

Let us work with priests who can embrace this new personal responsibility of the Inverted Pyramid. Let us join with priests and religious groups so that they, like others, can share their ideas and frustrations and say what they think needs to happen. And then, just like everyone else, let us work together to build our Inverted Pyramid Teams.

A PRAYER FOR PRIESTS, NUNS AND RELIGIOUS CONGREGATIONS

Please accept our invitation to work with you
to build our personal Inverted Pyramids
of Synodality, in all the ways that we can.
Help us to build new relationships
and work with you in new ways.

Please reach out and invite us
to be part of your personal Inverted Pyramids.
Work with us and help us
so that we can all grow,
personally and together, in new ways.

Please pray that all of us will join with
one another to create new arrangements
and new ways of working that reach
into every part of our communities,
our workplaces and our world.

CHAPTER 18: Time to harvest

Please take a moment to reflect and capture any initial thoughts, ideas, questions or action points that you wish to note and take forward. You will be able to gather these from each chapter for your personal development Action Plan at the end of the book.

Notes

1 ....

2 ....

3 ....

4 ....

5 ....

CHAPTER 19

Working together at a local level

In this chapter, we reflect on what this new process of working together locally might look like. What are the essential next steps for individuals, clergy, organisations and communities as we seek to build our Inverted Pyramids?

What next for the Catholic Church and the Inverted Pyramid of Pope Francis?

The timescale outlined for the initial phase of Synodality by the Synod of Bishops has now been extended to October 2024. The first phase of this process was an initial Consultation with local communities, completed in April 2022 with the results (Diocesan Synthesis) fed back to Rome. An Episcopal Conference will have produced seven draft documents by March 2023, prior to the Synod of Bishops in Rome agreeing these final documents in October 2023 and October 2024.

Questions

The initial Synodality Consultations raised many important questions, including:

- What happens next at a local level?

- Do we have to wait to see the final documents before we can discuss what happens next?
- Why were we not encouraged, enabled or empowered to continue the process at a local level?
- Can we set up specific interest/task groups to explore particular issues, ideas, needs or topics in more detail?
- Can we use this opportunity of Synodality to build community links and develop projects/initiatives that help those most in need?
- Can we use this process as an ongoing opportunity for personal/team spiritual development?
- And what might our evolving process look like?
- Can we reinvent/reinvigorate our local process so that we build on the tentative links that have been made? How might we become much more inclusive in welcoming everyone into our discussions?
- How might we invite the bishops and clergy to be part of our local processes? How might we use the Synodality process as an opportunity to meet people, build new relationships and create a framework for developing an ongoing dialogue?
- Can we create local or online meetings that enable all sectors and groups to join our discussions?
- If we were to kickstart this process, how could we do this? What is our first step?
- What are we looking to produce from these sessions (the outcomes)? A vision (of what)? A report (for whom)? A plan (to do what)? A team (to deliver what)? A network (to share what)? A community (to be what)? etc.

Given these and many other questions, it is important to ask '*What should we do next?*' How can we all be faithful to the methodology of the Inverted Pyramid?

The need to start again

Two of the primary questions arising at the local Consultation sessions were, *'What happens after the initial meetings when the findings have been submitted to the Vatican?'* and, *'What do local people do next?'*

The Inverted Pyramid of Inclusion calls on each of us to act now to shape this process. The initial process has thankfully been extended to October 2024. We must hope that the next steps are informed from where we all are now, and not where the bishops were when they designed the process. This is not about sitting around and waiting to see what the hierarchy does next. It's about recognising our role, our opportunity to contribute and build our individual Inverted Pyramid.

Synodality is, first and foremost, an invitation to all of us to start, to begin again better, and to keep reaching out to others as we journey. This journey is only beginning and we are at the heart of this. It's time to go now, and then go again, in our way.

How can we begin again, better?

We are all invited:

- To reflect on initial consultations that have taken place locally, whether we were there or not
- To think about how we might begin again, better, so that we are inclusive of everyone
- To create, continue to build or to join a local Inverted Pyramid process for journeying together
- To connect with all others and so continue to play our part in an interactive and dynamic worldwide journey of Synodality.

This is particularly relevant to all those who were not invited and who have not been involved to date. We desperately need your participation, now. The needs of those who are hungry, the young and the elderly, those who are lonely and those who are struggling in any way, are the focus of this work.

The urgent need for local leaders

One of the notable absences in many communities is the lack of leadership for Synodality. The process is seen as owned and overseen by bishops and priests, many of whom did not take an active part in the initial consultations, or even attend the sessions.

Some bishops did well. They attended the initial consultations and adapted the questions as best they could. They tried to make the process real. Some came along to genuinely help with a sense of purpose, humour and a little humility. But the process still ended there.

The leadership space has been left vacant. These roles will be welcomed by those who refuse to accept outdated behaviours and an out-of-touch Church. Isolation can be replaced with new project management frameworks, people development strategies, resourcing plans and emerging vision boards across all parts of our communities.

The 12 principles of Synodality

Here are twelve suggested operating principles to define the process of Synodality:

1. EQUAL
We are not subjects waiting to be told what to do. We are all partners working together on an equal basis.

2. BOTTOM-UP
We are responsible for journeying with others. This is a bottom-up process. The onus is on us to reach out from where we are.

3. INCLUSIVE
We try to be fully inclusive of everyone, without exception.

4. ONGOING

Synodality is an ongoing process that continues, from now. Every day, we continue to start again, better.

5. BUILD

We work with others to build Inverted Pyramids together. We encourage and support each other.

6. ASK

We ask the questions that matter to us. We are people who listen.

7. PRIORITY

We reach out to those who are most in need. We respond to the needs we see.

8. HUMILITY

We seek to engage those who are negative or apathetic. We have the humility to welcome criticism and critique.

9. PROFESSIONAL

We are working to build a professional, organised and joined-up inclusive global community in our homes, businesses, schools, colleges, communities, organisations and faith groups.

10. PERSONAL ASSETS

We bring our skills, experience and energy to the process and the groups that we work with in our efforts to build a better world for all.

11. SPIRITUALITY

We continue to develop our personal spirituality as an integral part of this journey.

12. GLOBAL

We recognise that we are all connected as parts of the same journey, individually, locally and internationally. We are all part of one global community of inclusion. Synodality can help us to add value to every aspect of our lives. It can provide a bridge linking our passions, interests and experience with all those we know and work with.

Personal responsibility

It would make sense to create a complementary and collaborative way for ordinary people to engage with clerical structures. To do so, we must shift the framework from control and authority to one of working together, building on all of our strengths, and cherishing all individual input.

There are no proper structures in place to develop Synodality locally, beyond the few people the bishop may have appointed from his inner circle. Where are the roles, responsibilities, job titles, projects, training programs, areas of responsibility, key objectives, plans, events, activities and schedules? Where is the excitement that Synodality should be building? Is this local inertia, frustration and more of the same old behaviours really what Pope Francis hoped for or intended?

So, we need to be different. We need to find local leadership. We need to support those who will step up and make something happen. We need outliers, the ones who are going to help us to create new models and different approaches that reach into all parts of our community.

The train is leaving the station

It seems clear that additional infrastructure needs to be created if we are to engage with and empower all individuals to act across our local communities. Here are some discussion questions:

- Are we ready to build Synodality now from the bottom-up rather than the top-down?
- Can we link local parish organisations and religious communities together at a local level to share experiences and journey together as one?

- Can we encourage local people in all sections of society, including business, education, community and public sector, to be actively involved and to claim their role in the Synodality process, and share their key skills, expertise and experience to help build a world of inclusion?
- Will we help young people, the elderly, the sick, the lonely, the ones left behind and all those who are struggling, to find a way to make their voice heard? Who is going to invite them in?
- Are we looking at sectors which cut across geographical boundaries and link people as communities of practice, with their own areas of interest and organic development process?
- Will bishops and priests reach out now to encourage us to continue building Synodality at a local level, on an equal and fully inclusive basis? Will they welcome this collaboration from local people in the management and ongoing development of the process, so that we can all move forward together in a new spirit of collaboration?
- Will local groups step up and invite the bishop, priest or local religious congregation to join their initiatives?

Bishops have an opportunity to link with each other and begin to empower others to build a comprehensive bottom-up strategy around the Inverted Pyramid frameworks of inclusion and personal responsibility. The practicalities of empowering people are easy.

What's our local plan?

So, have we a mission for what inclusion means to us? Can we imagine a modern Inverted Pyramid community of inclusion for our fast-changing world? What does it look like? If we don't know where we are going, then how will we get there?

What do we see happening? What will success look like? What are the key needs we're looking to address over the next twelve months?

What do we want to be radically different? What does love and service mean for us?

What exactly are we trying to build? What are we trying to change? Who are we seeking to help – and how? What will our community, our business or our Church look like in two years' time? What will be different? What do we need to do first to get the process moving? How can we help to make this happen?

CHAPTER 19: Time to harvest

Please take a moment to reflect and capture any initial thoughts, ideas, questions or action points that you wish to note and take forward. You will be able to gather these from each chapter for your personal development Action Plan at the end of the book.

Notes

1 ....

2 ....

3 ....

4 ....

5 ....

CHAPTER 20

Vocational guidance and career development

There is an old-fashioned idea within the Church that we should be praying for and encouraging vocations as if this was something restricted to young men setting out on the journey of priesthood. The reality is that we all have a vocation, and so prayer for vocations is just as much about ourselves and each other. In this chapter we will explore what vocation might mean to each of us.

An inclusive call for vocations

The Church has a very narrow field for active engagement. The very use of the word *vocation*, in the specific context of young males studying for the priesthood and young females entering the religious life, excludes over 99% of the population. It also says that resource-planning for the future of the Church is with these young people. We have placed an amazing burden on a few young shoulders.

This is not the journeying together that Francis envisages. Nor is it the reality of vocation today. Our wish must be to help us uncover and realise our own vocation and indeed the collective vocation of everyone working together. The call from priests and bishops must be for them also, to allow them to realise and uncover their true vocation as we journey together. This is a collective journey. For the future of the Church is how each of us can reimagine and rediscover our own vocation, and through this, how we build a global community of love.

A vocation does not have to be in a clerical role or Church setting. Vocation is made visible in our role as parent, caregiver, trainer or manager, as someone who is unemployed or has retired. We all have much to discover about each other and our contribution as we journey together.

Vocational guidance

When I was young, I used to think of vocation in career terms. In my case, it might have been about becoming a doctor, teacher or even a priest. But now I think that vocation is a direction of travel that shows every day who and where we are. I've learnt that vocation is also dynamic and of this moment. It grows and shifts as we learn and build on our experience.

Vocation is a lifelong journey made up of two elements: a journey outwards to others and a journey inwards to our inner selves. These dual aspects of vocation intersect, overlap and become one in all that we are, as we journey with others. This is where vocation finds its common purpose, in everyone together. For our ultimate vocation is to spread love, build love and become love as one.

All that we experience today is a gift for us to take forward in new ways, as we continue to become all that we are intended to be. It's our constant call to follow our vocation each day, outwards and inwards. To sit in silence, to help others, to be grateful and to do the work that matters.

What do you really want to do?

The Inverted Pyramid recognises that we are each on a different journey and that each journey matters. It also offers a different success framework to that of the world. We are not judged by the job we do or the money we make. What matters in the Inverted Pyramid is who we are, what we're about and how we work with others. The key question for each of us is, 'What do I really want to do?'

Each of us is unique. So, how will I use the skills, gifts and talents that I've been given? What's my purpose? What's my personal mission? How can I contribute to building a worldwide community of kindness? How might I pay it forward and give back to others? What's the legacy that I will leave behind? It's time to be ambitious for all that we can be. We are only here once. So, go for it! Do something every day.

Millions of journeys

Synodality is made up of millions of journeys coming together. It's how each of us makes real our vocation, purpose or mission, and builds love. Synodality is visible in the way we behave. It's in the way we reach out and offer to work with others, and actively encourage each other to collaborate in new and different ways. It's how we inspire and encourage our local groups, organisations, businesses, colleges and universities, charities, sports clubs and societies to create their own unique process and journeys of Synodality.

Personal spiritual development

The Inverted Pyramid is not just about a different way of interacting. It's actually about a different way of being. It's when we turn our lives upside down and inside out that we can embrace what love (or God) truly is.

And this is the spiritual journey that accompanies the process of Synodality. So let us not reduce the Inverted Pyramid to a tactical process when in fact it is a major shift from organisational to individual Church. And let us not miss the fact that this is not just another role for us but an opportunity to live our lives as intended.

Your journey is part of someone else's journey

Can the process of journeying together be a successful one? To do this means bishops and priests not only engaging with the faithful but also encouraging them to participate in this process and inspiring them to bring others on board as part of our collective mission.

Synods are a time to dream and 'spend time with the future': we are encouraged to create a local process that inspires people, with no one excluded, to create a vision of the future filled with the joy of the Gospel.

Restore my Church

The concept of an Inverted Pyramid invites us to reframe and totally rebuild a Church for today and tomorrow. The foundations are strong, but I am no longer confident that this is a structure that can be fixed up. This looks like a new build.

This gives us an opportunity to reconceive of what we want our Church to be.

So let us not sit idly by while others ignore rotting windows and crumbling mortar or disagree about the colour of the walls. Instead, let us, individually and collectively, build our own piece of community where we are, here and now – starting today.

Let us reach out to our friends, colleagues and families, and begin to discuss how we can build a kinder and more compassionate world in simple and yet ambitious ways. Let us all have a vision worthy of our vocation and journey together as we build a worldwide community of love.

Future Church

The future supply of sufficient priests may not come from the Church's current approach. Experience over recent years tells us this bluntly and repeatedly. The Church must focus on empowering everyone so that we can build a community that is outward-looking, adventurous and confident. It is a community that discards the shackles of the past, one that asks and encourages everyone, without exception, to play a part and to work together.

The Church does not need to pray for vocations. The Church already has all the people it needs. The spirit of love is already present in all of us. What is missing is the framework and permission to allow us all to be ministers, and to play our part fully in the work of service and helping all others.

Vocation is not simply a narrow call about recruiting priests and nuns. It is about building an effective and fully inclusive, collaborative Church that inspires us to fully live our vocation where we are now. Our prayer is no longer for priests to prop up an outdated and detached institution. Our prayer is for a new type of discipleship to emerge, one which is fully inclusive, participative and representative of all those we seek to serve.

INVERTED PYRAMID EXERCISE

What about the laity?

A NEW DISCIPLESHIP

Priests and clergy wear clothes
that clearly identify them
as people committed to God.
We expect, welcome or tolerate them
speaking about God.
That's their job.
Even if we disagree with their message,
we recognise their role.

For the rest of us,
it's not as easy as this.
We do not have uniforms
to identify whose side we are on.
The only way we can be recognised
as people committed to love
is by our behaviour and our words.

We are not seen as having a
similar vocation or commitment
that 'religious' people have.
We are out in the world
with no visible protection or defence,
except our trust in
the one who loves us.

Bishops and priests are at
the top of the Church.
They have an organisation
that holds them together,
and a legitimacy to act,
through their defined roles and authority.

But we do not have
an organisation to protect us,
a clear role, or permission to act.
We are out on our own
making our way in the world,
alone with
the one who loves us.

Priests and clergy have
a holy place where they can
talk about God
and the Christian message safely,
usually without ridicule or
being seen as a 'religious nutter'.

We do not have the security
of a holy place
or a welcoming space
to discuss our journey with God.

How can we promote a gospel of love
when we have no uniform
to show who we are,
no organisation to hold us,
and no place to speak,
in a world that does not even wish
to hear or talk about God?

The journey of Synodality
for the laity,
(as we were once labelled),
requires a different way.

This is a new calling,
where uniform is not needed,
where we are welcomed,
and where everyone is heard

as we journey together,
to all places, with
the one who loves us.

PERSONAL DEVELOPMENT REFLECTION
1. What is your 'calling' in the Inverted Pyramid?
2. What does this exercise mean for you personally?

Who is responsible for Synodality?

An inclusive process must involve everyone. That is our personal quest and responsibility – and not a parish, diocesan or Vatican one. This is not a process that is owned by the clergy. Synodality is an invitation to us, to reach out and to meet others in our upper room. We are invited to build a community of kindness locally, wherever we are.

INVERTED PYRAMID EXERCISE

What should we build?

INCLUSION ARCHITECT

We are all Inclusion Architects.
We build the future each day
through our interactions with others.
We can dream of a different world
and we can offer encouragement.
We can help others to dream.

We are all Inclusion Architects.
This is our vocation given to us
when we were born,
to make the world a better place.
And so, every day we awaken
to this opportunity and invitation.

286

We are all Inclusion Architects.
We use our skills, gifts and talents,
our knowledge, contacts and experience,
our links, friendships, and relationships
to build projects and initiatives
and construct a better future together.

We are all Inclusion Architects.
Take your role seriously.
Have your plan and act every single day.
Be ambitious for a better world.
A kind and safe place
where we can all live in peace and joy.

PERSONAL DEVELOPMENT REFLECTION

1. What are you designing at the moment as an Inclusion Architect?
2. Who is on your building team?

Career development opportunities for all of us

- The skills that we need locally to deliver important and worthwhile initiatives may fall into many key areas. Don't just look for helpers! Actively seek out people with the skills and experience you need, such as:
- Project management
- Community sector engagement
- Marketing/business development
- Social media/PR/promotion
- Facilitation
- Business and finance
- Building cross-community/cross-sector partnerships
- Video/graphics
- Event management/organisation
- Administration/liaison

- Training/education

This is an excellent opportunity for people to get involved in the work, to 'give back', to develop their career, and to help create something special in the local community.

Reach out and find the best project managers, the best marketing people, the best social media specialists, the best facilitators, the best coordinators and the best administrators!

INVERTED PYRAMID EXERCISE

What's your local collaborative project?

COLLABORATION

Jesus was a carpenter,
a joiner as we say.
This was his mission
and his message.

His vocation was
the same as ours.
To build and fix,
and join us all together.

PERSONAL DEVELOPMENT REFLECTION
1. What is your vocation?
2. How are you also a joiner?

CHAPTER 20: Time to harvest

Please take a moment to reflect and capture any initial thoughts, ideas, questions or action points that you wish to note and take forward. You will be able to gather these from each chapter for your personal development Action Plan at the end of the book.

Notes

1 ....

2 ....

3 ....

4 ....

5 ....

Vatican 3 – towards an inclusive Inverted Pyramid Christianity

In this chapter we ask whether the Inverted Pyramid methodology of Francis is the beginning of Vatican 3? Are we seeing the early stages of transformation from a hierarchal institutional Church to one in which individuals build their local Inverted Pyramids and link together to create a kinder world? Has Francis given us a framework that extends beyond the confines of religion to empower us all to work together to build inclusion for the benefit of everyone?

Back to Church?

As the Covid pandemic eased, I was surprised to see a note in the Church bulletin from the local bishops saying that from next Sunday they were restoring *'the obligation for people to come back to Mass in Church'*.

There was no explanation around this, just an instruction. Clearly, the bishops were keen to reinstate things as they were, as indeed were many employers as they called people back to the office.

But everything had moved on. We had gone beyond whatever we thought the new normal might be. In the two-plus years of Covid, people had to find their own way of developing their spirituality. They juggled with the challenge of trying to make their work fit within the fabric of their (much changed) day-to-day lives.

Of course, we can encourage people to come together for communal worship but let us not negate or dismiss the new roles that individuals and families have created for themselves. And to lay down the law without discussion or understanding of the new hybrid context of working seemed like a clumsy attempt to try to bring us back to an outdated, authoritarian Church.

A mobile faith

The upside here is that the web has opened up the Church to the world. What was once hidden behind walls can now be on our kitchen table, in our office or in our bedroom. We can create our own timetable for prayer or services to meet the needs of our families and responsibilities. We can journey to different churches. We can find the priests with good homilies which really speak to us. We can enjoy the choirs that literally sing with us. While many of our local churches are closed throughout the day, we can now sit in quiet churches all over the world.

The Internet enabled the Mass to become readily accessible for people, rather than a physical place that they must go to on Sundays. Why should the old hierarchal Church seek to minimise this opportunity or take this gift away from people? Our faith can now be integrated on our laptops and phones, wherever we are. Our community prayer has gained a new dimension, for we can now literally reach across the world and be with others. We will learn new ways to grow from here. We can get together in our homes with others and literally build Church, community and our Inverted Pyramids together.

Our inclusive worldwide Inverted Pyramid community will embrace this. Everyone, including bishops, priests and clergy, are important contributors to this new outward-looking engagement, with new conversations and creative collaborations. This offers career development opportunities that leverage the expertise and skills of those who have dedicated their lives to the service of others. It provides a creative and participatory canvas for our clerical companions far beyond the fiefdom of their local bishop. They can, with the rest of us, begin to work out how we can all work together.

We no longer expect a journey to our local church to largely define our faith journey. Retailing, for example, has learned that you can only offer a limited selection in every shop and that each shop manager can only do so much with their budget and resources. But by going online, retail outlets can offer everything customers need, and people can shop whenever they want.

An inclusive Inverted Pyramid Christianity

Our online services can offer the opportunity to focus on needs, make new conversations and be with each other in our various online breakout rooms. We can link with all others, irrespective of religion or belief. An inclusive Inverted Pyramid Christianity says that you don't have to be part of the club to take part in its activities. We should all be there, building relationships and playing a full part.

Within an inclusive Inverted Pyramid Christianity, there is no difference between traditional Christians, those from other faiths and those who do not believe in God. An inclusive Inverted Pyramid Christianity is underpinned not by theology but by Dual Responsibility, where we all look after each other.

The Second Vatican Council (1962–65) effectively turned the Catholic Church inside out when it sought to engage the congregation in the services rather than treat them as viewers. Up to then, the priest had his back to the congregation and spoke in Latin during Mass. After Vatican 2, the priest faced people, speaking to them in their own language, and everyone joined in the ceremony. Vatican 2 also promoted the concept of religious freedom and started a dialogue with other religions. Over a three-year period, some 2,000 bishops from all over the world, with their advisers, issued 16 landmark documents.

That was over 50 years ago, and it seems like another major shift is now underway. Whereas Vatican 2 turned the Church inside out, the Third Vatican Council (V3) will aim, as Pope Francis envisages, to turn the Church upside down by becoming an Inverted Pyramid. The spirit of love can reach out from each of us in so many ways. We can open our laptops and phones with each other. For we (not the institutional Church, bishops or advisors) are the architects of a new, inclusive Inverted Pyramid Christianity. I think that V3 has already begun.

V3 shows us that this is no longer an inward-looking Christianity, for there is no top to the Inverted Pyramid. It is an inclusive Christianity, not limited by rules and theology, but one which is about each of us offering a gift of love and practical help – unconditionally to all.

V3 encourages us not to be restricted or limited by an institutional Church, for the transactions (organising and delivering Church services and sacraments) are distinct and separate from the interpersonal role we have with love and with each other. V3 tells us that we are at last a bottom-up Church and that each of us has a key role to play in building a world of inclusion.

Francis has become our modern-day role model. He has stepped out of the transactional Church to invite all of us, whoever and wherever we are, irrespective of our religion or belief, to journey with him. He has bypassed the institution of Church to connect directly with the love that we all are. This is his personal Inverted Pyramid invitation of inclusion to each of us.

Giving away our religious treasure

Inclusive Inverted Pyramid Christianity is not a negotiated amalgamation of different beliefs or non-beliefs. Inclusive Inverted Pyramid Christianity is a collaborative celebration of all that is most precious to each of us.

This takes us beyond the rules of religion and goes back to the basic message of the Golden Rule where we love one another. For we are love. God is love. Love is all. We are one.

INVERTED PYRAMID EXERCISE

How can faith be inclusive?

INCLUSIVE CHRISTIANITY

To bring everyone together
we must give away
that which we hold most dear.
For this is true love.

When we hold onto something
it is of no use to others.
It is only when we give to others
that which is most precious
that we can become one with all.

PERSONAL DEVELOPMENT REFLECTION

1. What are you holding onto?
2. What is the most precious thing you can give?

Inclusive Inverted Pyramid Christianity removes all theological restrictions and rules that may hinder others from joining together. It takes us back to a guy walking by the shore of the Sea of Galilee and calling to us to love one another and to follow him.

The future of Church

As we journey together with whoever is on the journey, we create the future of Church. Systems, rules and structures can restrict us. History can take us off at a tangent. Power, ego and fear can hold us back. So, the process of Synodality is a gentle one. It's one of humility and vulnerability, of recognising that we have all got it wrong in some way.

The process of building our Inverted Pyramids is about reaching out, listening and journeying together in a profound way, for each of us holds each other. We all share responsibility for looking after others. We cannot just sit back and be organisers or onlookers on this journey. We have to walk as equals, for who knows who we will meet along the way?

Review

At the beginning of this section, we set out three key questions as part of this live case study that we should address. Please make a note of your answers to these questions:

1. How would you respond and what would you do if this scenario was unfolding in your organisation, business or community?
2. What specific advice would you give to Francis, the bishops, the clergy and the people they are seeking to serve in local communities?
3. What would you say to others who are interested in building inclusion? How might they respond in a positive way to add a different kind of leverage and a greater critical mass that can take the journey forward in ways not yet imagined?

CHAPTER 21: Time to harvest

Please take a moment to reflect and capture any initial thoughts, ideas, questions or action points that you wish to note and take forward. What are your main reflections from Section Four?

Notes

1 ....

2 ....

3 ....

4 ....

5 ....

SECTION 5

Future Work – the Emerging Inverted Pyramid Workplace

What does the emerging Inverted Pyramid workplace look like for us? How can we invert our leadership thinking, transform our Human Resources departments and provide training for all staff? Section Five invites us to play a key role in building an Inverted Pyramid workplace of the future that meets the needs of everyone.

CHAPTER 22

Inverted Pyramid employment

We're going to look at the evolution of Inverted Pyramid employment in this chapter. A lot of what we're talking about here isn't actually new. It's been well signposted over the last forty years, but recent events have provided the catalyst for accelerating the need for Inverted Pyramid organisations.

As we have discussed, the Internet, global warming, war, food/energy sustainability, migration, poverty, pandemics and global food supply have all brought home to us that we live in a totally interconnected and interdependent world. All of this now requires a much greater collaborative effort in every sphere. We can no longer just stick our heads in the sand and say that we are okay in our own bubble.

A clear example of all this development is the way in which remote and hybrid working have given individuals responsibility for managing themselves. There is no requirement that someone is looking over our shoulder. And we're actually working *at home* a lot of the time, if not all the time. We have taken responsibility seriously. Indeed, much of the time and cost savings of not going into the office have been translated into goodwill and added value for our employment relationship. Our flexibility and freedom to work at home is essentially rewarded by us making a greater effort and putting in more time.

You see, the Inverted Pyramid is also changing the way that we manage people. We are moving away from measuring what people do to looking at measuring outputs and what we can achieve together.

Individuals already work in an Inverted Pyramid way

If we look at how society has developed over recent years, we can see how most of us have taken on greater responsibility for managing all aspects of our life. We manage all the pieces. We work with others as freelancers, project workers, remote teams and so on. This is an almost prerequisite set of skills for ensuring that we can function and survive in the world today. The old idea from 40 years ago of somebody giving you a job effectively meant that many people were sorted for life. You had your work and your home life. Done.

Since then, this has changed dramatically. Now, we effectively manage our work life and our career ourselves. The idea of a job for life is long gone. Now, we have a team of people who work with us. Now, we do everything! We hire freelancers. We use the gig economy. We link up and chat online with people in different cities and in different countries. We book our own flights and produce our own books. We've all become Inverted Pyramid managers in our own right. And technology has enabled us to do all of this.

We are now working as much from home as we are in the office, as the lines between work and home are no longer fixed in the same way. Our larger organisations haven't caught on yet to what is happening to their staff. Many businesses are still panicking about hybrid working and trying to get people back to the office. But that bus has already gone.

Many senior managers are struggling to make sense of the traditional hierarchal organisation structure in terms of the Inverted Pyramid players we have become. It's no longer as easy to recruit people. Slowly, businesses are beginning to see the gap in expectations and the need for different types of relationships. Hybrid flexibility, part-time working, partnership arrangements, outsourcing, gigs, freelancing, joint ventures and project work are all replacing the old one-dimensional and fixed definition of employee. The Inverted Pyramid structure is not only the organisation of the future. It is the way that we organise the present.

A methodology for building your Inverted Pyramid organisation

What we're setting out to do is to create the methodology for making our organisation an Inverted Pyramid. It's about delivering on a bigger vision, with more connections and greater participation and inclusion from those inside and outside the business. It's about the fulfilment of opportunities for all of our people to build and develop their roles in all the ways that are important to them.

And all of this must sit within the operational structure of the business, because this has to add, not reduce, value. This has to make the business much more sustainable, relevant and effective in all that it does.

It's no longer about the person responsible for a project knowing all the answers. It's about each of us knowing who the experts are in every area of our organisation. This is not just in terms of their organisational role but also the skills, expertise and knowledge that they already have and may not yet be using within our business. This is the on-tap potential that every employee brings and most organisations never ever use. We all have a responsibility to know what others might be able to bring if we are to fully understand the potential of our Inverted Pyramids and our organisational effectiveness.

Work is us

The employment model, with its zero-hours contracts, has further accelerated the detachment of the business from its workers. Many businesses and organisations now only need to pay people when they need them. If it's raining, they can tell staff to stay at home, and they don't get paid. If the shop gets busy, they can call people into work.

This may sound like a great cost-saving approach, but effectively it has further loosened the bonds between business structure and the traditional employer-employee relationship.

It's easy to see why working from home, freelancing, working online, the gig economy and zero-hours contracts have enabled individuals to take greater control of their working life. More and more workers now structure their workpieces in terms of income needs, personal satisfaction and practical home demands. They move their career forward by changing their workpieces to achieve what is important to them.

In essence, the workplace has continued to shift from the mill owners of the 18th century to factories, manufacturing, offices, automation, and now beyond the Internet of the 20th century. The emerging 21st century workplace is now individual. It is each one of us. We are going back to our pre-industrial mindset of collaboration and community-building. Only this time, it's different. We take the benefits of the Internet with us. We see the needs of a worldwide community and understand the needs of our planet. This time, we can do the work really matters to us. Our relatives in the 18th century had no air travel or Internet. We, in contrast, can link and work with all others as we build on our Inverted Pyramid priorities – and not only those we can reach by horse. Inverted Pyramid employment is available to us all.

The Inverted Pyramid workplace

For many of us, our work has become detached from our real selves. If we had to choose what we really wanted to do, this probably wouldn't be it. We continue to settle for what we have and count our blessings.

Remember how our parents used to talk about work-life balance? Some of us in secure or traditional sectors still talk in this way. For many others, work has now become fragmented into an array of potential income generation activities that we manage as we juggle employers, tasks and roles, and try to pay the bills. It is not surprising that mental health and well-being conversations have become so prevalent, as we have left so many people to fend for themselves. This is one consequence of our transaction-driven economy.

The individual workplace, as we've seen from home working, can be a lonely place, and we know as humans that we need interaction, encouragement, positive support, camaraderie, kindness and joy. The Inverted Pyramid workplace is one where each of us can now grow and develop with each other as we build our initiatives with colleagues, contacts, friends and partners.

INVERTED PYRAMID EXERCISE

What is our work?

THE EMERGING WORKPLACE

I remember the fields
and the farm,
where my grandparents
used to work.

I remember the factory
and the garage,
where my parents
used to work.

I remember the offices,
hotels and training centres,
where I
used to work.

I remember the Internet,
phones and homes,
where we all
used to work.

And now our children live
in a different way,
where they can choose
to make their life work.

PERSONAL DEVELOPMENT REFLECTION

1. What is your life's work?
2. How is your way of work evolving?
3. How are you being proactive rather than reactive in doing the
   work that is important for you?

Hybrid living

Hybrid living is not just a combination of working from home or working in the office. Hybrid living effectively integrates the personal and business aspects of who we are, what is important to us and where we are going. No longer is our work life separate from our home life. Hybrid living addresses our personal needs, career ambitions, family responsibilities, close relationships, personal purpose and all the things that make up who we really are.

The Inverted Pyramid methodology helps us to build an all-inclusive framework for effective hybrid working which fully integrates and drives both the personal and work aspects of who we are.

There is no line between the personal and business, for we are the business. We look after one another so that everybody does well. If something is important to one of our colleagues then it should matter to us. The business is built on relationships rather than relationships being dictated by work systems and processes.

Hybrid working means each of us achieving what is important for us in a way that supports all others. Within this context, we build effective businesses, organisations, education frameworks, projects, networks and initiatives that benefit everyone.

The great disconnect

Have you ever thought about the disconnect between the work you do and the problems in the world? Have you ever felt the disconnect between the work you do and what you would really like to do? Have you ever felt the disconnect between the quality of your life and what you really want? It doesn't have to be this way. We do not have to continue to fit into other peoples' traditional top-down hierarchies of power and control.

INVERTED PYRAMID EXERCISE

What's the alternative to the Rat Race?

RAT RACE

We have inherited a world
where jobs and work
are allocated to people.

Employers decide on the tasks
that need to be done
and carve up the activity.

It's an outdated economic model
where we are paid to do what we are told,
and where many people have no jobs.

With technology we can now
create work in different ways,
driven by what really matters.

We can link up with others
and collaborate on projects
that are important to us as individuals.

We can take responsibility
for creating and shaping all of our futures
and a better world.

We can share resources
rather than waiting, like rats,
for the food pellet to arrive.

PERSONAL DEVELOPMENT REFLECTION

1. How can you use your skills, experience and passions in new ways?
2. Who can you start to work with today to create your new projects?

CHAPTER 22: Time to harvest

Please take a moment to reflect and capture any initial thoughts, ideas, questions or action points that you wish to note and take forward. You will be able to gather these from each chapter for your personal development Action Plan at the end of the book.

Notes

1 ....

2 ....

3 ....

4 ....

5 ....

CHAPTER 23

An interpersonal workplace

In this chapter we will outline a few emerging and challenging themes in our interpersonal workplaces, including the primacy of profit in business, the *God* word and making kindness real.

A worldwide community of inclusion

In building our Inverted Pyramid, we are developing pieces of inclusion. Pieces of inclusion can be formed by millions of people across the world, wherever they are, in line with the Inverted Pyramid principles of Dual Responsibility, kindness and collaboration. All of our pieces of community can come together to build a worldwide community of inclusion.

Many organisations are beginning to embrace the Inverted Pyramid for they can see the growth potential of global engagement and the business benefits of inclusion. But this is a much broader definition of business than simply share price or profit. For money is only a by-product of our effectiveness in building the fabric of collaboration, where we all work effectively together and look after everyone.

The primary purpose of our emerging Inverted Pyramid businesses is not to sell more and make more money. The purpose of business is to help build a global community of kindness and collaboration supported by the products and services that we offer. And we do this through the development of interpersonal relationships rather than impersonal transactions. It's our people who make this happen through their way of working and by being free to work seamlessly within their own Inverted Pyramids. This is how we build inclusion in, through and beyond our workplaces.

Organisations such as businesses or religious institutions that are unable or unwilling to embrace this, be part of the change and help to make this happen will simply be left behind.

When you turn your pyramid upside down, you've already changed your direction. You reach outwards, you look upwards, and you journey with others.

INVERTED PYRAMID EXERCISE

Where do you see yourself, right now?

IN THE PYRAMID

We are all caught up
in our own story.
We look inwards
and we see only ourselves
in the middle of everything.

But we are part
of a bigger picture.
And if we look outwards,
we can see ourselves
as part of everything.

PERSONAL DEVELOPMENT REFLECTION

1. What do you see when you look upwards?
2. What do you see when you look outwards?

Top-down hierarchy or bottom-up Inverted Pyramid

The implications of the Inverted Pyramid methodology for organisations and businesses is significant. Continuation of a traditional hierarchal approach, rather than a collaborative way of working, is likely to cause significant and increasing pressures on businesses being able to find, keep and develop the best talent. Individuals will become more likely to go off and do their own thing, with others, through their own range of Inverted Pyramid Teams working as part of more progressive initiatives.

We have to welcome the fact that we are all different, seek to embrace individual strengths and back individuals as they take ownership of their own development. We have to create a culture that actively encourages people to grow rather than ask for permission. Most of all, we have to allow people to lead our organisations from where they are. The idea of managing people as a resource is gradually shifting towards people bringing their expertise together to form new types of working arrangements. Ownership will take on a completely new meaning. As employers, we have an opportunity to promote this change. As individuals, we have a responsibility to make it happen.

Inclusive conversations

As I mentioned earlier, when I began delivering religion and belief workshops to companies in-house, one of the common questions at the end was always, '*Do we need a prayer room?*'

My response was always to say, '*Have you asked the people concerned what they think?*'

When I was writing the course, I was working with a leading Muslim who would simply find an excuse to go off for a short break at the required prayer time. Some people are very traditional in their faith practices while others may be very relaxed about the way they celebrate their tradition.

Many of us are told that we should not talk about religion at work. It's okay to talk about diversity but not religion. It's okay to make assumptions about our colleagues but not actually ask them what they really think.

So, how do we ask them? This is the question they put to me. Well, since you already ask about people's dietary requirements and accessibility needs, you should also be asking them about their faith or spiritual needs. This is an obvious question during the induction process and also as part of ongoing performance reviews or appraisals in place. After all, what is the point of a prayer room that is never used, or one that just divides us further?

Taking this further, should such a space be a single denomination prayer room, or a genuine multifaith prayer room? If you want to see examples of some good and also some very unwelcoming prayer rooms, pop into one next time you go through an airport.

Many organisations now simply have a Quiet Room where people can take a little time to reflect in peace or just escape for a few moments. Well-being and personal spirituality go well together. A Quiet Room can be a place that brings us together, whatever our belief, non-belief, background or position.

Let's deal with the *God* word

Some of us have difficulty using the God word or are very uncomfortable talking about God. 'It's just not done at work,' 'It's not something I'm interested in,' 'It's against company policy to talk about religion,' 'We don't do religion and politics here,' 'God is not relevant for me,' 'I don't feel comfortable talking about God.'

And from a senior manager: 'It's okay for people to practice their faith and talk about this airy-fairy stuff, as long as they do it in their own time. You see, that's not what business is for. We are here to make money. We are here to make a return to our shareholders.'

But if we change the word God to love (or inclusion) then perhaps we have a different way of linking up and working together with others with different beliefs. For God is just another word for love. It's the totality of all of us working together to help everyone. It is us giving of ourselves in all the everyday ways that we can. It is this love that is at the heart of who we are as human beings. It is a love that holds and unites us all as one, for we all live on the one planet, breathing the same air and sharing resources. We're slowly learning how we must look after our planet and each other.

But the reality is that these words are part of the lives of many of our people. When we do not enable people to grow in all the ways that they can, we become restrictive and exclusive. We are effectively telling staff to talk only about what we allow and to do only what we demand of them, rather than unleashing what they are capable of and have the potential to achieve.

INVERTED PYRAMID EXERCISE

What is your job?

THE PURPOSE OF WORK

The purpose of work
is not to make money,
build a business, deliver a service
or sell products.
These are simply activities.

The purpose of work
is to help others,
by giving of who we are,
so that we can all
grow together, now.

PERSONAL DEVELOPMENT REFLECTION
1. What are your work activities?
2. What is the purpose of the work that you do?

Other words around the periphery of the *God* or *love* word, such as spirituality, blessings, grace, compassion, are beginning to find their ways into more caring workplaces. This has been driven over the last 20 years by equality legislation which encourages respect for all beliefs and none, and for people with disabilities or different ethnic origin or sexuality. In more recent years, we've also seen the emergence of a well-being agenda which recognises the mental health issues that many people are facing.

And so, inclusion is now becoming the key concept to underpin the way that our organisations and businesses work. Inclusion was not a familiar concept in our business language 20 years ago. If we follow this trajectory, it's easy to see how kindness, compassion and caring for one another will be mainstreamed in the next 10 years. These 'softer concepts' will become essential values (and measures) in our collaborative way of working. It is already in the interest of every organisation to implement new Inverted Pyramid models of working together and supporting each other.

INVERTED PYRAMID EXERCISE

What is your belief?

RELIGIOUS BELIEF

Talking about God
is not easy in our world.
It's a conversation
that gets closed down quickly.

> It singles us out
> and we get placed in a camp.
> It's them and me.
> It becomes about exclusion.
>
> But their view of God and mine
> are worlds apart.
> They talk of religion or belief.
> I talk of love.

PERSONAL DEVELOPMENT REFLECTION
1. What does the word *love* mean to you?

When inclusion isn't working

I was asked to advise the senior team of a leading UK university on how to make inclusion work. They had four values – *innovation, collaboration, determination* and *diversity and inclusion* – in their strategy. But inclusion wasn't happening.

My queries seemed like a strange language to them. They totally disagreed with kindness and didn't see it as relevant. They had no place for caring, compassion or helping.

This was the view of the Head of Marketing and Communication. And the People Director.

Others stayed quiet. It seemed a strange position for a student-led business.

But this university is not alone. Many organisations are trying to bolt-on inclusion as a corporate behaviour, when really, it's a personal one. It's human values that we must cherish, as well as corporate ones.

Inclusion, in practice, is about behaviours that encourage and enable us to help each other, as we work and learn together. We must care for one another. We must be compassionate and kind. For none of us, whether staff or students, know what others are carrying, or going through.

INVERTED PYRAMID EXERCISE

How can we build a kinder world?

KINDNESS POLICY

Personal development
is not about me alone.
For my personal development
is dependent upon many others,
especially those I interact with for food, work, safety,
security, energy, health, friendship and love.

Personal development
is therefore about all of us.
It's about us working together
and looking after each other,
in ways that enable us all
to live happily, and to grow, together.

Personal development
is about us reaching out
and giving to others,
so that we can all be safe and well.
And yet, in our world we see so many
living and dying in shocking conditions.

We have been taught
to strive for more, put ourselves first
and hold onto everything.
But in our interconnected world,
this approach only serves to make life less secure
for ourselves, for our children and for others.

Kindness is much more
than a nice thing to do.
It is our emotional, rational and practical selves
acting through initiatives, responses and actions
to uncover who we are
and to discover what we can become.

Kindness is uncompromising and demanding.
It causes us to make choices.
It takes us out of our comfort zone.
It makes us look at the needs of others.
It enables us to understand who we really are.
Kindness is the heart of personal development.

It's time to put kindness on our curriculum.
It's time for kindness policies to drive our
workplaces, schools, universities and governments.
And it's time for us to build
a collaboration of kindness in our schools,
in our community, in our family and in our world.

PERSONAL DEVELOPMENT REFLECTION
1. Where is kindness in your life and in your workplace?
2. How can you personally become part of the collaboration of kindness in the world?

CHAPTER 23: Time to harvest

Please take a moment to reflect and capture any initial thoughts, ideas, questions or action points that you wish to note and take forward. You will be able to gather these from each chapter for your personal development Action Plan at the end of the book.

Notes

1 ....

2 ....

3 ....

4 ....

5 ....

CHAPTER 24

The leadership of common purpose

Personal leadership is at the heart of the Inverted Pyramid, for it all starts with us. This chapter seeks to help us to reposition traditional leadership thinking with a practical leadership that is common to us all. In this chapter we will reflect on Francis talking about leadership and the Inverted Pyramid.

Old school leadership thinking

Let us explore three stereotypical views of leadership and leaders that Francis turns upside down:

1. We must lead from the front

The danger with having a traditional leader mindset and leading from the front is that we have to keep looking over our shoulder to see if people are still following us.

And if we keep looking over our shoulder to see if people are still following us, then people see us checking that they are still there! This tells them that we are not a very good leader. So, I think leadership is actually about being with and behind others and trying to move forward from a place of service rather than control. And this is not just having a 'servant mentality'. It's about understanding that the strength of leadership is to be present in the situation, to be able to take everything into account and to move forward as one with people, rather than giving instructions from the front.

2. Leaders are prominent and visible

Sometimes we tend to think of leaders in an organisational sense, but the true leaders in our day (and probably in days gone by) are the people not limited by the culture, constraints or demands of an organisation. It's often the quiet people who don't seek or get any credit. It could be a nurse, a mother or father looking after a child, a caregiver, a youth community worker.

I see these people as amazing leaders because they don't need incentives or recognition. They don't need to be told what to do. They can see the whole situation. They're working alongside others and helping to move everything forward. I think leadership is directly connected to who we are journeying with, the situation we're in and who we really are.

3. Leadership is from the top

For Francis and the Inverted Pyramid, leadership isn't so much coming from the top as emerging from the inside out. For leadership is within each of us, and therefore the potential for leadership exists with every person and within every organisation, irrespective of role, position or situation.

The purpose of the Inverted Pyramid is effectively to build a worldwide community of love.

This is a compelling vision that doesn't exist at the moment because we live in a competitive world. We live in a world of wars. We live in a world of hunger. We live, so far, with global warming. This is a vision from a man who sees things as they are. We need change and this vision of inclusion is empowering and liberating for each of us.

What Francis is doing is totally subversive. He's flipping over and exploding the institutional pyramid of Church from the inside out – or he's trying to. He is giving the Church to everyone in the world, without preconditions. The name he took as Pope was the clue. Like his namesake, this is not about the maintenance of buildings. It is about rebuilding the whole of humanity, together, as one.

'*It's a task for all of us, to which each one of us is invited. But it's a time especially for the restless of heart, that healthy restlessness that spurs us into action.* Francis goes on to say that making light of ethical considerations and living at a superficial level have not served us well, and that: '*We need to proclaim that being kind, having faith, and working for the common good are great life goals that need courage and vigor.*'[xii]

INVERTED PYRAMID EXERCISE

What is the purpose of leadership?

PILGRIM LEADERSHIP

Leadership is not about changing roles
or shifting direction.
It is not about team development
or business strategy.

Leadership is a fundamental shift
in our being – what we are, how we think,
the priorities we set
and how we behave.

Leadership is a behavioural,
emotional and spiritual process.
It's rewiring the hard disk of our being
for a completely different output.

We are no longer
mass-market products
of the consumer age
but pilgrims with a purpose.

Executive leadership

On a recent Inverted Pyramid workshop with CEOs and senior managers, we explored how they could begin to develop Inverted Pyramid thinking and activities within their organisations. At the end of the workshop, in small groups, I asked them to share their personal key messages for other CEOs. Here are their top 12 messages:

1. Do not wait
'We cannot afford to wait until we sort out all our business ambitions before we do what is most important for us. The reality is that when we start to do what we really want to do, our business ambitions become realised much quicker.'

2. It's time to change the world
'To leave the world a better place is a desire of many. We are creating an Inverted Pyramid community as a practical framework and mechanism to enable us to do this. We would encourage others to have a think about how they might help to build a better world.'

3. What do you really want to do?
'The question, "What do you really want to do?" is a great one! What is it that you are passionate about? Is it success, fame, wealth, power, or is it cancer, inequality, lack of opportunity, healthcare, poverty, global warming, education, sustainability, peace, a better way to do something...?'

4. Think about the staff iceberg
'80% of the iceberg is hidden under water. Your staff only use a small percentage of their abilities to do the job you pay them for. So

much of their expertise, interests, skills and experience is not utilised in your workplace. Imagine if you could harness all this confidence, creativity, capability, commitment and collaboration (the 5 Cs) in your Inverted Pyramid community.'

5. Build a real community

'Some businesses compare their customers and contacts to a community that they serve. In reality they are a database of sales prospects and customers that do not relate to each other. In Inverted Pyramid communities, people work together and mutually support each other. They collaborate in new ways. They help each other. They actively look after one another.'

6. Work out the value of your business

'The real value of businesses today is beyond the P & L account, the balance sheet, the customer base, the email list, the brand and the goodwill. The real value now includes the contribution (and potential) of the Inverted Pyramid community you create – stakeholders, staff, customers, investors, the public etc., all working together for a vision bigger than the business.'

7. Make it part of your legacy

'Don't forget that the Inverted Pyramid community that you create will still exist and continue to grow after you have gone or the business is sold. The chain reaction of the relationships that are created will continue to grow upwards and outwards, reaching more and more people.'

8. We are unique

'Our Inverted Pyramid community will deliver something that has never been conceived of before – simply because we all want this to happen. We have amazing skills, expertise and experience. We are learning to create a new reality where people are free to imagine, collaborate and build a new form of togetherness.'

9. Start with the end in mind

'Many of us see our futures as developing from here, instead of beginning with the end in sight. Go beyond your current business constraints to be all you can be.'

10. Don't lose your biggest asset

'Because of the vision of the CEO/founders, their community is committed to something bigger than the business. But this Inverted Pyramid community value can be lost in the sale of the business.'

11. We need a business that works for all of us

'CEOs and founders typically spend over 95% of their energy on business growth activities and less than 5% on their personal vision or priorities. In virtually all the businesses represented here today, our staff are not aware of what really drives the CEO. As a result of this, all staff end up working for the business rather than the business working for all of us.'

12. We must stop selling stuff

'Our businesses will always be trying to SELL MORE and chasing customers until we finally offer people a vision which they identify closely with. It's a future which energises and engages them and one that they want to be part of. The old business model depends on products and services. The new Inverted Pyramid methodology is about vision, leadership and belonging. As CEOs we need to work with others to build a vision that everyone can be part of.'

'Far and away, the best prize that life offers is the chance to work hard at work worth doing.'

– Theodore Roosevelt

> *'Imagination is everything. It is the preview of life's coming attractions.'*
>
> – Albert Einstein

INVERTED PYRAMID EXERCISE

Are you ready to fill your bucket?

SANDPIT

We are but a grain of sand
in the history of the universe.
Tiny and insignificant.

No matter how wonderful our work is,
or how kind we are, or how successful we become,
we will all soon die.

Let us not focus on ourselves all the time
and miss the bigger picture.
We have another role to play.

For if God is Love and we are Love,
then we are not only a grain of sand but
the co-owners of an amazing sandpit.

And once we see our true relationship
with love, everything changes.
We can all build sandcastles.

PERSONAL DEVELOPMENT REFLECTION
1. What can we build together?
2. What is your sandcastle?

A kind business

Imagine a business philosophy based on kindness, compassion and love. It seems a long way from the traditional, lonely corporate model of greed, competition and money.

The Inverted Pyramid puts kindness, compassion and love centre stage. Our success is built with, through and alongside others.

When we report our successes we're not just reporting them for ourselves, but highlighting successes in terms of group interactions and the contribution of others. Who did you link up with? Who did you offer to help? It is this ongoing upward searching and action that enables us to build effective networks and leverages our expertise and experience in the very best ways.

This is a philosophy and a strategy based on maximising success for everyone. It's about collaboration, not competition. It's thinking about and supporting those who are struggling most. It's about everybody being able to share their ideas with everyone else.

Respect is at the heart of this approach: loving yourself; being grateful for your gifts; cherishing all that you've learned and experienced and become. It's love of others. It's love of what you do together – the excitement, challenge and achievements. It's about the struggle. It's about ongoing learning and development.

The key thing here is that the old business model defines us by what we do – getting a job, building a business, making a million. But we know that all of this is only temporary. The Inverted Pyramid, on the other hand, is a framework that we learn and then develop and grow with. We are always moving forward steadily step by step, doing something every day to realise our potential, help others and provide for those we love and care for.

INVERTED PYRAMID EXERCISE

How can we all find joy?

JOURNEYING TOGETHER

Journeying means
that we are moving.
We do not stay static.
Life changes, grows for us
and for those around us.

Our journey is the direction
that we want to go in our life.
It is our choice.
We do not need permission.
We can start from here.
We set out afresh each day.

Journeying together
means that we reach out
to others in different ways,
and at different times.
For we can all help others,
just as others help us.

It is these two words of
'journeying together'
that enable us all to move forward as one.
For we are individual
and indispensable parts
of a worldwide community of love.

We speak with those we meet.
We become role models for others.
We encourage many along the way.
We invite some to work with us.

And we share, together,
our skills, experience and ideas.

For two heads are better than one,
and the total is greater
than the sum of the parts.
It is in this coming together
that we build the fabric of love
that unites and guides us all.

We can do more
of what gives us joy.
We can do more
of what is important to us.
We can do more
of what we are called to do.

For all of us rest together
in the worldwide community of love
to which we are invited,
to which we all belong
and in which we play our part
in becoming all that we are.

PERSONAL DEVELOPMENT REFLECTION
1. What gives you joy?

CHAPTER 24: Time to harvest

Please take a moment to reflect and capture any initial thoughts, ideas, questions or action points that you wish to note and take forward. You will be able to gather these from each chapter for your personal development Action Plan at the end of the book.

Notes

1 ....

2 ....

3 ....

4 ....

5 ....

CHAPTER 25

A new discipline for HR and training professionals

The Inverted Pyramid is about all that we are, all that we do and all that we become, individually and together. It offers us a fresh new canvas for what we still call Human Resources (HR). In this chapter we have an opportunity to play with and imagine the future development of HR and training in our businesses and organisations.

A different role for the HR Department

Alex, a senior HR Director, said to me recently, 'HR has become the keeper of the book of rules. We are the guardians of policies and procedures. We are the ones to hold people to account if they break the rules. We have become corporate police departments.

'Rather than being an empowering and creative engine to help uncover and explore the true potential of our staff, we hardly talk to people. Rather than showcasing the successes of staff, or bringing people together in new ways, or promoting and encouraging participation in initiatives which represent and reflect our values, we hide away.

'Years ago, HR managers knew every person by name and we smiled and greeted each other when we met. We were on first-name friendly terms. This is no longer the case.

'I think that HR has lost the trust of staff. We have lost our personal touch. We have lost our way. What we really need to do is to urgently shift our own thinking and look at what HR can contribute to the organisation. My own view is that we must be the enablers that allow our people to shift from being passive employees to becoming more fully themselves. I think HR needs to regain its soul and connect directly to those it seeks to look after.'

Human Resource Management is an outdated concept

Contrary to Inverted Pyramid principles, in which we seek to serve and work with all others, many businesses and organisations continue to operate in a traditional hierarchal structure, in which people are there as hired hands. We are saying that the type of business we are building excludes love, God, spirituality, grace, kindness and blessings. Our model of business remains like the mill owners of the 19th century or something from *Downton Abbey*.

Most of our workplaces still maintain a very old-fashioned view of Human Resource Management, whereby we treat people as instruments to make money for us. It says that we're not really interested in people in their own right. We look for staff who can help make us more profitable, deliver better services, save money or improve efficiency.

Of course, these days we dress up the mill by talking about equality, discrimination, well-being, diversity and inclusion, but we are really only tinkering with a broken-down machine. There's not much positive and empowering language in most contracts of employment.

The Inverted Pyramid department

The future of HR is no longer about managing human resources, but about facilitating the development of Inverted Pyramid collaboration. We can free our training departments to be the enablers of inclusion. And we can start by renaming HR as IP.

In a discussion with a group of trainers and HR specialists, I asked them what they thought their new priorities around inclusion should be. Here are their responses:

- *We need to train our staff and explain how the Inverted Pyramid works*
- *We need to rethink our inclusion strategy*
- *We need to build a culture of collaboration*
- *We need to begin to develop a bigger vision for our businesses and our workplaces*
- *We need to review the approach and effectiveness of our DEI team*
- *We need to connect who we are as individuals to what we do*
- *We need to connect all that we work on to the bigger world*
- *We need to find a way to bring the senior management team on board*
- *We need to radically rethink our HR strategy*
- *We need to help people to become agents of change*
- *We need to build joy in our workplaces*
- *We need to treat our people as colleagues as full human beings and not just people who provide work for us*

Inverted Pyramid training

If we are to keep the Inverted Pyramid growing upwards, then we need to explain to people what we're doing. Otherwise, it will just sit apart from what is happening within traditional hierarchal structures. Building inclusion is not just about helping people, reaching out, developing initiatives and involving everybody in those initiatives. It's also about explaining how the process works, so that everyone becomes a practitioner and a player.

We are empowering others to become partners rather than subjects in all that we do. We are striving to involve others as architects of the process. For this is how they can continue in their own way to develop their own inverted presence. We are cascading upwards.

Inverted Pyramid communities are like free-flowing processes responding to individual ideas, as people take on new and different roles. New teams are formed by people coming together in a way that the traditional business or organisation cannot foresee, plan or control. For the business has a different way of operating.

Training itself must become an Inverted Pyramid

Training has become transactional rather than developmental. The onslaught of online courses in the last five years has turned training into a product, rather than a process for developing the potential of the people we work with. We have turned our training courses into hierarchal pyramids where the trainer sits at the top with all the expertise and the participants sit at the bottom. There is little human interaction beyond the subject matter. There is little relationship-building. There is little real continuity or growth. In so many cases, the delivery of training has become functional, sterile and stale. It's certainly not fit for purpose in many of the organisations looking to build inclusion.

Inclusion calls on trainers, managers, consultants and HR specialists to invert their professional pyramids. Training courses can offer us the potential to bring people together to discover more about each other and find solutions, and also provide a platform for them to continue the work beyond the course. For so often it is perceived that the training finishes at the end of the workshop or the course, and so effectively, we are stopping the development of further relationships.

If we present the opportunity of an Inverted Pyramid approach, then we are saying you must continue to develop your work, your relationships and build the impact of what we can achieve together. Every training workshop is an Inverted Pyramid of potential and possibilities. Every training activity becomes about personal and interpersonal development, strengthening the fabric of inclusion within our Inverted Pyramids.

Rethinking your training sessions

We build global inclusion by enabling and encouraging every person to create and grow their Inverted Pyramid.

Our role as trainers and managers is not the passive delivery of material but:

- to bring people together to learn about each other
- to encourage the development of new linkages and relationships
- to share experience from those we are working with and to learn from each other
- to develop new initiatives and arrangements that can be taken beyond the training situation as we each build our personal Inverted Pyramids and collective initiatives
- to link these new arrangements and initiatives together so that we build a body of inclusion across departments, functions and, of course, beyond the organisation itself.

Building inclusion in your organisation

It's easy to see why so many organisations struggle with the concept of inclusion – they're stuck providing policies and training courses on equality and diversity. They are seeking to get representation and equality in their process and procedures. They are looking to deal with unconscious bias, to close the gender pay gap or to ensure that minority groups are fully represented in all aspects of the business or organisation.

Although all of this is so important in promoting and sustaining the rights of each individual person, it does not in itself build inclusion. As trainers and managers, we are simply keeping people in their place while talking to them about equality. If we are truly to build an inclusive workplace, then we need a bigger vision of who we all are together. We need to enable people to link up together and build a raft of Inverted Pyramids. We as trainers and managers must become Inverted Pyramid role models – not just talk about it or stay at the top of our training pyramids. And then, with others, we can all come together in ways we could never imagine or predict.

How to build inclusion into every training course or meeting you deliver

People will assume that we are acting in a traditional hierarchal way unless we signal and specify that we are working differently. We can do this with an Inverted Pyramid diagram.

We can enable individuals to link up and discuss what's important to them. We can encourage staff to build relationships with each other that cut across departments and go beyond their defined job roles. We can invite and encourage them to be creative, to look at the needs that are not being addressed and to explore ways of making things better et cetera.

So, as trainers, we need to flip the pyramid at the start of our training sessions. Irrespective of the topic, we can create a bigger canvas where people can link together and build a greater context of needs, possibilities, constraints and a host of personal situations affecting our colleagues. We can root our training in the reality of people's lives and the world we live in, and in doing so, build greater resilience, capability and personal fulfilment in all that we do.

We can explain to participants that they are in charge of their learning, how they can grow and develop and work with others and how they take this forward. The days of sitting passively listening to the trainer, I hope, are long gone.

A new discipline

The Inverted Pyramid approach requires a new learning framework that enables staff to develop their interpersonal skillset, a proactive, collaborative mindset and agreed inclusive behaviours. HR and training professionals within organisations have a key role to play in ensuring that all staff are effectively trained and able to contribute from the outset.

If we are to successfully implement the Inverted Pyramid ethos and processes into our organisations then of course we need customer care people to link up with distribution people to link up with IT people, but we also need the fabric of HR to support the training and implementation process in a way that can be validated and the outcomes captured.

The senior management team must all be 100% behind the implementation of the Inverted Pyramid approach, otherwise it will fail. Indeed, the CEO has to be the role model. This is not a 'Let's try it and see' scenario. This is who we are.

Where we have implemented the Inverted Pyramid approach, it has worked incredibly well. Staff love the process because at long last they are valued for all that they are. They weren't just talking to the same people in the same team every day. They were constantly looking for new opportunities, better ways of working, more effective ways to utilise resources. We saw new levels of integration and engagement across departments such as engineering, manufacturing, design and distribution – with people of mixed levels working together effectively in teams.

INVERTED PYRAMID EXERCISE

What's the purpose of Human Resources?

INCLUSION DICTIONARY

Community development
means all of us together.

Business development
means all of us together.

Organisation development
means all of us together.

Management development
means all of us together.

Personal development
means all of us together.

PERSONAL DEVELOPMENT REFLECTION

1. What should Human Resources mean?
2. How would you like to see HR develop in your organisation?

The soul of HR

How might we respond to Alex's comments earlier in this chapter? Here are ten topics that we may need to consider to help us to shift our organisations to the Inverted Pyramid of Inclusion way of working:

1. Freedom to act

One of the key points to emphasise around the new enhanced work roles in the Inverted Pyramid structure is our extended freedom to act. This needs to be a key part of each individual's job description and person specification. Each role must detail the freedom to act that we have in building new relationships, along with the expectation and the responsibility for doing so.

2. Person specifications

Our person specifications need to be clear about the personal values we look for, along with the behaviours which will help each person to be successful. We want to find and keep the very best people. Our recruitment process sends a clear message likely to attract those looking for more than just a job. We want to offer them an organisation where they have a direct role in building its success, where they will be responsible for helping all others and where they can build a career that is aligned to their passion and interests.

3. Job descriptions

The job description now needs to include the key element of building our Inverted Pyramids with colleagues in the business. It needs to be more than a list of transactional activities. It should detail our individual responsibility for supporting others on a one-to-one basis, working collaboratively and playing a role in developing effective Inverted Pyramid teams. What's more, it should clearly specify the processes, measurement and targets for all aspects of our Inverted Pyramid role.

4. Culture shift

We can say to staff that one of their key responsibilities is to be kind to other people or to help other people. But what does that mean? What are the action points and deliverables around that? What are the behaviours that we expect to see? How do we redefine our culture so that these behaviours become our normal way of working?

The activities of reaching out, linking up, working with others, addressing new needs, developing alternative approaches and making things better are not a 'nice to have'. These are essential behaviours for all staff and for building the business. We all assess our own performance against these Inverted Pyramid criteria.

The behaviours of kindness, reaching out to help others, giving back, paying it forward and sharing are just some of the key behaviours we are trying to encourage. So, how do you define these as outcomes in your business or organisation? Instead of a list of meaningless tasks filling up pages on the job description, let us put in the key behaviours and measures that we expect from all our staff.

5. Value statement

There is little point in having a value statement in your corporate plan that nobody knows or implements. And it's of little use having an aspirational statement unless it is translated into specific behaviours day after day, by every single person. These are the behaviours and measures that become our new way of working. These are the actions that drive who we are, enable us to grow and build the strength of fabric within our Inverted Pyramids.

If we treat our values simply as aspirations rather than distinct measurable behaviours, then we will remain rooted within our traditional hierarchal structure and our organisations will be left behind to stagnate as good people are snapped up by those with a bigger vision for a better world.

6. Induction training

Our induction training will focus on exactly how we work in an Inverted Pyramid way, and how staff are expected to contribute to and build on this. We can give clear examples, processes for linking up, case studies and a personal awareness process that introduces new individuals directly to a range of colleagues across the organisation.

7. Welcome note

When you join us, you also become an Inverted Pyramid community builder. You immediately become part of something more than our business. Our community is an inclusive, ever-expanding, outward-looking, proactive team that looks after each other, drives individual purpose, reaches out first, and works on the basis of abundance rather than scarcity.

We encourage you to create, build and be part of Inverted Pyramid Teams that matter to you. For us, inclusion is at the heart of the way that we work together, for we believe that the total is greater than the sum of the parts.

8. Dream job

Our Inverted Pyramid workplace can be a launchpad for individual development rather than a box that constrains our growth. Our ongoing personal development support, training options and Inverted Pyramid behaviours must help to meet the personal aspirations of the individual rather than simply support their practical, job or technical needs. We have to ask each other, *'How are you? How can I help? What do you really want to do? What's your priority at the moment? What else do you think we should be doing? Is there anything outside of work that you need help with? Can you think of a better way to do this?'*

9. Looking outwards

There are people in need across the world and in our local communities. The real opportunity here is to help to address physical, well-being or technical need – for example food, a home or entrepreneurship training to help people to build their own Inverted Pyramid. This can start with the people on the workshop you're running. Colleagues can provide a platform for exploring how to use this new information, how to support each other and how we might journey to the next stage together.

10. Celebrating success

Every day, our staff do wonderful things, both with and for their colleagues. Every day, our staff sort out problems for our customers and make life easier for so many people. So much of this good news gets lost in the transactional nature of our workplaces and organisations. That's our job, isn't it? Yes, but many of us in these fleeting transactions make a personal connection, have a sense of satisfaction or even get a thank you. Imagine the impact if we were all building these connections 'on purpose'? With the Inverted Pyramid methodology we, as individuals, have a responsibility for reporting and promoting these successes. For this is what encourages others, helps to build a culture of inclusion and drives our pyramids upwards as frameworks of possibility, positivity and success.

The Inverted Pyramid curriculum

There's a whole new management discipline here. The Inverted Pyramid of Inclusion responds to the need for a much more interconnected world. It's about the future of work and, indeed, the way we work. It's about the way we train everyone as leaders to help us build organisations for our present challenges and a future that is still unknown. It's about how we move away from the traditional individual model of career development to one that is based on collaborative working, personal contribution and the welfare of all.

We need a new curriculum to address collaborative training, learning and development. This is a completely new area for teachers, trainers and college professors. We need to unleash our knowledge-givers to test and champion new ways of engagement and empowerment.

INVERTED PYRAMID EXERCISE

What is the deficit of inclusion?

WORKPLACE DEFICIT

Sin seems like an
old-fashioned word.
It's not one we typically find
in our management training
and business processes.
Sin means absence.
Absence of love.
Absence of compassion.
Absence of gratitude.
Absence of giving.

This absence means
we are less than we can be.
It lessens our potential
to grow into what we should be.
Sin is a deficit.

Inclusion addresses this deficit
when we build kindness and compassion,
gratitude and giving
into our management training
and business processes.

PERSONAL DEVELOPMENT REFLECTION

1. How is inclusion made real in your management training and business processes?
2. What is the deficit in your workplace?

CHAPTER 25: Time to harvest

Please take a moment to reflect and capture any initial thoughts, ideas, questions or action points that you wish to note and take forward. You will be able to gather these from each chapter for your personal development Action Plan at the end of the book.

Notes

1 ....

2 ....

3 ....

4 ....

5 ....

How can we provide Inverted Pyramid training and support for everyone?

In this chapter we outline some of the training and support available to help individuals and organisations to learn more and to build their Inverted Pyramids.

We are just beginning!

The Inverted Pyramid is an amazing invitation for ALL of us to work together from here. We can contribute and be part of this process from now. We can link up with our colleagues and discuss all that is important to us. This may be a practical project to train others in the Inverted Pyramid methodology, help those in need, build Inverted Pyramids in our workplaces or explore the many ways that we can look after each other and our planet. It is never too late to begin or restart your Inverted Pyramid journey.

Support

Diversiton offers a training and support infrastructure to help build a worldwide network of Inverted Pyramid Licensed Facilitators and Centres. Diversiton is a not-for-profit training body established for over 20 years and well-known for its work internationally in diversity and inclusion. Diversiton developed the first training workshop on religion and belief in line with equality legislation across the world. It also created and delivers the world's leading inclusion calendar for business and public sector bodies every year. Diversiton has delivered a wide range of Inverted Pyramid pilots for businesses and the public sector over the last eight years.

Workshop

The Inverted Pyramid of Inclusion

An initial three-hour online workshop open to all individuals. Learn and explore with others how the Inverted Pyramid relates to you, the work that you do and your future plans.

Available online – see www.invertedpyramid.info for details of upcoming sessions.

Become a Licensed Facilitator for the Inverted Pyramid and join our worldwide team

Diversiton is supporting the development of a worldwide network of individuals and organisations to deliver our range of workshops and courses. We need facilitators who will help us in this rollout, wherever you live or whatever your workplace. You and/or your organisation can become a Licensed Facilitator in this process.

Our worldwide network of Licensed Facilitators will help to spread the methodology of the Inverted Pyramid and support the development of learning at an individual, organisational and local level.

We are looking for people with good communication skills who want to give back, pay it forward and add a whole new level of meaning to their current role or career. We are especially looking for positive and enthusiastic trainers and managers with a business or education background, and those who have worked in the community, Government and charity sectors.

We are seeking to partner with those who wish to use their skills and experience to play an active role in helping to fulfil our vision of an inclusive worldwide community. As a Licensed Inverted Pyramid Facilitator, you will be part of our worldwide support network.

Training and support for our Licensed Facilitators

This is a six-week online development process consisting of one live two-hour session each week. This is where we support our Licensed Facilitators to help individuals to build and grow their Inverted Pyramid relationships and initiatives. Available online – see www.invertedpyramid.info for details.

Licensed Facilitator opportunities are available worldwide to deliver the initial workshop and help local initiatives to become established.

As one of our Licensed Partners you can work with us in four ways:

1. **INDEPENDENT FACILITATORS** who offer training for individuals and organisations

Could you help to establish a local Inverted Pyramid Development Team in your area? Could you help to train, encourage and link others so that they can build their own Inverted Pyramids?

As an independent Inverted Pyramid Licensed Facilitator you can:

- Provide training for all individuals and organisations on the Inverted Pyramid methodology
- Develop a plan to systematically reach your priority groups and organisations
- Support the creation and development of Inverted Pyramid projects and initiatives

- Bring individuals together to leverage best practice and drive growth
- Capture learning and success stories
- Work with other independent licensed facilitators on our worldwide monthly development sessions.

Your input can be full-time or part-time, one day a week or two days a month, or whatever works for your situation. The important point to note here is that we will help you to create a role that works for you.

We encourage all our facilitators to work in pairs. Have you a colleague you could work with at the local level, or would you like to team up with someone in a different location? Online delivery of our workshops allows us to support each other wherever we are training! Our paired approach ensures that each of our trainers has practical day-to-day support and encouragement, as well as assistance in facilitating the workshops.

Further information, including dates of forthcoming programmes, licencing arrangements and costs, can be found at www.invertedpyramid.info. Applications can also be made online.

2. **TRAINING ORGANISATION FACILITATORS** who offer support and build links with individuals and organisations in their region, industry or sector (private, public and community)

This is any organisation wishing to utilise the experience and expertise of its staff to help other organisations and individuals to learn about the Inverted Pyramid methodology, and so build inclusion. Your organisation can join our worldwide team of Training Organisation Facilitators and:

- Provide training and ongoing support for other organisations and personnel on the Inverted Pyramid methodology
- Develop a plan to systematically address the needs of specific sectors, geographical areas or local/international issues

- Support the creation and development of Inverted Pyramid projects and initiatives
- Bring teams together to leverage best practice and drive growth
- Capture learning and success stories
- Work with licensed facilitators from other organisations on our worldwide monthly development sessions.

Diversiton will help you to develop frameworks to link Facilitators from different organisations to build wider support networks, capture best practice and to share learning, case studies and successes.

Further information, including dates of forthcoming programmes, licencing arrangements and costs, can be found at www.invertedpyramid.info. Applications can also be made online.

3. IN-HOUSE FACILITATORS – organisations and businesses offering training to staff

Is your organisation ready to explore and embrace inclusion in its fullest sense? Are you keen to connect your staff in new ways, uncover and leverage untapped potential, explore new areas, offer opportunities for creativity and innovation, support holistic personal development and become a workplace of the future?

Join our worldwide team of Licensed Facilitators and develop the Inverted Pyramid methodology with all those connected to your organisation.

As an in-house Inverted Pyramid Licensed Facilitator you can:

- Provide training for all your staff on the Inverted Pyramid methodology
- Develop a plan to systematically bring different departments and personnel on board
- Support the creation and development of Inverted Pyramid projects and initiatives

- Bring teams together to leverage best practice and drive growth
- Capture learning and success stories
- Work with Licensed Facilitators from other organisations on our worldwide monthly development sessions.

Diversiton will provide a framework to link Facilitators from different organisations so as to build wider support networks, capture best practice and to share learning, case studies and successes.

Further information, including dates of forthcoming programmes, licencing arrangements and costs, can be found at www.invertedpyramid.info. Applications can also be made online.

4. **COMMUNITY FACILITATORS** – typically supported by government departments, local agencies and local authorities who train their staff and sponsor local community organisations

These are Licensed Facilitators funded by central government departments, local government agencies or local authorities. They can work within one organisation on an ongoing basis or across a number of organisations.

The Inverted Pyramid methodology has been piloted successfully over the last six years at the central government level and within local authorities. Your department or agency can support organisations within your area to address key issues through the building of a more inclusive, joined-up and effective community infrastructure.

Government departments or local authorities can sponsor a number of organisations and/or a number of local Facilitators to become licenced to deliver the Inverted Pyramid process. By linking your local Facilitators, you will help to build critical mass (community capacity) that is effective, sustainable and growing.

Further information, including dates of forthcoming programmes, licencing arrangements and costs, can be found at www.invertedpyramid.info. Applications can also be made online.

CHAPTER 26: Time to harvest

Please take a moment to reflect and capture any initial thoughts, ideas, questions or action points that you wish to note and take forward. What are your main reflections from Section Five?

Notes

1 ....

2 ....

3 ....

4 ....

5 ....

SECTION 6

Personal Review and Action Plan

What are the Inverted Pyramid opportunities for each of us? How can we begin to develop initiatives with colleagues in our organisations and communities? Section Six helps us to review our priorities, create a personal Action Plan and explore how we can begin today, with others, in a new way.

CHAPTER 27

Personal Review and Action Plan

We are all called to do big stuff in a small way

Are you ready to pull together your Action Plan? Can you capture your initial ideas below, or create a section in your Journal? Begin now to map out the key actions and activities, colleagues and contacts that can help you to grow and develop.

Please set aside some time to do justice to your thinking and ideas. Use this Action Plan as your personal development growth plan for, as we know, inclusion is all about us and what we do.

So complete all the parts of the Action Plan that are important to you. This is not meant to be a one-off or static document. Come back to your Plan, review your progress and be grateful for your achievements. Enjoy the process that has already started to unfold...

Personal Review

Let's do a quick check together and see where you are, now that you have completed this book:

- You should be able to specify clearly the difference between diversity, equality and inclusion

- You should be able to explain the difference between a traditional organisation structure and an Inverted Pyramid process
- You should be able to explain what Dual Responsibility is
- You should be able to recognise the difference between transactional working and interpersonal relationship-building
- You will have had the opportunity to reflect on your own personal approach to building inclusion using the INVERTED PYRAMID EXERCISES throughout this book
- You should be able to explain how the Inverted Pyramid creates inclusive communities by enabling people to reach out and work with each other
- You should have a clear idea for beginning to build your own Inverted Pyramid
- You should have had an opportunity to reflect on your own workplace and potential priorities for training others in the Inverted Pyramid methodology and building a range of initiatives
- You should now be ready to take the first steps in introducing others to the Inverted Pyramid and working with them
- You should know who you are going to talk to now, and what you are going to share with them.

So, let's see if we can use some of this to build your Action Plan…

PART 1: Let's start with you

Look through your notes from the various chapters. What are the key messages you have written? What do you want to follow up on? Who do you want to talk to? How are you going to move your ideas forward? Look back at the notes you've made and the ideas that resonated with you.

Key notes / action points

1 ....

2 ....

3 ....

4 ....

5 ....

6 ....

7 ....

8 ....

9 ....

10 ....

PART 2: Think about your 8 points of personal impact

Remember, the Inverted Pyramid is an approach that encompasses and makes real all that is important for each of us to build our future. Who will you reach out to, to discuss the Inverted Pyramid with? What ideas do you have to build your first initiative? What need will you be addressing? Where do you think you might make an impact?

Use the checklist below to begin to explore opportunities and map out a framework for action:

1. Your personal purpose

What's your big dream? What do you really want to do? We're only here once, so what is it that you want to see happen?

Key notes / action points

1 ....

2 ....

2. Your organisation

What is the potential for your team, your clients, your colleagues, and how can you all play a bigger and more significant role in what you do? Where will you start with your organisation and colleagues?

Key notes / action points

1 ....

2 ....

3. Your other workplaces

Many of us work with more than one set of work colleagues. What is the potential for you to link with these individuals beyond the usual transactions – and help them to link together?

Key notes / action points

1 ....

2 ....

4. Your career development

Will you be able to fulfil all that you want to through your current organisation or work structure? What additions or changes might you need to look at? Who might help you with this?

Key notes / action points

1 ....

2 ....

5. Your family and friends

How can you link with and support those close to you? How can you all work together in new ways to help each other? Who should you really reach out to? Who have you not spoken with for ages?

Key notes / action points

1 ....

2 ....

6. The wider world

What are the key issues and challenges in our world that resonate for you? Where would you like to see real change happening? What do you want to learn more about? Where can you start and take a small step? How might you inspire and encourage others to join you?

Key notes / action points

1 ....

2 ....

7. Your local community

Who is struggling in your local community? How can Inverted Pyramid projects include them? What organisations would you like to learn more about? How might you connect your workplace and colleagues to local needs?

Key notes / action points

1 ....

2 ....

8. Your values and behaviours

How will you explore the potential for collaboration with those you would not normally work with, who have different beliefs or are different to you? What are your inclusion behaviours?

Key notes / action points

1 ....

2 ....

PRIORITIES

Set out your ideas. Make notes of specific project ideas. List the people you want to talk with. What are your priority tasks? Set yourself some targets and timescales. Use this book as an invitation for others to work with you.

Key notes / action points

1 ....

2 ....

PART 3: Help your organisation to become an Inverted Pyramid workplace

Inverted Pyramid thinking is about inclusion, working together and trying to build a kinder and fairer world. The Inverted Pyramid process is about unlocking the potential of each person so that everyone can benefit. This is what we are trying to free up. This is why we are trying to turn the traditional organisation structure on its head, to go beyond transactions and encourage our colleagues in our workplaces to build real and meaningful relationships.

See if you can pull together some ideas for your workplaces from the points below:

1. Where would you start?

You and your colleagues know your organisation well. You know what it could do to make a bigger impact. You have ideas for how your organisation could reach out and work with other groups and bodies. You can see opportunities for serving customers or the public in better ways. You know where situations could be improved.

You know what you would like to do, if asked your opinion or invited to lead on a project. Why are you waiting?

2. Begin with yourself

If there is no knowledge of the Inverted Pyramid methodology in your organisation, start to think about what you can do. How might you develop your approach, the way you work and the way you interact with others or set an example? How can you encourage others to be part of what you are doing, trying to solve, or keen to move forward?

3. Find a colleague

We have to start from the bottom up. So, begin with your closest colleague in the organisation, wherever they may be. Share some of your thoughts from this book and your ideas for the organisation. See how you might begin to explore something together. And then continue to journey together – learning, encouraging one another and creating possibilities.

4. Harvest from everything

After each client encounter, work meeting, completed report, phone discussion or online session, don't just move straight onto the next task. Ask yourself what you might do differently or better. What are the key points from this that you need to capture or take forward? How does this link with other aspects of what you are doing? From all your activities, remember to pause and harvest, reflect, imagine and create and so move forward, better. Use an Inverted Pyramid Work Journal to capture ideas and thoughts on an ongoing basis.

5. Apply Inverted Pyramid thinking

How can some of the principles and ideas in this book be applied to a current project or process or procedure that you are working with? Is there a small step you could take? Is there a big shift you should make? Work with what you have and where you are to explore, build success and develop a process of trust.

6. Work with people of influence

Who in your organisation will be open to building and promoting inclusivity? Who will be keen to empower all staff and build greater collaboration and innovation? Is this the boss, a senior manager, a specialist team or group, a training manager or someone in HR? Why not send them a note about the book you've just read and request a short meeting to discuss one or two of your thoughts?

7. Opportunities and challenges

Every organisation has a range of challenges and opportunities at any given time. There are always things that need to be resolved and problems to be addressed. What challenges does your organisation face at the moment? Using the Inverted Pyramid approach, could you get together with two or three of your colleagues and put your creative hats on? What ideas might you come up with?

8. Introduce the concept of the Inverted Pyramid to others

Send an email: I've just read an amazing book on inclusion and would like to...

Organise a briefing session to explain what the Inverted Pyramid is

Put the Inverted Pyramid as an item on the agenda of your next team meeting.

9. Partner with us

Arrange for staff to attend an Inverted Pyramid workshop

Explore the possibility for internal staff in your organisation or business to be trained as Licensed Inverted Pyramid Facilitators

Get the Inverted Pyramid book for each member of staff. What a great way to get some conversations happening!

Let us customise and co-brand this book with your organisation.

10. The values and behaviour question

Ask the question internally about values and behaviours in a positive way. How can we seek to improve the way we work with each other and help one another? What are the interpersonal behaviours we are seeking to instil?

11. Become a role model

Be clear about your own behaviour and be the person that you want to work with. Smile, help others, reach out, always be positive, have the energy to want to move things forward, be the one who is determined to include others, never be negative about those who are struggling or underperforming but seek to involve them, have time to listen, ask others how they are. Encourage them to move from passive transactional employees to energised, proactive relationship-builders.

PRIORITIES

Set out your ideas. Make notes of specific project ideas. List the people you want to talk with. What are your priority tasks? Set yourself some targets and timescales. Use this book as an invitation for others to work with you.

Key notes / action points

1 ....

2 ....

3 ....

4 ....

5 ....

6 ....

7 ....

8 ....

9 ....

10 ....

PART 4: Let's build new links everywhere!

Continue building your Inverted Pyramid process inside and outside of work and then share the learning with your different contacts and colleagues. Our collective aim is to move from parallel working to collaborative working, joined-up initiatives and new connections.

Imagine the potential of how your different Inverted Pyramid projects will grow as you bring different people, initiatives, groups, organisations and sectors together.

The call is for each of us to build our own personal Inverted Pyramid. This is how we journey with others. Our whole ethos becomes about reaching out, linking up and working together to help others.

Once we recognise how our workplaces and daily routine can trap and limit us within manmade structures, this is the moment when we allow ourselves to see a different array of possibilities. This is the moment when we have an opportunity to flip our pyramid and to begin again in a better way. It's a daily call of renewal.

And we are never alone on this journey. For there are millions of others seeking to build their personal Inverted Pyramids also. It is sometimes so difficult to make things happen on our own, despite all our best efforts. And yet, if we link up with others and work with them in a bigger way, we find that what is important for us can quickly become our joint reality.

Key notes / action points

1 ....

2 ....

3 ....

4 ....

5 ....

6 ....

7 ....

8 ....

9 ....

10 ....

INVERTED PYRAMID EXERCISE

Have you escaped?

DON'T LET THEM PIGEONHOLE YOU...

They want to pigeonhole you.
Not just what you do, but who you are.
'*What exactly do you do?*', they ask,
ready to put you into one of their boxes.

You could give them five answers,
but instead, you say
'*I'm working to build inclusion.*'
They look blank, and the pigeon escapes.

PERSONAL DEVELOPMENT REFLECTION
1. What are your five answers?
2. Have you escaped yet?

PART 5: Inverted Pyramid exercises

I hope that you have been able to take the opportunity to spend a little time reading some of the Inverted Pyramid exercises in this book. They are a learning format which offers an additional perspective about various topics. Most of all, they allow us a personal opportunity to reflect, to ask our own questions, to build our understanding and to connect the many pieces of our own lives.

To assist our journey of personal development together, I have compiled a series of books, each containing 200 Inverted Pyramid exercises. These can help you to explore, free up and reframe your thinking, and are designed as a personal support structure to help you to develop, build and maintain your own personal Inverted Pyramid process.

Many people take one exercise each day, and so build a habit of spending a little time with themselves and their own personal development.

The range of Inverted Pyramid exercises covers 24 important topics, including Work, Business, Gratitude, Daily Routine, Spirituality, Kindness, Love, Leadership, Harvesting, Inclusion, Gratitude, Happiness, Creativity, Purpose, Inner Learning, Collaborative Working, Well-being, Education, Future Planning, Career, Personal Effectiveness, Dying, Life Journey, and Special Times of the Year.

You can find more details on the Inverted Pyramid website or on Amazon.

Which Inverted Pyramid exercises in this book did you find helpful? What notes or ideas would you like to capture here as part of your Action Plan?

Key notes / action points

1 ....

2 ....

3 ....

4 ....

5 ....

6 ....

7 ....

8 ....

9 ....

10 ....

PART 6: We can continue to develop our personal spiritual journey

Our invitation to be part of the Inverted Pyramid process is a personal one and a community one. It's about reaching in (to ourselves) and reaching out (to others). How might your personal spiritual development (however you conceive this) grow with the Inverted Pyramid process?

How might you develop your own spirituality? What would you like to learn more about? What would you like to discuss? Which aspects of the Inverted Pyramid process can support your personal spiritual development?

Key notes / action points

1 ....

2 ....

3 ....

4 ....

5 ....

6 ....

7 ....

8 ....

9 ....

10 ....

PART 7: Do something every day

One of the key messages from the Inverted Pyramid process is to *do something every day*. This is an important habit because it focuses us on what is most important for us. By doing something every day, we take another step forward in achieving our purpose.

If we don't do something for *ourselves*, the world will quickly swamp us with activities, media, tasks and things that aren't really a priority. Our day will be lost.

There is no greater role for all of us than helping to build a worldwide community of inclusion, so let us do something every day to help make this happen.

It can begin with a coffee with friends. It can be capturing and writing about your ideas or sharing your experience. It can be working on a project idea. It can be a meeting with a colleague online. It can be suggesting ideas for your organisation's inclusion strategy for next year. It can be a private thought or short prayer any time, for someone in need. It can be sending an email relating to some of the thoughts or ideas raised by this book. It can be a chat to look at the next steps in developing Inverted Pyramid thinking in your department or workplace.

How can you move forward with growing your Inverted Pyramid in some small way today? How can you share some of this with others in your school, college or workplace, your family, local community, club/group/association, church, or with those you meet online?

What's the focus of your Inverted Pyramid initiative? Is it health, education, technology, finance, spiritual development? Who might you talk to? What could you write? What should you research? Who can you encourage? What do you need to read? How could you share your skills and experience? What training could you offer? Who should you meet or reconnect with? What can you sort out? What could you arrange? Who needs your help or advice? Where will you go?

This book has failed if you do not continue with your own personal journey and become an inspiration and encouragement for others. In other words, you should be creating your own Inverted Pyramid Team or looking to join a team. That's what this whole process is for: trying to build a kinder, more inclusive, collaborative and sustainable world.

This is not just another set of tasks to do. This is our core activity. This is who we are. For it is in helping to build an inclusive worldwide community that we can discover our own way. Let us encourage each other to do something every day!

Key notes / action points

1 ....

2 ....

3 ....

4 ....

5 ....

6 ....

7 ....

8 ....

9 ....

10 ....

Thank You

I hope that you will work with us as we all build our Inverted Pyramids and journey together.

Please look for ways to join us, whatever it is you do and wherever you are.

Let us remember that we are dealing with hundreds of years of conditioned behaviours, set structures and established ways of working. Be patient and stick to your own process. Be gentle with yourself. Reach out to others and encourage them. This is more than enough!

Feedback

Thank you for reading and working through the book. It is, of course, only a beginning. Please share your thoughts, successes and plans with others. Ask for help, collaboration and input. Any feedback, suggestions for improvement or further ideas are especially welcome.

Leave a word of encouragement for others on Amazon

Please take a moment to leave a short review on Amazon – just a sentence or two can encourage others to join us as we all journey together.

Thank you, talk soon!

Des McCabe

Email: _diversiton@gmail.com_
Call / Text: _(44) 7717 203325_
Visit: _www.invertedpyramid.info_
Connect _with me on LinkedIn:_ _https://www.linkedin.com/in/desmccabe_

APPENDIX 1

Sustainable Development Goals

Connecting us all together

The 2030 Agenda for Sustainable Development (https://sdgs.un.org/2030agenda), adopted by all United Nations Member States in 2015, provides a shared blueprint for peace and prosperity for people and the planet, now and into the future. There are 17 Sustainable Development Goals which represent an urgent call for action by all countries in a global partnership. They recognise that ending poverty and other deprivations must go hand-in-hand with strategies which improve health and education, reduce inequality and spur economic growth – all while tackling climate change and working to preserve our oceans and forests. It's a framework to link all Inverted Pyramids together and to focus our efforts on agreed global priorities.

The 17 Sustainable Development Goals to transform our world are:

GOAL 1:   No poverty
GOAL 2:   Zero hunger
GOAL 3:   Good health and well-being
GOAL 4:   Quality education
GOAL 5:   Gender equality
GOAL 6:   Clean water and sanitation

GOAL 7:   Affordable and clean energy
GOAL 8:   Decent work and economic growth
GOAL 9:   Industry, innovation and infrastructure
GOAL 10:   Reduced inequality
GOAL 11:   Sustainable cities and communities
GOAL 12:   Responsible consumption and production
GOAL 13:   Climate action
GOAL 14:   Life below water
GOAL 15:   Life on land
GOAL 16:   Peace and justice – strong institutions
GOAL 17:   Partnerships to achieve the goal

Five strategic questions for measuring the effectiveness of our inclusion initiatives:

In line with the 2030 Agenda for Sustainable Development, how can we respond to the five priorities of people, planet, prosperity, peace and global partnership?

People

'We are determined to end poverty and hunger, in all their forms and dimensions, and to ensure that all human beings can fulfil their potential in dignity and equality and in a healthy environment.'

Can we create Inverted Pyramid Initiatives for People?

Planet

'We are determined to protect the planet from degradation, including through sustainable consumption and production, sustainably managing its natural resources and taking urgent action on climate change, so that it can support the needs of the present and future generations.'

Can we create Inverted Pyramid Initiatives for our Planet?

Prosperity

'We are determined to ensure that all human beings can enjoy prosperous and fulfilling lives and that economic, social and technological progress occurs in harmony with nature.'

Can we create Inverted Pyramid Initiatives for Prosperity?

Peace

'We are determined to foster peaceful, just and inclusive societies which are free from fear and violence. There can be no sustainable development without peace and no peace without sustainable development.'

Can we create an Inverted Pyramid Initiative for Peace?

A Global Partnership

'We are determined to mobilize the means required to implement this Agenda through a revitalised Global Partnership for Sustainable Development, based on a spirit of strengthened global solidarity, focussed in particular on the needs of the poorest and most vulnerable and with the participation of all countries, all stakeholders and all people.'

Can our Inverted Pyramid Initiatives contribute to a Global Partnership?

Further information:

https://sdgs.un.org/goals
https://sdgs.un.org/2030agenda
https://unstats.un.org/sdgs/indicators/Global%20Indicator%20Fram ework%20after%202022%20refinement_Eng.pdf
https://unstats.un.org/sdgs

APPENDIX 2

Building an Inverted Pyramid organisation - checklist

1. Have a corporate vision and purpose that encourages staff and colleagues to reach out beyond the business and connect to the world in a bigger way. Make this explicit, write it down and communicate it to all staff.

2. Have visible and consistent 'buy-in' from the business owner, CEO and all of the senior management team.

3. Produce a clear statement of behaviours expected, ensure regular measurement of Inverted Pyramid performance and reward individual accountability for delivering on Inverted Pyramid activities.

4. Ensure that Inverted Pyramid training is given so that all staff understand their new enhanced roles.

5. Have a clear framework that enables people to share their passions and expertise with others.

6. Have a system for people to meet up with others at different levels and in different departments of the business.

7. Ensure that all personnel have time to work on community initiatives.

8. Be ambitious around the growth and development of the community

9. Empower individuals so that the work of the community flows seamlessly within the business and outside of the business at the same time.

10. Do not be constrained by traditional organisational thinking such as reporting, structures, effectiveness et cetera.

11. Make sure that there is regular updating and promotion of our success stories, case studies and assessments of the impact that we are making to help others in the world.

12. Make sure we restructure and enhance all roles and job descriptions to reflect the importance and implementation of Inverted Pyramid behaviours.

13. Remember that our Inverted Pyramid community is a dynamic collaboration, capable of changing instantly, responding rapidly and embracing freely.

14. Aim to make our organisation simply a servant of our overall Inverted Pyramid.

APPENDIX 3

Main benefits of an Inverted Pyramid approach - checklist

1. It's our silo-busting strategy! Getting individuals to work together across the organisation.

2. It develops cross-disciplinary thinking. Helping individuals to gain a greater understanding of all aspects of the work we do.

3. It builds teams and strong personal networks. Enabling people to meet new people and work in new ways on new initiatives.

4. It harnesses individual skills, passions and interests. Being able to leverage individual expertise across the whole organisation.

5. It helps to meet client and customer needs in a bigger and better way. Bringing the full potential of all parts of the organisation to the issues that matter to users.

6. It offers a different approach to business and personal development. Empowering individual members of staff to take responsibility for their own development.

7. It helps to develop innovation, creativity and thought-leadership skills. Ensuring that we are tackling the issues that are important – harvesting from the group and not just presenting the corporate view.

PLUS:

- We build motivation
- We offer opportunities to take part in new initiatives
- We uncover hidden skills and experience
- We build new links across the organisation
- We extend the reach of the business into new areas
- We refine our values and brand identity in a practical and impactful way
- We empower our teams to become proactive and outcome-driven problem solvers
- We develop project management skills, build personal responsibility and facilitate empowerment
- We embed a new way of working which drives new opportunities to do what really matters
- We make an impact outside our business that directly connects our people to those who need our help
- We create our stories and case studies to share with others as we link and work together to build a world of inclusion.

APPENDIX 4

An organisational Inverted Pyramid transformation audit - checklist

Here are ten key questions to help you guide your organisation:

1. What is the purpose of our organisation? Are we explicit about building inclusion?

2. Are we actively seeking to create a better world? Does this include encouraging

3. others to reach out and make connections and build links across and beyond our organisation?

4. What are our values? Are these written down and communicated to everyone?

5. What are the specific behaviours that we require from all staff to demonstrate and live these values?

6. Are these values and behaviours stated explicitly in job specifications, recruitment and induction processes and maintained through ongoing personal and professional development?

7. How do we reward and recognise those efforts and initiatives which are helping us to build an inclusive organisation?

8. How are we training our people to build inclusion through an Inverted Pyramid methodology?

9. How are we embedding Inverted Pyramid thinking alongside daily job roles?

10. How are we actively encouraging people through daily working processes to continue to reach out, build links and become better at all we do?

11. How are we reaching out and building wider linkages to many other Inverted Pyramid initiatives and so becoming part of something bigger?

APPENDIX 5

Helping your organisation to become more inclusive - checklist

If there is little or no knowledge about the Inverted Pyramid methodology in your organisation, then do start now! There is much that you can do! Here are 12 ideas for you to consider. See if a few of these can help you to move forward.

1. Begin with yourself
How might you develop your Inverted Pyramid approach, in the way that you work and interact with others and in the example that you set? How can you enable and encourage others to be part of what you are doing, the situation you want to address, or the idea that you've had?

2. Find a colleague
We have to start from the bottom up. So, begin with your closest colleague in the organisation, wherever they may be. Share some of your thoughts from this book and your ideas for the organisation. See how you might begin to explore something together.

3. Harvest from everything
Don't just move onto the next task after a client encounter, a work meeting, a report you've just finished, a phone discussion or an online session. Ask yourself, *What might we do differently or better moving*

forward? What are the key points from this that I need to capture or think about? How does this link with other aspects of what we are doing? From all your activities remember to pause, reflect, harvest, link ideas together and so move forward, better. Have an Inverted Pyramid work journal to capture ideas and thoughts on a daily basis.

4. Apply Inverted Pyramid thinking
How can some of the principles and ideas of the Inverted Pyramid be applied to a project, process or programme that you are currently working on? Is there a small step that you could take? Is there a big shift that you can make? Work with what you have and where you wish to build collaboration, success and so develop a process of trust.

5. Points of leverage
Who in our organisation will be open to building a more inclusive and empowering process in which staff can work more collaboratively? Is this someone in marketing, a training manager, someone in HR? Why not send them a note about the book you are reading and request a short meeting to discuss one or two of your thoughts?

6. Opportunities and challenges
Every organisation has a range of challenges and opportunities at any given time. There are always things that need to be resolved and problems to be addressed. What challenges does your organisation face at the moment? Could you get together with two or three of your colleagues and put your creative hats on? What ideas might you come up with? This can build stronger interpersonal relationships and perhaps the start of an Inverted Pyramid project.

7. Send an email about building inclusion in your organisation
'I've just read an interesting book about how we can build an inclusive organisation. I would be interested in your feedback.'

8. Mini training/briefing session
Organise a mini training or briefing session for other staff. You could ask a colleague to work with you on this – and so begin your personal

Inverted Pyramid process. Take an idea (or story) from a Chapter or use one of terms in the Glossary to introduce some new thinking.

9. On the agenda
Add the Inverted Pyramid as an agenda item to your next monthly / weekly meeting.

10. Parallel working
Continue building your Inverted Pyramid process outside of work and then share the learning with your colleagues internally. Imagine the potential of how your different Inverted Pyramid projects could come together and create new links.

11. The values and behaviour question
Ask the question internally about organisational values and behaviours in a positive way. What exactly are the values of your organisation? What then are the associated behaviours that are required of you in the way that you relate and work with each other?

12. Become a role model
Be the person that others want to work with. For example, smile, help others, reach out, always be positive, have the energy to want to move things forward, be the one who is determined to include others, not negative about those who are struggling or under-performing but seeking to involve them, having time to listen, asking others how they are. We have to ensure that we are not acting like passive wage-earners from the 19th century but claiming our place as energised stakeholders of the 21st century, wherever we work and whatever we do.

ABOUT DES

Des McCabe is one of the leading experts on inclusion and personal development.

In the early part of his career, Des founded TBG, which grew to become the largest independent training organisation in the UK. When the company was sold in 1995 it was finding jobs for 5,000 long-term unemployed and helping 4,000 people to get qualifications every year.

Des's expertise in the field of job creation led to him becoming an advisor to the British, Irish, US, Argentinian, Romanian and Albanian governments on employment and inclusion. He received formal recognition as one of the leading job-creation entrepreneurs from Europe's 500, Europe's most prominent bodies of entrepreneurs.

Des served as Chair of the European Union's cross-border Interreg training group in Northern Ireland, and as Chair of the EU Border Training Bureau. He was an advisor to the Irish and US Governments in the early stages of the Northern Ireland Peace Process and went on to design the *Peace Builder* training programme with US Special Envoy Senator George Mitchell's Northern Ireland Fund for Reconciliation.

Beyond his professional achievements, Des established and raised funding for The Training Trust, an international charity set up to meet the humanitarian needs of children in Romanian orphanages. He has assisted with Comic Relief projects in Kenya and supported a range of anti-poverty initiatives in Ghana and Madagascar.

In 2003 Des founded Diversiton as a social enterprise. Its Inclusion Calendar is used internationally by hundreds of organisations. The annual International Inclusion Awards and the Diversity Champion Awards are also administered by Diversiton.

As a Coach, Des is well known for his experience in licensing, helping many colleagues to license their training courses and services across the world.

In 2011 Hay House published Des's ground-breaking book, *Work it Out!: How to Find the Work You Always Wanted in a Shifting Jobs Market*, which led to the development of the Inverted Pyramid methodology.

From 2014 the Irish Government, as well as numerous agencies and businesses worldwide, supported a wide range of Inverted Pyramid pilot initiatives to build inclusion in communities and workplaces. Inverted Pyramid training licenses became available worldwide for individuals, organisations and government agencies in 2023. Des continues to support this.

VISIT - www.desmccabe.com / www.invertedpyramid.info / www.diversiton.com

CONTACT - diversiton@gmail.com / +44 7717 203325

BIBLIOGRAPHY

Bergmann, C, *Synodality: A Guide for the Perplexed*, Catholic Archdiocese of Melbourne, 30 September 2021

Canaris, M M, *Open minds, hearts key to fruitful synod process*, Catholic Star Herald, 21 October 2021

Canaris, M M, *Pope Francis through the eyes of a 'buen amigo'*, Catholic Star Herald, 14 April 2016

Canaris, M M, *The Pope's 'Inverted Pyramid' vision of the Church*, Catholic Star Herald, 2 August 2018

His Holiness Pope Francis, *Address of His Holiness Pope Francis to the Faithful of the Diocese of Rome*, Paul VI Audience Hall, 18 September 2021

His Holiness Pope Francis (Author), Morey A (narr.), *Let Us Dream: The Path to a Better Future*, Simon & Schuster Audio UK, London: 2020

International Theological Commission, Sub-commission for Religious freedom, *Religious Freedom for the Good of All Theological Approaches and Contemporary Challenges*, 21March 2019

Lamb, C, *Pope Francis plans synodal shake-up*, The Tablet, 21 May 2021

McCabe, D, *Work It Out!: How to Find the Work You Always Wanted in a Shifting Jobs Market*, Hay House UK Ltd, London: 2011

The Vatican: *For a Synodal Church: Communion, Participation, and Mission Vademecum for the Synod on Synodality*, 7 September 2021

ACKNOWLEDGEMENTS

I am so grateful to all those who have enabled me to be part of their amazing Inverted Pyramid journeys.

Special thanks to Pauline McCabe, Sharon Cowan, Jimmy Ryan, Diane Page, Seamus McCrory, Dean Minuto, Michael-Don Smith, Gail Cassidy, Tina Corner-Stolz, Clodagh McDonnell, Cathal McCabe, Lisa Rose, Shaunaka Rishi Das, Barry Kirby, Fiona McLeod, Eimear McCrory, Fiona Hammond, Cynthia Bostock, Neil Thorogood, Judith Kerr, Larry Ryan and Tim Bourke.

GLOSSARY

Diversity
Diversity includes everything that makes each of us unique, including our background, skills, personality, interests, history, physical make-up, experience, values and so much more! Diversity is our amazing individual toolbox.

Dual Responsibility
We have a responsibility to look after ourselves and we have a responsibility to look after every other person in the world.

Equality
Equality is essentially a legislative framework targeting key issues such as belief, sexuality, gender, race, et cetera. Equality labels people and groups by these characteristics to raise awareness, minimise discrimination and promote equality of treatment in our workplaces.

God
God is another word for love. It's the totality of all of us working together to help everyone. It is us giving of ourselves in all the everyday ways that we can. It is the love that is at the heart of who we are as human beings. This love holds and unites us all as one.

Golden Rule
Simply, for us to treat all others as we would like them to treat us.

Freestyle management
This is individuals as 'self-managers' working behind, alongside and in front of others in alternative ways with a variety of projects and priorities. We identify specialist coaches and mentors for this new

arrangement, who can help individuals to work though practical priorities and challenges in a collaborative spirit.

Harvesting

Harvesting is how we take additional value, insights and understanding from an experience such as a conversation, interaction, event or activity. We look backwards at the experience and capture insights and understanding from this. We then write down this new learning to create case studies, ideas, stories, concepts, training materials, articles and books from this.

Inclusion

Inclusion is both a personal development process whereby we can each play our part in making our world a better place, and a series of interpersonal relationships because this is how we make this real. Inclusion happens through our interactions with others, through our contribution with others and through the difference that we all make in each other's lives.

Inclusive Charity Model

The inclusive charity model is invoked when a business, organisation or individual links directly with those in need of help. It is a collaborative approach. It's about reaching out to help others with our skills, expertise and resources.

Interpersonal Christianity

Interpersonal Christianity is characterised by multi-ethnic, multicultural, multi-belief Inverted Pyramid teams which open themselves to everyone, are fully inclusive, are directly connected to the needs of local people and global issues and are joined up as a worldwide community of inclusion.

Francis has provided an invitation to an 'open door' Christianity which welcomes everyone and sees each individual as essential in building a worldwide community of love.

Interpersonal Relationships

Interpersonal means exactly what it says. It's a personal (not work) conversation and connection between (inter) two people. Interpersonal relationships are the foundation of inclusion.

Inverted Pyramid

A collaborative way of work initiated and led by individuals to build a world of inclusion. It's a bottom-up process in contrast with a hierarchal structure.

Inverted Pyramid Exercise

A short reflection on a particular concept or idea, usually with one or two questions to help us build our understanding and learning.

Leapfrogging

The process of accessing all parts of our organisation in order to make new contacts. This is not just a random 'Let's talk to anyone' process. It's a way of seeking to connect with people who may be able to help us to progress an initiative, who may have expertise in a particular area, who may be able to advise us or link us up with someone internally or externally that we should talk to.

Mexican Wave of Kindness

To build, grow and promote kindness as a force for good, we must be explicit about the goodness that we share. When we show kindness to others, we should also encourage them to be kind to others. Together we create a 'chain reaction' that becomes part of the Mexican Wave, passing the behaviours and benefits of kindness onto others.

New Space

The opportunity for us to come together and work together does not have to exist in our current arrangements. New space reminds us that we can look outwards beyond our situation, our roles and our organisation to find perhaps more significant or more important opportunities for collaboration.

Pick 'n' Mix

Our Pick 'n' Mix consists of all of our knowledge, skills, contacts, experience, expertise and passions that we build up over our lives. Our Pick 'n' Mix is like a bag of sweets or candy we can dip into at any stage and access what we already know – our bag of personal assets.

Social Meitheal

The old Irish tradition where people in rural communities gathered on a neighbour's farm to help save the hay or some other crop. Each person would help their neighbour, who would in turn reciprocate. They brought different levels and types of skills, experience and equipment (technology) to the endeavour.

Sustainable Development Goals

A collection of 17 interlinked global goals from the United Nations designed to be a 'shared blueprint for peace and prosperity for people and the planet, now and into the future'. The SDGs offer a practical framework for everyone to build Inverted Pyramid inclusion projects.

Synodality

The process of journeying with each other every day. Synodality is the development of our interpersonal Inverted Pyramid relationships and includes all aspects of our lives. Synodality is inclusive of everyone, for we can all journey together and help each other.

Transactional interactions

When we speak of transformational, we mean the series of steps required to complete a task or process, a bit like a recipe or a Google map.

Transformation

The process of moving from transactional behaviours to interpersonal relationships is called *transformation*. It's how we can transform any transactional interaction, using our initiative or style of response. We initiate, take control or respond in an unexpected way. In other words, we step outside the transaction with, for example, a comment, a smile, a facial expression, a question, a gesture or an offer of help.

Vatican 3 (V3)

This book suggest that the Third Vatican Council (V3) will, as Pope Francis envisages, aim to turn the Church upside down by becoming an Inverted Pyramid. V3 is the process of building an inclusive Christianity, inviting each of us to share our gift of love and practical help unconditionally to all others. V3 may have already begun.

Vocation

A lifelong journey made up of two elements: a journey (outwards) to others and a journey (inwards) to our inner selves. These dual aspects of vocation intersect, overlap and become one in all that we are, as we journey with others. This is where vocation finds its common purpose, in everyone together, as we spread love, build love and become love as one.

Work it Out!

A collaborative way of working which enables us to develop and manage our lives to give us the income we need and achieve all that is important to us.

Workpieces

The way that we spend our time becomes our workpieces. Some of these may be voluntary or paid work or looking after our loved ones.

REFERENCES

i His Holiness Pope Francis, *Address of His Holiness Pope Francis to the Faithful of the Diocese of Rome*, 18 September 2021, The Vatican, https://www.vatican.va/content/francesco/en/speeches/2021/september/documents/20210918-fedeli-diocesiroma.html

ii Mares, C, *Pope Francis: Synodality is What the Lord Expects of the Church*, 29 November 2019, Catholic News Agency, https://www.catholicnewsagency.com/news/42963/pope-francis-synodality-is-what-the-lord-expects-of-the-church

iii Pope Francis, *Address of His Holiness Pope Francis to the Faithful of the Diocese of Rome*

iv The Pillar, *Synod on Synodality reaches a 'due' date. What's next?*, 15 August 2022, https://www.pillarcatholic.com/synod-on-synodality-reaches-a-due/?action=share

v Pope Francis, *Address of His Holiness Pope Francis to the Faithful of the Diocese of Rome*

vi The Vatican, *For a Synodal Church: Communion, Participation, and Mission Vademecum for the Synod on Synodality*, 7 September 2021, https://press.vatican.va/content/salastampa/it/bollettino/pubblico/2021/09/07/0541/01166.html

vii His Holiness Pope Francis, *Let Us Dream: The Path to a Better Future*, narr. Morey, A, Simon & Schuster Audio UK: London, 1 December 2020, 6

viii Pope Francis, *Let Us Dream*, 51–3

ix Pope Francis, *Let Us Dream*, 81–2

x Annan, K, private letter to the Training Trust Trustees

xi The Vatican, *For a Synodal Church*

xiixii Pope Francis, *Let Us Dream*, 6

Printed in Great Britain
by Amazon

14704445R00230